Nights in the Forest

Nights in the Forest

Anthony Corbyn

Red Point Publications, Caithness

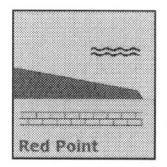

Copyright © 2024 Peter Haase

All rights reserved.

No part of this publication may be reproduced, stored in a retrieval system, or transmitted, in any form or by any means, electronic, mechanical, recording or otherwise without prior permission from the copyright holder.

This story is based on true events, although narrated with some degree of literary freedom. The original manuscript has been extensively edited and the names of the protagonists have been changed or are mentioned as nicknames or first names only.

First published 2024 by
Red Point Publications, Caithness

Cover illustration: Ben Frieden at Pixabay (rotated, clipped)

Table of Contents

Introduction – A little Market Town in the 1950s 1
Chapter One – A Broken Home 11
Chapter Two – A Juvenile Delinquent 31
Chapter Three – Caught by an Act of Treason 53
Chapter Four – Life at School – or playing Truant 69
Chapter Five – A Variety of Pets 89
Chapter Six – Dangerous Visits to the Underworld 113
Chapter Seven – Sinking the Battle Fleet 135
Chapter Eight – Homemade Fireworks for Guy Fawkes Night ... 157
Chapter Nine – The Canoe 175
Chapter Ten – Starfield House 189
Chapter Eleven – Back to the Forest 211
Chapter Twelve – Training to become a Seaman 231
Chapter Thirteen – In the Merchant Navy 251
Chapter Fourteen – The Gun 279
Chapter Fifteen – The Great Hare Shoot 297
Chapter Sixteen – My Nemesis 313
About the Author 325
All Titles by the Author 327

Introduction

A little Market Town in the 1950s

If one walked toward Corsham along the A4 road from Chippenham to Bath, there was no need to worry about traffic. Despite being the main road to London, it never became really busy. A drystone wall was built along the left hand side all the way up Chequers Hill. Undulating pastureland became interspaced with copses of horse chestnut and Spanish oaks. Cows would gather under them to shade from a blistering afternoon's summer sun. With a little patience you might catch a glimpse of rabbits scampering between tall tufts of grass. On top of Chequers, the road levelled out with large overhanging horse chestnut and smaller hazelnut trees camouflaging that drystone wall. Clusters of gangly stinging nettles, climbing weeds, swaying yellow dandelions, moss and fluttering miniature ferns contributed to its concealment as nature masked man's construction.

At the crossroads stood a pub called "The Cross Keys", a small, very old building with pale yellow stone from local mines reflecting a withered with age look where brackish grey infiltrated pale limestone to present an acquired "Olde World" appearance. Flat stone tiles formed neat shingles where a master roofer once worked. Two vertical poles supported a wooden gantry holding a loosely swinging jet-black signpost displaying a set of crossed keys, painted in gold. On dark nights, rushing wind rustled leaves and encouraged rusted iron hinges to squeak and groan. Splattering rain drops could not disguise their noises sounding like a criminal's ghost searching for freedom. A small car park behind the pub was available but three cars would be a maximum number it could hold. A Morris 1000, an Austin A40 and a Ford Consul would pack it to capacity. Thereafter, any additional drink drivers parked in the lane. On very dark motionless nights, a welcoming display of lights glinted from small lead lattice windows. Dog-eared calico cotton curtains had barely sufficient threads to dim 40-watt bulbs. Although a comforting sight for strangers, the lighted welcome could not mask a pungent aroma of stale urine coming from the men's toilet. A urinal had been built against the pub wall, which was surrounded by a shoulder-high stone partition. There was no roof to protect a man from rain while relieving himself. A call of nature could only be accessed by scuttling about in the dark. Any lighting, to guide someone who acquired an overloaded bladder associated with heavy beer drinkers, normally came from a streetlight. However, as with the publican's apparent concern for saving power, Wiltshire County Council decided not to repair that broken light. Steering one's way along a muddy pathway toward the Cross Keys' urinal on stormy nights proved very hazardous to unwary patrons.

Turning left at the crossroads led into the town itself. The gradually disappearing low drystone wall, being reclaimed by nature, continued for about fifty yards. On the other side stood a copse of leafy trees housing a rookery. Black shapes resembling vultures glided and fluttered above with persistent irritating cries. At the far end of that rookery, the drystone wall suddenly became grossly oversized. It towered above any walker striding along a narrow footpath. That height was deliberate. Its purpose was in excluding intruders from entering Lord Methuen's Estate.

On the right hand side was the first junction called Coulston Road meandering through a single-story prefabricated housing estate. The houses were built from concrete blocks and asbestos roofs. Asbestos was used extensively on all roofs, apparently no one knew about its inherent danger. If anyone did, they were keeping very quiet about it. Coulston Road's population consisted, for the most part, of large families. Or more precisely, they were poor families who lived off family allowances, unemployment benefits, or National Assistance. Many were fatherless military families with more than a few foreigners lumped in among barking dogs and screaming children playing in dilapidated gardens. Lack of finances prevented poor stony soil conditions being improved. Nonetheless, intrepid owners grew insipid looking cabbages, stringy string beans and carrots in crooked lines.

Nights in the Forest

Whatever could be grown was eaten. Freezing winters always left each garden looking like desolated wasteland in seemingly abandoned condition. Inadequate chain link fences restrained animals incapable of leaping over to attack unsuspecting passers-by. It gave the impression of a poorly maintained prison complex. There were no real television aerials, although one or two intrepid individuals with black and white television sets constructed lengths of steel-galvanized pipes and bolted them against a wall. Wire coat hangers protruded from the top in an attempt to catch any available signals. Whilst most families appeared destitute and living inside unheated concrete rooms, they were quite a friendly bunch. It was no surprise to discover, with so many children living under such adverse conditions, a cacophony of illnesses kept breaking out. This situation provided doctors Westfield and Henderson with very busy schedules subduing rasping coughs and high velocity sneezes with a variety of medicines. Boils were lanced and any puss squeezed out before being dosed with antiseptic ointment and bandaged. Spots, zits as they were commonly known, were normal teenage afflictions and treated with a variety of skin-cleaning ointments that never really worked. Nonetheless, it did not stop companies producing an inordinate number of lotions, soaps, creams and potions. The power of industry supplying a demand was put into full swing. Had we spotty teenagers known, all we had to do was wash in hot water with normal soap. Eating the right food also helped, but that as with everything else was in short supply. Heated classrooms were ideal breeding grounds, which ensured a complex scenario of miserable afflictions perpetuated for those unfortunates at school. Running red noses were blown into thin cotton handkerchiefs. These pieces of saturated material were crumpled up and stored in pockets. Nothing was wasted, not even bacteria-impregnated cotton. Needless to say, doctors, parents, interfering neighbours, friends and relatives who came to visit the sick imposed old-fashioned remedies on children. In effect, anyone who thought they knew the answer. It was amazing how many helpful souls came out the woodwork to aid a sick one, despite not having a clue what to do.

Anthony Corbyn

More often than not, Mother Nature and common sense cured all.

Just past that first junction was a line of cherry trees. For a limited period of time during the year, just when the blossoms were blooming, a fragrant scent of cherries smothered the atmosphere. For just over a week one could inhale freshly seasoned aromatic air. When every tree stood close to bursting from a colourful display, with the help of nature, they performed their ultimate spectacular show. In late spring or early summer a strong breeze rushing past overhanging canopies prompted them to shed millions of pale pink petals. The same gentle wind dispersed multitudes of pretty snowdrops across the road, pathway and any people under it. A large green patch of grass surrounding those trees became inundated with various shades of cerise. White-tipped cherry blossoms became intermixed with numerous shades of emerald. A magical atmosphere developed, although it only lasted while decorated snow was falling. It was not unusual to see parents and their offspring dancing about under a shower of pretty petals. Such an unusual event represented a colourful display provided by nature at no cost to those who enjoyed it.

The first houses one came across on the left when entering Corsham from Lacock were the Almshouses. These ancient monuments of a previous era had been built opposite an equally aged horse-drinking trough carved from a huge lump of stone. Between those Almshouses and horse trough, a pair of peacocks proudly strutted around looking as though they owned everything in sight. On special occasions, known only to them, they would lift their tail feathers in a beautiful multicoloured display. A rainbow's primary tints were pale in comparison to those tails.

The old post office had been another almshouse that was converted into a business premises and stood on a corner of High Street. Outside its front door was a universally acclaimed Post Office red telephone box. These communication devices were always placed in a position where they caught every ultraviolet ray the sun produced. At some stage, especially around midday, those small glass boxes became hot as an oven cooking chickens. The doors were spring-loaded, which made it impossible to talk on the phone with it open, unless one had extensions attached to a leg. Some older people, also known as grey tops, were apt to suffer from heat exhaustion after a ten-minute conversation. Those who survived being baked alive, practiced hyperventilation after emerging from their self-imposed cookery lesson. Making a phone call was relatively simple. One fed the coin box with an appropriate number of pennies, also known as coppers because that's what they were made of, and dialled the required number. When the phone at the other end was picked up, one pressed button A. At that stage, conversation could commence, providing one of an inordinate number of problems did not occur. If nobody answered, one pressed button B and like magic, pennies would tumble into the collect tray, providing any number of problems hadn't transpired. The primary factor blocking monetary returns was usually a bent coin or washer jammed tight in the coin chute. That was about as much as one could say about public phone boxes.

Down the side street, a church had been constructed on Lord Methuen's grounds, coincidentally, so was the local cemetery. Anyone wandering around reading epitaphs on tombstones could not fail to notice that all available spaces had long since been filled. Naturally, there was always plenty of room elsewhere. However, that was a mile down the road where the majority of Corsham's deceased were buried, including my brother Freddy and Uncle Willy. The town's main hotel had also been built on his Lordship's ground and as expected, it was named after him. The Methuen Arms had always been what most people in Corsham called a posh pub. It was and still is known as the best place to take special visitors or well off members of one's family for drinks and a meal. It contained a number of rooms, a good dining room with an excellent à la carte menu, a lounge bar, and a public bar with a skittle alley. In effect, an architect designed it to cater for every level of society's social classes. The lounge bar was sumptuously spacious with comfortable padded seating and table service with softly playing classical music filtering into a gracious atmosphere. Everything in that area was maintained in prestigious order. Softly spoken and very amicable conversations were entered into. Meanwhile, raucous laughter and fun could be heard emanating from the public bar. Those sounds often prompted some upper echelons of Corsham's social elite to desert their comfortable arena. Beer, skittles, bench seats and bare wooden tables, sawdust on the floor, barely comprehensible West Country dialogue and laughter constituted a powerful incentive for upper classes to slum it with the locals. They abandoned Gordon's Dry Gin and Schweppes tonic water with interesting conversations in salubrious surroundings. It was not uncommon to see a gentleman remove his jacket and tie during the serious business of competing with a local at skittles.

Lord Methuen's manor house consisted of a very large and impressive building standing in extensive grounds. A driveway leading to the front steps stretched to a side road leading out of town. Someone, who almost certainly occupied one of the graves in Corsham's churchyard, planted a line of horse chestnuts, which eventually grew to stand like enormous sentinels guarding the lane from one end to the other. As expected, a restriction to such an impressive driveway was represented by huge wrought iron gates. Methuen's extensive grounds were covered in trees with dozens of cows chewing up lush pastures to provide milk for a farmer renting the land. Somewhere near the centre of those undulating fields was a small lake. That lake acquired a reputation of housing a man-eating pike. Nobody actually knew where the pike's legend originated from but as with all mysteries, they could not be proved and grew beyond belief. According to one myth surrounding that notorious fish, it attacked a cow thirsty enough to risk drinking from the lake. Naturally, I became one among many attempting to catch that mysterious pike, which incidentally had a reputation of being at least six feet long. On the other hand, no one knew for sure how heavy it might have been. The only drawback to any successful fishing or poaching expedition on his Lordship's lake and grounds was that one became very reluctant to brag about it. Nonetheless, it never stopped this rebellious person making numerous unsuccessful attempts, despite knowing that poaching fish was considered an offence punishable by a heavy fine. That pike lies in wait for a human or anything else foolish enough to drink or attempt swimming in those murky waters. If the occupier of that lake fails to get you, the gamekeeper will. Although poaching fish was considered illegal, so was trapping hares and rabbits or shooting pigeons. Some were not afraid of keeping the population of those species down to a minimum. Silence came in the form of concealed traps, an air rifle or bow and arrow.

The weather was fine most times but there were a few rainy days, especially in the form of summer thunderstorms. These provided spectacular performances for anyone stupid enough to watch from outside. Dry open ground became saturated within minutes. If not millions, then billions of cascading water droplets the size of marbles were absorbed by cracked sunbaked ground. Others would splatter and rise in miniature fountains to cool sizzling tar macadam surface. A massive accumulation of droplets gathered into rushing rivulets that overcame roadside drainage systems. Gushing gurgling sounds erupted from gratings and those noises accompanied whistling wind creating horizontal rain amid rolling thunder. The orchestrated routine continued until the storm passed. Dark overcast skies filled with mountainous cumulus formations stretched across distant horizons. Overhead, golden beams penetrated broken clouds to reheat the ground and atmosphere. This caused drenched surroundings to start evaporating. Steam rose off warm roads and surrounding meadows to convert cooled air into a sauna. After summer rain cooled an overheated environment and made everything wet, humidity overtook any warm conditions that remained. By the end of a long afternoon, hot summer heat returned until sunset. Each scenario provided a mesmerizing array of aromas percolating into the air. Blistering heat gave a dry grass scented format until a downpour. This masked everything with a freshness of untainted rainwater that clung to nostrils. Humidity blended every available scent while adding its own stifling stickiness. After that, everything became dried out again by blistering sunlight.

The main road through Corsham was very narrow, particularly where L.R. Love & Son, the local butcher's shop, used to stand opposite the surgery. It's not a butcher's shop anymore but a tiny restaurant. Those with nothing better to occupy their minds could watch a double-decker bus driver attempting to negotiate that oversized vehicle through the bottleneck. On numerous occasions it was quite common to see why he failed. Passengers would disembark and roam the street while grumbling and making facetious remarks about their driver's inability to drive. More often than not, some idiot had parked his car too close to the narrowest section.

If one took a left turn at the Methuen Arms Hotel, it led out of town toward the cemetery. Taking a right turn led back toward the main A4 to Bath. Before the Severn Bridge was built, a trip to Cardiff on the other side of the river was by ferry and once there, that country was full of Welsh people. Some say the Severn Bridge was built to let the Welsh get out. On the other hand, others say it was for the English to get in.

A few nondescript little shops, the Halifax Building Society building and a small cinema littered the right hand side of the road leading out of Corsham. The popular Saturday nightspot stood for those not old enough to drink at one of the seven pubs. All the latest movies were shown and on those occasions almost seventy people packed into it. On the left, opposite the cinema and down Paul Street, was Corsham's Secondary Modern School. The town's newly built school quickly acquired a reputation for having the meanest male teenage students on planet earth. Teachers needed to become meaner than their students to retain control. Their attempt perpetuated a continuous battle between teachers and rebellious young males and promiscuous females. Without fear of contradiction, one can honestly say, there were plenty of us. In effect, we outnumbered our teachers by about thirty to one. Close to the school, a swimming pool had been built where excess youthful energy and rampaging hormones could be exhausted, or at the very least tempered for a while.

At the far end of town was another junction named Pickwick Road and at that turnoff, on a large patch of open ground, stood three enormous walnut trees. Those trees were a fantastic place for gathering my favourite nuts. Friends and I collected a variety of objects, usually lumps of rock, and hurtled them at nut-bearing branches. Big green, fruit-bearing objects tumbled to the ground. There was always an inherent danger in collecting those precious nuts while others were still throwing rocks into the branches. Falling nuts were relatively harmless compared to stones, lumps of wood, and various other projectiles cascading from the trees. These objects bounced and ricocheted off branches with no way of telling where they might end up. A friend of mine made the mistake of rushing in to collect some big green walnuts. My warning shout caused him to look up, but he was unable to avoid an alternative object tumbling out the tree. Lofty was escorted to the Corsham Surgery where a mass of residual blood was wiped off his face and a stitch used to sew up his forehead. The heroic Lofty staggered through Corsham ensuring everyone saw the damage perpetrated on him, by the person holding him up.

Not far from those walnut trees stood another pub called the "Hare and Hounds" with the main A4 running along one side. That made it impossible to pass, enter or leave Corsham without seeing at least one pub.

A short distance from the Hare and Hounds stood a Catholic church where sinners went on Saturday to ask Father Sullivan for forgiveness. Our good father was an Irishman with an infamous reputation that included a powerful voice, a belief in the holy trilogy and a fervent liking for Black Bush Irish whiskey. Sins committed during the week would be forgiven under the condition of atonement by accepting a penance from him. This usually amounted to saying every Hail Mary on a set of rosary beads. On Sunday mornings all sins were forgiven and every loyal Catholic was sure of a place in heaven. On the other hand, one had to pass a pub on the way home and a house of ill repute where an extremely attractive, very accommodating merry widow lived on immoral earnings.

When looking back on the traumatic experiences encountered during my juvenile years, one has good reason to wonder how I survived. Conversely, the compensation of freedom and abundant adventures, particularly in the forest, made it worthwhile, despite what adults told me. Besides, the Catholic Church provided an option clause for any sins committed. The good Father Sullivan, bound by a vow of privacy, always forgave sins committed, so long as one carried out any penance he handed out. However, none of the above was discovered until the remnants of my family left Germany.

Chapter One

A Broken Home

Leaving Germany came about from a chain of avoidable events committed by my father who joined the army before the Second World War. Not only was he bulky but stood six feet two inches in army socks. This height made everyone look up to him. It was whilst serving in Malta that he met mother and fell madly in love with her. At the time, mother was an innocent Catholic who had been brought up by nuns. Naturally, my mother was very flattered that such a great big fearless army sergeant should ask her out. Their dinner date was interrupted by air raid sirens, which prompted them to make a hurried departure from the restaurant. According to dad, they were hiding in a bomb shelter when he kissed her for the first time. That kiss, as he put it, was in reassurance of her safety while he held her in his arms. It meant their romance started with a bang made in Germany. That's what father told me.

After the war ended, a sort of peace settled between all warring nations and dad was sent to Egypt then to Germany to sort out the mess. That's something else he told me. At some stage he became so important, the generals in their infinite wisdom promoted him and he became a regimental sergeant major in the military police. That promotion was good for us and good for him because he earned it. After organizing Malta's defences and keeping the Germans out of Egypt, he led all the victory parades. The generals gave him several medals, all of which were well deserved and that's a fact because he told me.

We were in Germany for a couple of years and it appears that dad was doing rather well. Under his direction Hamburg was being rebuilt because, during the hostilities he organized England's Royal Air Force and, with the help of a few Americans, they bombed it flat. Although the Americans had a hand in it, apparently they were pretty ineffective and could not hit a barn door with a shotgun from ten paces.

There were many things dad told me that were hard to understand or believe. For example, why would anyone want to shoot at barn doors from a plane? Still, if that's what he said they did, it must be true.

In Hamburg father became responsible for traffic control in the city. Dad quickly emerged from being a domesticated sergeant to a big, seventeen stone, bombastic bastard who barked orders at everyone in a very loud voice. He ran the household like a set of traffic lights. Powerful demands were boomed out to anyone within the confines of our home. "Orders must be obeyed without question at all times" seemed the correct expression to describe how he imposed his will. It must have been something to do with his training, or the promotion went to his head.

My elder sister Laura and mother lived in trepidation at his homecoming, particularly after a bad day at the office. On those occasions Laura and I would be commanded to comb his hair and clean his enormous feet. To indicate how huge his feet were, he wore size twelve hobnailed boots. The submissive treatment of dad's head and feet effectively calmed him down although my personal choice was in combing dad's lank black, Brilliantine-plastered hair. It was immeasurably preferable to cleaning big stinking, sweaty feet. Needless to say, our restraint was severely tested under those circumstances, but what could children do about that kind of treatment? After all, he was a regimental sergeant major whose orders must be obeyed without question at all times.

Father commanded respect and fear throughout Germany, that's what he told us, apart from which we were reasonably well off with no reason to complain. Our social standing must have gone up because the army gave mum permission to hire a maid. This was because mother had fallen pregnant again. Since father was responsible for mother's condition, a breadwinner, wore medals and the biggest member of our family, he naturally took the decision of choosing which woman would be our maid. After all, she would be looking after his family. The house needed cleaning, meals to cook, there would be laundry duties, his daughter and two sons needed their clothes pressing. No ordinary maid would do.

The moment Freda came into the kitchen, mother and I stood open-mouthed in stunned admiration. We were astonished that father should pick such a tall, slim, long-legged, educated, good-looking blond. She represented the absolute opposite of mother. Not only that, in my opinion she looked a bit young for a maid. It made no difference to my brother Freddy, my sister Laura or me, although, from the look in her eyes, mother was very suspicious.

There were four bedrooms in the house and our new, very young maid moved into the spare. I had no idea why she had the larger room with a double bed but my younger brother Freddy and I shared a single, while Laura had one to herself. Mum and dad naturally slept on a big king-size bed in what everyone called "the emperor's bedroom".

Before long, everyone settled into a routine with Freda making breakfast every morning and dinner in the evening. My sister and I went off to school while Freddy stayed at home. Father organized mother's visits to the military doctor for regular check-ups. After all, he was a regimental sergeant major and who better than him to arrange important appointments. Each afternoon, I returned from school to find the house spick and span. Every window was wide open to let fresh air flow through the rooms. Mother was out shopping while pushing Freddy around in a pushchair. There were always fresh flowers on the dining room table and some in a vase on the bedside table next to the king-size bed in the emperor's bedroom.

I was a good boy at that stage because dad kept everything and everyone under control. That's what good fathers do, that's a fact because he said it while pointing his enormous nicotine-coated finger at my nose. Regimental sergeant majors have an overpowering presence and the authority to match. They need it, and have to practice that power at every opportunity, wherever they are and to whomever they speak.

Not long after Freda arrived, mum and dad had a big argument. Mother may have been a short, black-haired, illiterate woman but being a pushover could not be entertained in her persona. Mediterranean women have a reputation for being somewhat volatile and short on temper. Having discovered dad's sudden preference for tall, blond-haired, blue-eyed Germans, she decided to empty the spare bedroom. The first step came about by throwing Freda's clothing out the window into pouring rain, which I thought was a bit mean. An overcast sky provided thunder and lightning during that process, although it never dampened mum's enthusiasm. On the contrary, it seemed to help speed things up and her constant cackling chuckle while she dispensed all those lovely clothes out the window made me wonder if she had gone round the bend. Colourful underwear and nylon see-through blouses floated on swirling wind. Those flimsy items of female apparel eventually landed on the lawn. They presented a vibrant colour scheme interspaced by a wet emerald backdrop. Freda's two full-length fur coats and leather jacket, however, were made of heavier material and plummeted vertically until they plopped onto a wet concrete footpath. During the proceedings dad went berserk. He rampaged through the house using his powerful voice to its ultimate pitch. Actually it was so high and loud, nothing could be understood. He represented a monstrous gargoyle that ranted and raved with arms rotating like windmills in a storm. What words could be understood confused me because if father claimed he was an atheist, what did Jesus Christ have to do with anything during the mayhem going on? In the meantime, Freda burst into tears and ran off. Laura, Freddy, and I watched until those heavy plopping sounds prompted us to hide in our bedrooms.

It was a defiant yet futile gesture from mother because within days of that fiasco, my oversized mum, who had reached the waddling stage, Laura, Freddy, and I were dispatched to Hamburg airport, bound for England. We were cast off to fend for ourselves. At the same time, I acquired a sudden sense of freedom. Having the sensation of being dominated by an overpowering monolith called father taken away, felt good. Although mother did not seem too happy about it, my feelings were bordering on ecstatic. There was only one problem with freedom for a boy my age, and I quickly discovered it – adults do not listen when he says, "It wasn't my fault." However, reminiscing about those hectic, bad-tempered, turbulent days just before the family broke up prompts a smile to open my lips.

On a miserable early spring morning we departed Hamburg. The plane's engines roared and rotated its propellers into whirring circles. It lumbered and bounced along an undulating runway until my stomach dropped and we were airborne. Misty surroundings disappeared under clouds in exchange for clear sunny skies as our pilot guided his aircraft toward London. By the time we arrived in England, it was my fourth country and I instantly became a seasoned traveller. Springtime in Germany must have been working on a different setting because a darkened overcast sky greeted our arrival at Heathrow before it emptied buckets on us all the way to Lypiatt Camp in Wiltshire. Adults used the expression "it's raining cats and dogs", although I never saw a single one. All the residential buildings at Lypiatt Camp were prefabricated and in typical army manner, they stood in neat rows with the exception standing at one end of the estate. In their infinite wisdom, the army built a large building where everyone congregated during meal times. We queued up to collect our share of food on large china plates, just like children at school. The food was metered out from stainless steel bains-marie and actually plopped onto plates in a very reminiscing sound and tasted much the same as the stuff at school. Our family lacked a father, so anything handed out for free was appreciated. On the other hand, this ritual of being fed once a day barely contributed sufficient calories for an energetic, rapidly growing, skinny little runt whose ambition was – to become a juvenile delinquent.

On entering a single-story building we called home, I headed toward the kitchen for something to eat. Whilst mother was never considered a good cook, she always made sure a pot of simmering stew remained on the stove with a sufficient supply of bread in the bread bin. That idea was excellent because it ensured that whatever else happened, none of us would ever go hungry.

It remained a constant source of wonder to me, why the bread never stayed fresh for more than a day. It must have been something to do with the delivery system. Fresh bread always arrived before any stale bread had been eaten. Everyone knows fresh bread's delicious aroma tempts hungry people into eating it before any stale leftovers. Whenever I reached that bread bin, there was never a conflict of interest. A large chunk of fresh bread was sliced off before being smothered in Echo margarine. The margarine may have looked yucky but tasted pretty good, especially to anyone with an uncompromising appetite. Whatever it might have been, if it was edible, I ate it.

Butter, on the other hand, was another luxury we were unable to afford. Nonetheless, there was always a plentiful supply of margarine to spread over whatever bread remained. The stuff looked and smelled like axle grease. In fact, Uncle Willy, who appeared soon after our arrival in England, actually used it for that purpose. He also used it to slick down my unruly, unpredictable, rebellious locks. Real hair cream, such as Brylcreem, was another item that disappeared off mother's shopping list. That's to say her memorized list because mother was illiterate.

Having long, Echo margarine-saturated hair must have been one of the many reasons why adults began pointing and calling me a hooligan. Parents became reluctant to let their children play with me for fear of influencing them into behaving badly. I had no idea why Echo margarine, plastered on one's head, should have such a negative influence on people. On reflection, most adults reacted that way toward me whatever I had on my head. In spite of many parents' reluctances, there were numerous ways of getting around restrictions imposed on their children in futile attempts to stop them playing with me.

To keep things in perspective, one must revert to the circumstances of my parents' meeting.

Mother came from a large impoverished Catholic family who never received the benefit of schooling. She attended a convent where nuns considered devout prayer as the answer to every problem. It was quite common to see mother making a sign of the cross while muttering Maltese incantations and performing these entreaties to God. Her faith remained staunchly defiant against any odds, be they unavoidable inconveniences, insurmountable problems or unprecedented disasters. Any overwhelming odds had no chance against a Christian kneeling in prayer. Her Catholic education provided an answer to everything except an ability to read and write. Insofar as those nuns were concerned, that aspect of life belonged to the ruling classes or priests. Except the priesthood learned Latin and dispensed the service in that tongue, which only they could understand.

When mother met father, who was an atheist, the entire world was close to oblivion. Nonetheless, they married during an air raid. According to dad's recollections, my parents' wedding took place with the sirens wailing a mournful warning. At the same time, hundreds of thousands of German and Italian warplanes were dropping millions of bombs on the island. Father went on to say, every bomb crew's effort were a direct result of Hitler and a character called Mussolini ordering their aircrews to stop the wedding at all costs. Dad's descriptions were very specific and included trembling walls with bits of plaster falling onto the congregation like confetti, especially when the ring was slipped onto mother's finger. Meanwhile, one gathering stood to attention, they wore shiny boots with smartly pressed, highly decorated uniforms whilst retaining stiff upper lips. According to dad, the priest concluded the marriage ceremony in double quick time while other guests kneeled in fervent prayer. Most of those appealing for God's protection were on mother's side of the gathering. These included family and relatives, two dozen nuns in their habits, a priest or two mingled among numerous beggars and thieves praying for a free meal at the reception. Proof positive, as if any were needed, the nuns who educated mum were absolutely correct. None of the hundred thousand bombs dropped that day actually landed on the church. By an odd coincidence, the wedding ceremony ended at the conclusion of a flypast by bombers. From the look on father's face, it made me wonder if the ongoing celebration was a way of thanking God for sparing him or for being married.

I entered my first teenage year just after our arrival at Lypiatt Camp with a sense of freedom enveloping me. I felt liberated from the many constraints father imposed on my natural propensity to wander, create mayhem, alarm and despondency. In effect, enjoy myself. Whilst at Lypiatt, the remnants of my family survived on National Assistance, which was just enough to keep us from poverty but close to the bread line. Nonetheless, as with all people in the same situation, an element of survival takes over. An input of initiative takes over. Mother either made or procured hand-me-downs given by other families or purchased clothing from second-hand shops. There were lots of those shops around with more than enough customers to keep the businesses going on a thriving base.

Laura had already reached the right age to attend Corsham Secondary Modern, while I went to Regis Junior School. It would take several months before the authorities decided to move me to the same school as my sister. Apparently my birthday fell after the beginning of term. This created problems in calculating a maths permutation, which included minus two weeks from one month. Calculators were in their infancy, so was the local maths teacher's brain.

My younger brother Fred was the most unfortunate member of our family by being born with a hole in his heart. Adults called him blue baby because any kind of exertion, including a brief walk, made him gasp for breath and go blue around the lips. Father remained adamant about Freddy by claiming, "That boy is not my son because there isn't anything wrong with my own heart." The fact that Freddy looked more like father than the rest of us was purely coincidental, according to dad.

Freddy ended up going to St Martin's Hospital in Bath for a heart operation. There were high hopes of a half-decent repair job being accomplished or at the very least Fred's life would be extended beyond our local doctor's predictions. According to Doctor Westfield, "as long as Freddy didn't move, he had a reasonably good chance of surviving for six months give or take a month." Doctors have always been very good at that sort of prognosis. At the time, St Martin's acquired a reputation for being where doctors sent their "not a hope in hell's chance of surviving" patients to die. That kind of unfounded rumour did nothing to inspire confidence in doctors or their patients. Apart from which I went there with a serious illness and there's nothing wrong with me. At least I don't think there is. Every member of my family went to church on Sunday to pray for Fred's recovery. Mother naturally claimed her son's recovery was due in no small measure to our prayers. The doctors had nothing to do with it. God had intervened, according to mum. After the operation Freddy went to a recovery hospital in Marlborough for rest and recuperation. Visiting him remained out of the question for the duration, since money for such events could not be acquired, not even from the National Assistance people. The government and charity organizations were a tight-fisted bunch that claimed it was due to contending with a soaring influx of refugees from war-torn countries. In reality it meant, I had no chance of visiting my brother because a few million foreigners were scrounging all the available money. Meantime, Fred remained miles away lying on a sickbed. Still, everyone assured me that my brother would return, once he recovered.

Being born Catholic carries a huge responsibility. Not only did one get the given name everyone called you but one became lumbered with two more. Saints' names have always been a dominant feature in the Catholic faith, particularly when parents are choosing one for their offspring. In my case, mother decided to give me three. Father had no say in what to call his first son because he was an atheist, apparently they don't believe in anything. On the other hand, his parents must have been Catholics or at least Christians because they named him David. Except, when one thinks about it that name is also related to Judaism. No wonder dad found it hard to believe in anything. No one told me who Anthony was, other than he was a saint. I remained confused because so were David and Paul. One must assume the name David was given as some sort of consolation to dad's pride. Uncertainty seemed the byword for everyone and everything during those initial and very confusing years.

Actually the entire world remained in a state of doubt, flux and instability during its approach to 1959. The Prime Minister of England was Harold Macmillan while President Dwight D. Eisenhower held power in the United States of America. Meanwhile the musical world teetered on the verge of a great revolution. Big bands were being phased out. The Glenn Miller era was closing down, despite a strong reluctance by a generation fed on and became inspired by its elegant influence. There was a newer, younger, more vibrant generation developing its revolutionary music. One of the major contributors to the revolution, Buddy Holly, was killed in a plane crash along with a couple of his friends. Buddy's looks had no chance of fitting the personification of a rebellious teenager. He had funny looking features and not in the least bit handsome, he was skinny with oversized horn-rimmed glasses emphasizing wild eyes. His death simply enhanced the growing reputation of rock and roll as it bludgeoned itself onto expectant post-war baby boomers and into a burgeoning teenage market. Buddy Holly's songs "That'll Be the Day" and "Rave On" ideally suited his unique style of singing. I thought he had permanent hiccups, except "That'll be the day-ay-ay that I die" still made it into the Top Ten. It reached Top of the Pops, a recent innovation shown on black and white television, and it accompanied Bill Haley and the Comets who "Rocked Around the Clock". Bill Haley could not be described as a teenager, since he was an overweight middle-aged man. His head was sparsely covered in hair with what was described as a kiss curl hanging over his high forehead. Some people said he could sing, while others, including me, said he made a lot of noise. There was only one rock singer the others were trying to emulate, that was Elvis Presley. He became known as the King of Rock and Roll. Multitudes of impersonators leaped about the stage thrashing guitar strings and were attempting to influence and change the cultural standard of music around the world.

At about the same time, a major motor vehicle manufacturing company, Austin and Morris, launched a new concept car. The Mini became an icon to rival every small car on the market. This name even influenced the way clothes designers described women's clothing in the following years. Not only did garment manufacturers produce a miniskirt, by the following year alternative fashion designers produced a micro mini. This latest female apparel competed directly with the miniskirt. The mini represented a moderate if negligible level of decorum in dress sense compared with the micro mini. That fashion garment permitted any person walking behind to view the female's buttocks. Naturally, the female gender felt obliged to rebel as much as their counterparts who rode motor bikes and called themselves Rockers. These young men rode big, British built bikes under the flag names of Triumph, Matchless, Norton, Velocette and BSA among many others. Riding on a pillion seat, the moll was always held in high esteem within the ranks of insurgent males. Whilst helmets had not reached the compulsory stage in legislation, leather jackets with superimposed lettering did. This included an illuminated painting of a skull and crossbones on the back, which constituted a rudimentary detail for gang identification. Naturally, if one had a moll dressed in a micro mini on the pillion seat, one gained higher accolades from one's acquaintances or gang members.

While all that was going on, Harold Macmillan contended with a cod war between English fishermen and their competitors in Icelandic waters. When the British Navy intervened, brandishing shotguns, malicious attempts at sinking each other's fishing boats and cutting nets actually stopped.

In England there were over six hundred thousand people unemployed. I naturally assumed most were either ex-services personnel because the war had been over for some time and they had nothing to do, and there were thousands of refugees seeking employment. A lot of them lived in and around Corsham. In fact, Uncle Willy claimed he was one. Any permanent industrial work was located in large cities like London, Coventry, Liverpool, Manchester, Plymouth and Birmingham. These places were rebuilding factories and houses, which were a priority. Those of us in the peripheries, we country yokels, were left to get by as best we could. Actually, all country folk have always been able to get by very well without lumbering dorks from cities getting in the way.

As already mentioned, unfortunately for my brother Fred, God gave him a hole in the heart before he was born. I took him to Hawthorn Cinema in a pushchair and although it was a two-mile hike, most of the journey was downhill. Getting to the pictures across derelict ground was easy. Negotiating the pushchair around clumps of overgrown earth and potholes at speed was exciting for both of us. Returning uphill via the shortcut, however, was another matter. After our arrival at the cinema, the usher looked after the pram while Fred and I watched Flash Gordon flying rockets and saving the earth from alien invasion. Nothing much has changed in that continuum of human entertainment although the special effects have improved dramatically since those early days. Flash Gordon's rocket looked like a rocket and it landed on a distant planet that looked identical to Weston-super-Mare's beach with the tide out.

After leaving school, Laura acquired a job as a waitress at Sandridge Park Hotel just outside Melksham. The hotel was built on top of a hill and surrounded by extensive lawns, rose gardens and trees. It can best be described as the elegant proportions of a mansion and owned by a graceful Lady, but eventually closed down, allegedly due to poor financial administration. Things were tough all round and everyone suffered to some degree during those intermediate years.

Uncle Willy, who arrived at our house as a lodger, came from a place called Silesia, which he claimed was part of Poland. There was some disagreement about that declaration, particularly from Germany. Since, from what I can recall, Silesia was their primary reason for starting the Second World War. Nonetheless, whomever it was supposed to belong, it ended up in German hands and according to Uncle, if one could not speak their language or worked in their coalmines, you didn't eat. He also claimed to have escaped from the German Army after storm troops invaded his country. Much to their credit for tenacity, they managed to conscript him into their army and made him fight on their side. Any show of resistance to orders was suppressed by a threat of sending him to the Russian front. Uncle knew the Russians and what kind of people they were. The thought of campaigning against them was something he did not look forward to. That idea kept him in line. He clicked his heels and saluted anyone who looked like a German, sounded like he might be a German, was wearing a German uniform or what might have been a German uniform. That's what he told me. In reality, Uncle was not particularly good soldierly material. In fact, he used to brag about how several hundred rounds of ammunition, supplied by the Germans, were used for target practice. This practice was carried out on a bridge he had been subjected to guard when no one else was around. Punching holes through steel-reinforced girders with German bullets was his way of getting back at them and the bridge could not shoot back. Apart from that, he was more of a poacher than anything. He resented the fact that Germany not only invaded his country but set up an administration which conscripted him into the Wehrmacht. I've never been able to figure out how they did that. At the first opportunity, Uncle Willy stuck his hands into the air and became incarcerated by the liberators. He never knew whom he surrendered to but when they took him away from the fighting and any possibility of confronting die-hard communists, he couldn't care less. Uncle Willy was sent to England as a person in exile being hunted by the Gestapo. I've never been able to figure out how he managed that either.

After moving from Lypiatt Camp to Rudloe Estate, Hawthorn, just outside Corsham, I attended Corsham Secondary Modern. That big modern building contained more than its fair share of rowdy students. One teacher, a Mister Macy, was beaten up for giving one of his students a hundred lines for talking in class. The delinquent student informed his big brother of the punishment but neglected to disclose the mitigating circumstances. Needless to say, his elder brother was a hard-nosed rocker who rode a Triumph Bonneville and confronted the teacher one dark stormy night, beat seven bells of shit out of him and threw him down a flight of stairs. Our heroic teacher ended up with numerous bruises, lacerations and a broken leg. Retribution, however, was not carried out after he left hospital. According to him, the hostile assailant was wearing a helmet and visor and therefore could not be recognized.

The educational institution had a pretty tough reputation by any standards with severe punishment administered to students by a special instrument called a cane. Six whacks across a bum stretched tight by bending over bloody hurts. Take my word for it. The idea of stuffing paper inside one's pants doesn't work. A Yellow Pages phone book, borrowed from a public phone box, is obvious enough for a blind teacher to spot. The best method of reducing pain, providing one received advance warning, was wearing two pairs of pants. Regardless of the torture and method of dispensing it, no pupil ever found a way of winning. If one was humiliated into crying in front of classmates, male students labelled you a wimp although some compensation came in the form of sympathy provided by the girls. However, on the upside, the teacher who dispensed such punishment felt he'd done a good job. If one refrained from crying, both genders of classmates considered you a tough guy, but the teacher felt deprived. This prompted him into giving a little extra effort in the last strokes to extract a tearful ending.

One schoolmate of mine had to take six of the best across his hand for something he adamantly denied doing. His strenuous denials caused his face to redden and eyes bulge. He quite obviously had a very low pain threshold. Fear of it and the thought of being punished for something he had not done showed on his face. Getting him to stand still with his hand out was a protracted affair consisting of teacher yelling and student protesting.

Actually I did the dirty deed, flicking a pellet of chewing gum at the teacher and scoring a direct hit on the back of the head felt exceptionally good but to hell with accepting punishment if it was administered to someone else. Some students called me sneaky for not owning up. Any disparaging remarks were confirmed by admitting my cowardice and sneaky nature while at the same time keeping my nose in the air.

The innocent managed to avoid several attempts of the teacher's cane to make contact by withdrawing his hand whilst the cane was descending. There were repeated whooshing sounds without a sudden smack, which annoyed the teacher. It seemed I was not the only sneaky coward in the room. This naturally amused the class, infuriated the art teacher and resulted in my friend having to bend over. For those who do not know, it is impossible to avoid the stinging punishment from a slender bamboo across one's buttocks while touching one's toes.

That barbaric method was intended to impress other students what happened if they were up for punishment. In any event that procedure became transferred to the privacy of a headmaster's office. Thus the infamous threatening remark, "If you don't behave I'll send you to the headmaster's office," evolved. Everyone knew what that meant. The adult world perpetuates its power over underlings by using threats. Not much has changed in that hemisphere of life.

Christmas has always been a time of cheer and goodwill to all men. The festive season, however, contains many opportunities for taking advantage of kind-hearted people. Teachers commended the act of singing carols in the town square under a Christmas tree to collect funds for charities. Conversely, they didn't condone the act of carol singing at people's doors to collect money, in their opinion it constituted nothing more than begging. As it happens, I went begging at every available opportunity. Singing carols five days before Christmas usually gave one the drop on those who followed. My philosophies at the time included, get in first and if you can't win fair and square cheat until you do. When one had friends to accompany any pre-emptive deed it provided an assurance and a measure of safety in numbers should any inadvertent competition be met.

John Pilchard (Kipper) lived in Boxfields, about a mile away from my home. He was a solidly built youth with ginger hair. With a combination of having such a ridiculous surname and ginger hair, he could not avoid being called Kipper and became my best friend. Our friendship survived, despite his mother's persistent directives that he was not permitted to associate with me and called me a disreputable reprobate, whatever that meant. John's parents were separated and as an only son, he became a mummy's boy. On reflection, his faults were perpetrated by parental guidance and in due time I managed to influence his good nature into following an alternative course. One must take into consideration it's what he really wanted anyway, so it really wasn't my fault.

Anthony Corbyn

Laurence Lofters (Lofty) lived at the end of our terraced block and no genius was required to figure out where his nickname came from. He had five younger brothers, which meant there were eight in the family. Dear God in heaven help us all, there were eight Lofterses, eight! That excessive number kept them in the poorhouse. Mister Lofters was an unemployed builder's labourer who could do nothing better to occupy his time. He decided to keep procreating siblings until his wife produced a girl. I honestly thought they were either doing something wrong or were Catholics. Everyone knew Catholics were forbidden to use artificial birth control methods. Condoms were not allowed but Catholic roulette was. I did not have a proper understanding of that expression until much later. Although, at the time, everyone knew Catholic roulette was a very risky business and closely resembled Russian roulette. However, regardless of which roulette game was being played, the use of condoms or birth control pills was not permitted. According to the Catholic faith it constituted an act of depriving life to exist before it was given the chance of being born. That would be a mortal sin. On the other hand, it provided the world with lots of hungry mouths to feed, which was okay because they would all be good Catholics.

"God will punish those who commit such an abomination. For such a repugnant act he will condemn your soul to burn in the eternal fires of hell." Father Sullivan, a rotund Catholic priest mentioned earlier, conveyed this message vehemently during one of his sermons before describing what it felt like to burn for eternity. Apparently, it's the same feeling one gets when you burn your finger with a match. "That's the feeling you get all over your body, forever and ever, for eternity and it never ends." His Irish accent boomed through the small Catholic church. Heavy wooden pillars supporting the tower vibrated. Pictures of Christ's twelve stations to his crucifixion rattled against the walls. A pungent scent of frankincense filled everyone's lungs. Hearts beat faster. There were no doubts in my mind, from the way several of that kneeling congregation were clutching their hands together and praying faster than anyone else, they must have committed that dreaded sin. Without wishing to cause any alarm or despon-

Nights in the Forest

dency to the faithful, I refrained from asking Father Sullivan how he knew because I never saw anyone stand up in church to query a priest's oration. Apart from that, I always thought a soul couldn't feel pain. The Catholic clergy has an uncompromisingly powerful grip on its followers. Fear and wonder keep us all in check.

Dave Clark (not to be confused with Dave Clark from the Dave Clark Five) was also known as Clarky. The simplistic addition of a "y" to his surname provided my next-door neighbour with a nickname. He had two sisters and like myself, came from a broken home. One would think with such similar family circumstances he could be trusted, although, when it came right down to it, Dave let me down. Being sneaky was one thing, being a traitor was something else.

Vladimir Kalousek (Vlad), he never had a nickname just an abbreviated Christian name. Vlad was a tall blond youth who also came from a large family and yet another refugee from Czechoslovakia. He also belonged to the remains of another broken family because, according to him, when the Red Army "liberated" his country they shot his dad, before his mother, two sisters and a brother escaped to England for their own safety. Vlad couldn't recall why the Russians shot his father. This gave the rest of us plenty of room to hypothesize. Freedom fighter, assassin, spy, in the wrong army, wrong place at the wrong time, mistaken identity or an accident were a few of the speculative thoughts that came to mind.

All five of us went round the estate singing carols. This was specifically to collect money so we could purchase pint bottles of Ushers Brown Ale from the British Legion Club. If one knew the bartender, he never asked who the beer was for because it meant listening to a lie. That would have been true except one has to take several circumstances into consideration. Most of us did not have a father and Uncle Willy would rather die than drink brown ale. He made his own Polish spirit and therefore, telling the bartender it was for my father would have been a double lie. There was no father, it was for me. Only one friend had a father, who was unemployed and unable to afford buying beer anyway.

Anthony Corbyn

"Silent Night" and "The Twelve Days of Christmas" was usually followed by a chorus or two of "Christmas Is Coming" while rattling a collection box under the noses of any person listening, to induce some sort of payment. This worked for a variety of reasons, not the least of which was the out of tune singing and rattling coins in a rusty baked bean tin. Any hesitation from the house owner simply provoked louder singing and harder rattling of copper coins against tin.

> Christmas is coming, the goose is getting fat
> Please put a penny in the old man's hat
> If you haven't got a penny, a ha'penny will do
> If you haven't got a ha'penny, then God bless you!

Much later I discovered what significance a goose had in that Christmas carol. It seems geese had been traditional English Christmas fare on the table before gobble, gobble turkey came along. It goes without saying that one or two derogatory words became incorporated into the last lyrics, particularly after a couple of illicit brown ales.

Doctor Westfield, our family practitioner, was an ex-military medic reputedly accustomed to pulling bullets out of wounded soldiers with his fingers. That was no surprise, since he considered pain as something people suffered from and couldn't possibly be attributed to anything he might be doing to them. Any expression of discomfort one became subjected to by his hands usually brought about a dismissive "Pooh, pooh." Doctor Westfield is mentioned at this point because he was directly linked with mother's method of cooking and a related excruciatingly painful experience of mine.

The electric meter at home took coins – pennies, threepenny bits or sixpences. It actually took a shilling coin if one could ever be found. In effect, that meter took almost anything round and shiny. There were occasions when Uncle Willy attempted obtaining free electricity by using shiny washers. He even fashioned a steel pipe with the same inner diameter of a shilling. The idea was to punch out a series of round, shilling-sized pieces of steel and feed them into the meter. It never worked but not for the want of trying. Whenever the electric meter collector mentioned that an inordinate number of illegal coins in the shape of washers and distorted rounds of steel had been discovered in the meter, Uncle would jabber in Polish and mother carried out an equally incomprehensible conversation in Maltese. The bemused look on that meter man's face always made me smile. Whenever washers of the right configuration were not available, mother remained on constant lookout for precious coins. If these were unavailable she used a paraffin heater close to the kitchen door to cook on. There was only enough room for one pot and almost certainly the reason why a solitary pot of stew claimed a dominant role in any cooking schedule during winter. Summer feeding consisted of sandwiches or bread and dripping made from fatty, cheap cuts of beef purchased from L.R. Love & Son, the town butcher. I particularly liked the dark, jelly-like substance that settled on the bottom of the pan. Although it contained less fat, it was saltier and much tastier.

Exiting our kitchen into the backyard became a very hazardous affair. There wasn't much room in such a small kitchen and it compounded my failed attempt to bypass that heater. The contents of a pot of simmering stew splattered down the calf of my right leg. I could describe the pain except words fail me as they did at the time. A long howl, similar to a wolf that had just been shot up the bum, would be closest to a description as makes no odds.

Doctor Westfield rushed round the same day to dress my wound with a dry dressing and while he attended this wounded hero, mother was busy making hot sweet tea for everyone. This, according to mother, is a formula, generally known as a method, of calming people suffering from shock. Meantime, our next-door neighbour, the mother of Dave Clark, otherwise known as Clarky and not to be confused with the pop singing leader of the group named after him, had a perverted interest in everyone else's business and tut-tutted our good doctor's philosophy of dry dressings. She made numerous suggestions of smothering the partially cooked flesh with beef dripping, butter, margarine or cooking oil.

From her descriptions one imagined she was basting a lump of beef rotating on a spit. Her unwanted interruptions were dismissed by our infamous family doctor as old wives' tales. Somebody should have told Westfield that many of those old women knew what they were talking about.

Within a couple of days my dry dressing became congealed with blood, hair, burned skin and flesh. That didn't deter Doctor Westfield, oh no! He smiled knowingly at the expected result of his handiwork, grasped one end of the dressing firmly in his fist and ripped it away with what he described as, "One quick, painless flick of the wrist." That flick may have been painless to him but it hurt me like those burning fires of hell Father Sullivan warned his congregation about. A breathtaking scream would be a mild description of my reaction to that episode. Not to mention a variety of crude swear words I directed toward the perpetrator of such deliberately inflicted pain. The old women's message must have got through because a fresh dressing on the open wound was wrapped over a thick layer of antiseptic cream. Nonetheless, I still cringe at the thought of removing a Band Aid.

Chapter Two

A Juvenile Delinquent

The entire problem wasn't my fault. People who didn't know and understand me were prone to exaggerating the troublesome reputation I acquired. These people included parents, teachers and other grown-ups, particularly those in authority. Their lives obviously centred on putting every rebellious child in its proper place. Whilst that may have sounded very mature, I was never able to figure out where that place was, other than being seen and not heard because it's what dad used to say all the time. Most things I got up to were never out of a desire to deliberately hurt anyone, although once in a while it became necessary to carry out revenge attacks. However, that particular response was always carried out in a justified cause. Adults, politicians and those in authority frequently use similar kinds of reactions to excuse their actions.

On one particular day in question I hadn't gone far, just down the road, across a field and up a tree. Everyone knows, any rebellious juvenile delinquent running away from home, usually causes concern to parents, mayhem and full-scale searches. My escapades always did. It was tremendous fun watching the goings on from my lofty hideout.

There were lots of people involved in the scenario including other parents, a number of army personnel and several policemen. The searchers were spread out in an extended line. They trudged across the sopping wet open fields known as Knapp's Farm while calling my name. That struck me as very odd. Why should I answer? At that moment in time, my sole purpose in life was in avoiding contact with anybody whilst enjoying a newly established freedom. On the other hand, I acquired a tremendous sense of achievement in gaining so much attention. After about an hour up the tree I began thinking of food. Apart from that it became terribly uncomfortable sitting on a branch. During such a short stay up that tree I learned a very valuable lesson in life and reflected on my days in the Wolf Cubs while living in Germany. The Cub motto was memorised by verbally repeating it over and over while standing to attention in a group and giving the two-fingered salute.

> Dib dib dib. Dob dob dob.
> I promise to Do My Best.
> To do my duty to God, and the Queen,
> To keep the Law of the Wolf Cub Pack,
> and to do a good turn to somebody every day.

Whenever contemplating a journey, for whatever reason, be prepared. After all, it's the best rule of any Boy Scout or Cub that's worth remembering.

My so-called unruly appearance, uncontrollable and disruptive nature advanced to a stage where authorities warned mother that one day men in white coats would come and take me away. Many adults who came to visit predicted the same ending. I scoffed at their ideas of self-discipline by giving them a universally known gesture. My defiance simply confirmed the predictions our neighbours had been making for some time. They were a bunch of self-righteous individuals who acquired their pleasures and amusements from seeing someone fall down. I have never been able to understand people who jumped up and down shouting, "I told you so." Many adults informed me that self-praise is no recommendation. Nevertheless, the know-alls were happy they finally got something right.

The houses at Rudloe Estate were constructed in much the same way as the ones at Lypiatt, concrete block walls with asbestos roofs. They were identical to every house built by the military, with no central heating, just a tiny pot-bellied stove in the front room. Concrete floors were covered with lino and small, thinly woven rugs beside the bed were used for stepping onto in the morning. If a fire wasn't lit, the air became damp with condensation forming on walls and windows. However, cold winter days had their compensations and these included sharing a bed with a warm companion and the decimation of insects.

Arachnophobia is not something I'd wish on my worst enemy. Spiders have always given me the creeps but freezing cold winters provided the advantage of killing them off. Except, summer months countered any effect of coldness by allowing, even promoting those horrible creatures to breed faster. Any big, brown, hairy house spiders reduced their life expectancy whenever they appeared within range of my shoe or rolled-up newspaper. Life for me became an undulating sense of fear and pleasure according to the season.

Mother purchased a small, second-hand single bar electric heater. A solitary penny slotted into the meter didn't last long when that thing was on. Any visitor would be gently harassed into parting with a spare copper or two. Mother perfected her search for non-existent personal money to the point where a visitor would make offers mum found hard to refuse. "Oh no, the electricity has run out and there is no money left, what are we going to do. It is so cold!" mum would exclaim.

Our visitors would cringe and pull scarves a little tighter round their necks as mother made furtive attempts looking for money. There would be intermittent apologies until the visitor said, "Josie, if you don't mind my helping, I do have a spare sixpence."

The gleaming sixpence coin would be taken post haste and popped into the meter while mum pronounced a place in heaven waited for such generous-hearted people. It meant another couple of hours keeping warm by hovering over the heater. The coldest winter nights saw everyone congregated in the front room. We surrounded a fire in that pot-bellied stove while listening to the radio. A large teapot stood on the stove to keep its contents and us warm. Body warmth was shared with any member of the family one hadn't argued with. The only double bed in the house was moved into the front room and everyone piled onto it. Although classified as a double, at a pinch, everyone could be accommodated comfortably under a layer of threadbare ex-army blankets. On really cold winter nights, when the fire had gone out and there was no more firewood or coke, those thin concrete walls were unable to retain any residual heat, so we dressed for bed. My recollections are of freezing nights when my only consolation, due to an unforgivable misdemeanour with a fellow family member, was an extra pullover. The cold weather became a huge incentive to stay friendly with members of the family one would have been happier to see dead.

Mother and Uncle were of the old school. They believed in old-fashioned remedies handed down by grandmothers, grandfathers and anyone from the ancient world. If a member of our family suffered from a cough, head cold or bronchitis, with Grim Reaper knocking at the door, an old folk remedy was called upon. One such treatment included deep breathing of peeled onion fumes. It not only cleared the nose by making it run like mad and opened bronchial tubes by making one gasp for clean air, it also made one's eyes water like a tap.

Any good Christian will tell you, Sunday is a day of rest. It's when people go to church, go fishing, go on picnics or mooch around the house and generally take things easy. Sunday also meant listening to a weekly compilation of The Archers, an everyday story of country folk, big band music or Mario Lanza singing on the radio. Televisions were expensive, they were few and far between, which, for normal people, meant entertainment came from conversation, playing board games or listening to one's favourite program on the radio. In my case, going on a hunting trip, fishing and swimming filled long sunny days. I have always been in favour of Sunday, which became a habit developed with dedication. The priority was in having a long lie-in till late morning or perhaps early afternoon if the fancy took me. One particular Sunday I was accompanying Bill Haley singing "Rock Around the Clock" while mother fussed about doing housework.

> Put your glad rags on and join me, hon
> We'll have some fun when the clock strikes one
> We're gonna rock around the clock tonight
> ...

Nights in the Forest

It wasn't even midday when mum cut short my accompaniment by shouting, "Get out of bed, you lazy little sod!"

I found that instruction difficult to understand. What should I do after getting out of bed? Everybody knew it was Sunday, surely that meant a day of rest. My quotation from the bible regarding God taking the seventh day off made little difference. Mother continued badgering me to get up.

During such a rebellious stage, friends, including adults, considered it dangerous to provoke an almost fourteen-year-old hooligan. In spite of that well-known fact, mother wasn't scared of a skinny little runt like me who, as she kept shouting at the top of her voice, was also a lazy little sod. Verbal abuses were piled on physical threats, all to no avail. I responded by rolling over whilst muttering a mild obscenity, which resulted in a very uncharacteristic violent reaction from mum. I had no idea she could muster so much strength in her throwing arm. Had I remained under the blanket, that hidden power would never have been revealed. After raising myself onto an elbow to protest at so much verbal abuse, a solid brass ashtray, all the way from Egypt, left mother's hand. The intended target had been the wall, so she told me later. Nevertheless, my surfacing came just in time to obstruct its flight path with my head.

The noise it created by crashing against the skull caused my brain to disintegrate into hypothetical fragments and was the reason my ears rang all day. The reason for my outburst can definitely be attributed to the pain. Nonetheless, for some reason, most people rarely want to hear a hooligan's side of the story. All they were interested in was why he smashed a window then discharged a shotgun with the intention of killing his mother beating a hasty retreat across the playing field. It's amazing how a simple thing like losing one's temper can be blown out of proportion. Elders have never been able to tolerate that sort of activity by a juvenile.

When that meteoritic flight of a brass ashtray collided with my forehead I screamed in pained surprise and added something about killing. People say it all the time with their intentions being no more than to scare one another. It doesn't actually mean they'll carry out their threat. Mother didn't hang around to discover what might happen. She saw me, screaming like a deranged lunatic with blood running down my forehead over an eyelid and onto my face while loading a small bore shotgun, and took me at my word. Her short legs began performing like pistons. True to the Wild West method seen in movies, I smashed my bedroom window with the shotgun butt before swinging its barrel through and firing into the air. By copying a cowboy's technique of displaying angry determination, it seems several by-laws were inadvertently broken at the same time as my bedroom window. These included, discharging a shotgun in a built-up area, pointing a weapon with intent to cause bodily harm or alarm and despondency, scaring the shit out of neighbours, wilful damage to property and showing no remorse to a distraught mother. Who, as someone informed me later, required numerous cups of strong sweet tea to calm shattered nerves. Of course I was remorseful but wasn't given the opportunity to say sorry.

Long before the police arrived, my school satchel was packed with a half loaf of stale bread, an almost full bottle of milk, box of matches, a tin of baked beans and an opened jar of jam without a golly stuck to it. Robinson's strawberry jam has always been my favourite. The remaining shotgun cartridges were stuffed into a pocket before a bow and quiver of arrows were slung over my shoulder. On the way out, my hand, which had a will of its own, grabbed a tin of Uncle's Old Holborn tobacco. True to the Cub Scouts' motto, I was prepared and set off at a run.

With the essentials for survival clasped closely under one arm, I headed for Wyvern Valley and the forest. Once there, an army couldn't find me and I put as much distance between myself and home as quickly as possible. On reaching Top Wood that grew along the main A4 road connecting Bath to London, my pace slowed to a steady jog. I opted for being on the run again, although this time better prepared and totally confident my hunting skills would see me through for however long they were required. My outburst on that occasion was far more serious than usual; nonetheless, given a little time, things would cool down. I reasoned everything should return to normal very quickly. Well, normal as possible under the circumstances.

Once inside the forest, safety felt assured. It represented a domain, a sanctuary where mind and body were at ease and one with nature. Left to my own devices among the trees, retaining self-control became easy and during late summer, the nights were warm. And from an abundance of game spotted during my trek toward the forest, the hunting would be good.

Soon after entering the forest I found myself heading down a long narrow lane toward Penny Pool, my favourite hideout when escaping from people. An overhanging canopy provided shade in that long meandering tunnel and it was followed until I stood still on a small stone bridge. A shallow clear stream ran underneath and trickled over a waterfall that spilled into deeper pools of water below. It was such a wonderful place, a feeling of freedom, of being alive and ready to take on the world swept over me. I sucked several deep breaths while taking in the surroundings. A fresh scent of lush grass mingled with flower blossoms. Deep in the valley there stood what remained of a dilapidated farm building everyone described as "the haunted farmhouse". In reality, it was just a broken-down, two-story building used as a barn to store hay. After moving across the bridge to a cluster of trees nearby, I checked to see if my fishing poles were still there. It wasn't the best time of day for fishing, which left nothing better to occupy myself with than settle down, rest and contemplate my dilemma.

First things first, time to take stock and work out how long it would be possible to remain hidden. I saw no reason why my meagre food supply couldn't be supplemented by hunting, so long as the ammunition lasted. My mind reflected on an alternative weapon to hunt with. More arrows could be made and some practice with the bow was needed to sharpen any skills in that area. There would also be fishing at the right time of day. "Ha!" I exclaimed quietly to myself. I saw no reason why an indefinite period of hiding couldn't be maintained. After all, I was a self-sufficient person who could hunt.

Anthony Corbyn

After cleaning the .410, counting ammo, checking the bow string and arrows in the quiver, I withdrew my multi-purpose hatchet from its sheath and set about cutting hazelnut stalks to make a few more. There were plenty to choose from and it simply remained a question of selecting straight ones with the right weight and thickness. A Bowie knife was used to strip off any bark and sharpen one end. At the other end, a small recess was cut to secure the bowstring. By late afternoon my total supply of arrows had grown to more than a dozen. With shafts cleaned and points hardened in fire before being weighted with fence wire wrapped tightly into a recess, they were ready and so was I. There were no materials for constructing flights, although the same method of production proved very successful in the past.

The time came to bait some fishing lines before dropping them into the stream, have a bite to eat, and then look for shelter. I had already checked where the fishing poles were left last time when prevailing circumstances prompted me to take a quick break. I put the bottle of milk in the stream to keep cool then set about building myself a lean-to from small branches interlaced with ferns.

Gnats always mustered in swarms once dusk fell, so the lean-to was built close to the fire. This allowed wisps of smoke to filter through the shelter and keep those damn insects away. With the shelter completed I crawled into my primitive refuge. By staying low and covering myself with a blanket of ferns it was almost comfortable. Recollections of the last time an escapade prompted my escape to the forest, rain made it absolutely awful. It was wet and miserable with torrents of rainwater cascading from dark grey skies soaking me to the skin. Mother's big, floppy, hand knitted woollen jumper made from hand-me-downs proved useless in keeping me dry. Waterproof garments like a gabardine mackintosh were items of attire made for rich people. Mother always recycled clothing too small to fit the youngest member of our family. Unravelling woollen garments before balling up the strands and knitting an alternative jumper big enough to fit an older offspring did this. Hand-me-downs that reached the end of their recycling life were also used. Some long-sleeved jumpers had the arms removed and the wool used to extend the length. One usually ended up with a sleeveless pullover for summer constructed from a winter jumper. On the other hand, or should I say "foot", shoes were a different kettle of fish altogether. A conflict of wearing shoes belonging to siblings that consisted of mixed genders occurred because there was no way anyone would see me wearing a pair of my sisters' strapless low heels. Contributions came from relatives, neighbours and second-hand shops and that usually put things right. It should be noted at this stage, that shoes were a major contribution to the poor condition of my feet, particularly the smallest toe. It acquired a resting place on top of the adjoining appendage to fit within the confines imposed upon it by ill-fitting, second-hand footwear.

Darkness arrives quickly in a forest. Noises from its inhabitants steadily become subdued until all is silent. It's at that moment realization dawned of being totally alone. During an extended silence, a feeling of aloneness overcame me. It was time to comprehend the seriousness of my actions while wondering what was happening back home. The main consideration invading a number of confused thoughts included, when would the inevitable search party come looking for me? The only comfort was a certainty it wouldn't happen till morning. My solitude would remain undisturbed until then. That thought pleased me and contributed to feeling relaxed. From my position under a pile of ferns I stared into flickering flames inside a hole dug for the fire. For a few moments my lungs filled with fresh, clean, cool evening air. The only contaminant came from slow burning wood producing an excellent accompaniment of sweet-smelling aroma. I closed my eyes. Concerns for the future were swept aside. Sleep came easy because the forest provided me with everything including security. During the night, I dreamed of a successful hunt that replenished a dwindling food supply. A juicy fat rabbit and a pair of pigeons were prepared and roasted slowly over an open fire. During the early hours I roused from sleep to feed the fire with just enough fuel to keep it smouldering without a flame. In the morning things would be different. Any smoke would reveal my position by providing a clear indication to the searchers where they could find me.

A pre-dawn chorus woke me with a sense of relaxed joy. My mind's eye registered each bird's position. The distinct sound of a pheasant quickened my heart in the knowledge it would soon be hunted. Imagination substituted the dream of that rabbit and pictured a pheasant's carcass rotating over a fire. I could almost smell the aroma of its gently cooked, soft, game-flavoured meat. Dinner would be a feast fit for the gentry. The only thing I needed to do was to catch it. I remained still in the darkness watching millions of stars disappearing while listening to an increasing volume of bird song until it was time to get up. I stretched slowly, and then kicked the pile of ferns away after emerging from my lair. The fire needed stoking into flame before I washed in the stream and made preparations for some early morning fishing.

Rusty fishing hooks were baited with bread paste and then lowered into the stream before I examined some traps made from old nylon stockings. One stocking was laid flat on the river bed with its wide neck held open by a circle made from a wire coat hanger. It would lie there until a fish swam over the circle. When that happened, it would be scooped up. The second stocking was stretched over a series of wire rings and remained suspended in a deeper part of the stream like a windsock. When any fish swam in, they became trapped in the foot, couldn't swim out and became something to eat. There weren't many fish caught with either trap but it didn't matter. Any number, no matter what size, tasted good when hunger knocked at the door.

By the time both traps were set, the fire burned fiercely and ready to cook a breakfast of toasted bread smothered in strawberry jam with a drink of cool milk. A cigarette complemented my first meal of the day. After smoking a roll-up, the milk bottle was replaced in the stream to keep its contents cool. An early morning sun peeked at me over the horizon and began warming my relaxed body. There was little, if anything to do but relax and enjoy the simple pleasures of life. I breathed in a musty forest floor aroma being warmed by an early morning rise in temperature, then fished and daydreamed of the luxurious lifestyle I wanted to become accustomed to. One visualized lazing back and being fed by a diminutive, very beautiful submissive female. Going hunting and swimming whenever I wanted was another. Not going to school ever again seemed like a good idea. Being rich would help. All I had to do was discover a hidden treasure chest full of gold. My imagination had no problem seeing a huge ironclad treasure chest being opened to display mountains of precious jewels. The purpose of life was to live it, that alternative idea worked its way into my brain and pushed all other thoughts aside. My fingers were unconsciously preparing another roll-up. I smoked while an alert mind meandered across a variety of alternatives. Despite those relaxing conditions promoting a sense of lethargy, my eyes remained on constant alert. They wandered along horizontal tree limbs and over forest floor covering noting their condition while ever watchful for game. Time passed slowly, my second cigarette was pressed into the earth. Thoughts pondered on it being time for those expected search parties and I speculated on which direction they were bound to come from.

Under normal circumstances, time and date were never a significant factor. Seasons were far more important. Nevertheless, I worked out what day it was. My current predicament started because of mother's Sunday morning ritual. The one day when everyone was home appeared the only time she set about the housework. Her busy bee attitude normally started with humming an unrecognisable song. As the work progressed, mother became more irritable. The humming would stutter to a stop and Maltese mutterings would ensue. Tiredness and lack of stopping for the obligatory tea break would compound her irritability. Not getting any help from a lazy son usually set the cat among the pigeons. A simmering temper would erupt like a volcano. It seemed reasonable to conclude it must be Monday morning. The recent incident seemed so far away it faded out of context. I wondered if the search party would have a day out looking for me. Maybe they'd leave me alone for a day. Let me stew in my own juices, as they say. In any event, the mystery remained, why should anyone come looking? Why attempt to capture me and force my return home?

All they had to do was wait. Given time, I always returned. It would save the authorities an awful lot of time, effort and money. My opinion of grown-ups could be summed up in three words. They're all daft!

During late summer, blackberries always formed with many ripe enough to eat. Hazelnut bushes were loaded with underdeveloped nuts, yet still worth collecting. My food gathering morning passed quickly. Whilst moving from hazelnut tree to blackberry bush, I made a selection and stored the gathered food in a school satchel. An occasional big juicy berry was popped into a grateful mouth and consumed with relish. Back at the campsite, two fish traps had been laid and although I remained hopeful, didn't expect to catch any.

Several times during my foraging expedition, I crouched close to the ground or took cover before slipping the shotgun off my shoulder and came up at the ready. On each occasion, any game took flight before the range could be closed. My attitude toward those disappointments was philosophical. I shrugged before continuing with fruit and nut picking until my bag was full. With that initial task accomplished, I returned to camp. The fire continued smouldering without much smoke and I sat down to enjoy some nuts and berries after checking the traps. There wouldn't be any fish on the à la carte menu for lunch and any expectations of that happening didn't amount to much anyway.

Green hazelnuts are easy to crack open with one's teeth and although they were very small, each one tasted sweeter than honey. Conversely the blackberries were still a bit sharp. Nonetheless, it was good to relax in the shade by a small campfire, enjoying the fruits nature provided. Meantime, the empty milk bottle was washed out, refilled with water and placed beside the fire. Lunch had been satisfactory. I relaxed in the sun while enjoying another cigarette, although my senses remained alert. Suddenly, voices in the distance echoed across the valley.

The sounds prompted a primitive animal instinct to take over. I scrambled about the campsite and poured that bottle of water onto the fire. It produced a hiss followed by a puff of ash-laden steam. A pungent smell of wet ashes masked the musky forest scent as that small pile of earth beside the fire was used to fill in the hole. My foot compressed loose soil tightly into the hole. No residual smoke was escaping. A swift kick at the heap of floor covering eliminated any visual appearance of where the fire had been. I set about spreading the lean-to around until nothing looked unusual. The fishing poles and traps were retrieved, then hidden and my school satchel was packed with any remaining possessions before I used the trees for cover while moving toward the voices.

It may seem odd that someone on the run should move closer to his pursuers. In my view, if I could watch whoever was looking for me, they were less likely to find me. For the next two hours a couple of young constables trudged about the valley in heavy boots. Their dark blue uniforms contrasted sharply with a variety of pale and dark green foliage. They were intermittently calling my name, which seemed pretty stupid for reasons I've already explained.

After two hours following the hunters, boredom set in. It also looked as though the policemen were about to give up looking for me and go home; at that point a devil inside rose to the surface. Whilst crouching behind a tree in the undergrowth I eased the straps over my shoulders to make them comfortable. A fly buzzed my face and although it was distracting, I didn't shoo it away or make any sudden moves. After sleeping in outdoor clothing I must have smelled pretty ripe while hunkered down under cover. Both hands were green from tearing up dozens of ferns. The denim jeans felt tight between the legs and irritated to the point of making a promise to have a good all-over wash later. A trickle of sweat ran down my back. I stowed the satchel and belt under a bush before stepping into the open to yell, "What do you want?"

Although some distance off, they were not too far enough away I couldn't see a sense of relief on their faces when they turned round. Both policemen were able to see whom they'd been searching for and could actually include "they saw me" in their report. One took a deep breath before shouting, "Come here!"

My response was to give them a dysfunctional Cub Scouts' salute or, as it is universally known, an intimidating gesture with a very loud raspberry. The constables looked at one another, then at me with my feet apart, one hand on hip with the other holding a shotgun over my shoulder. Before they gave chase someone should have told them it would be a valiant wasted effort for a number of reasons. The least of which, when it came to running, few if any could match me. Especially since all my gear had been unloaded in readiness for the anticipated speedy departure. However, they were duty-bound to try. I led the retreat at a steady pace knowing my pursuers would maintain the chase for some time and therefore I needed to conserve energy. It quickly became obvious they were having a hard time, since those heavy boots ploughing through long grass must have been a real handicap. By contrast, I was suitably attired with lightweight shoes, which provided an ability to lope over undergrowth like a gazelle. There were no doubts in my mind – they'd never be able to catch me.

At the top of a small knoll I watched both constables slip and slide down the river bank, splash their way across shallow water and begin a wholehearted assault on the hill. They slipped and slewed up the muddy bank and were about halfway up before stopping for a breather. Both were in obvious need of some encouragement, so I shouted, "Hey! Come on!" and waved a beckoning hand. That challenge prompted greater effort from them. Nonetheless, however hard they tried, on reaching the top I was out of sight and watching their descent while easing into denser foliage and it looked as though their day had been livened up a bit. After stopping to discuss what options were left, their heavy breathing and comments were clearly audible as they approached.

"Which way?" one policeman asked, as they stood at a narrow crossing in the track.

"Take your pick," the other answered.

"If I catch the little sod, I'll give him a damn good thrashing," the first policeman hissed between gasps of breath. His head swivelled while both eyes traversed the greenery seeking a gap that he could see through. His breathing slowed with his body movements.

Nights in the Forest

"Yeah, well, stand in line," his colleague muttered. His rapid agitated movements were also slowing down. Overhanging branches brushed their pointed helmets. The taller one waved an acrimonious hand at them before removing that dome from his head. A red face looked relieved. They were bending their knees and were shoulder-to-shoulder while moving stealthily along the narrow track. Dense green undergrowth began engulfing two dark blue blobs.

The policemen were getting closer and closer while walking directly toward me. An overstressed heart pounded from the effort of running. Meanwhile a concentrated effort was made to get heavy breathing under control. A bead of salty sweat plopped into my eye and stung. A fly buzzed in my ear before trying to crawl up my nose. With one eye shut, I blew short sharp puffs down my nose but couldn't move a muscle, so hung on. From what the open eye could see, if those policemen came any closer, they'd walk right over me. They stopped just in time, although much too close for comfort.

"I say we call it a day," one said.

"Me too," his colleague replied curtly before adding, "We'll never find him in this place. From the speed he was going he's more than likely on the other side of the forest by now."

A long pause in their conversation followed while a tear escaped from under a closed eyelid and rolled down my face. I held my breath. That inquisitive fly took a windless opportunity to have a look up the other nostril. Something up there must have been attractive. It crept inside. I wanted to sneeze or at the very least blow my nose. The policemen stood a few feet away with hands on hips. They were back-to-back and almost close enough to touch. For all the good it did them, one looked up the track while the other looked down it. The hardest part was in believing they couldn't hear the pounding in my chest. If they stood there for a minute longer I knew they would either hear my nose blowing or my chest exploding.

One finally broke the silence. "Come on, let's go."

A sense of relief swept over me. A throbbing heart began slowing to its normal rhythm; the tear was wiped off my face and that irritating fly brushed away. I watched their slow ambling walk for a minute before breaking cover to follow. At that stage, my considerations centred on all things being equal and enough was enough. But that devil inside wanted satisfaction. The bobbies were about fifty yards away and walking down a long tunnel of overhanging forest canopy when I attracted their attention with "Hey!"

They turned to see me cradling a shotgun. Two dark blue uniforms stood side by side with hands on hips seemingly unwilling to start another chase.

For reasons beyond my understanding, I fired into the air. From the distance they were standing, my small bore shotgun wouldn't punch a hole through tissue paper but neither seemed aware of that. They weren't taking any chances and dived headlong into the bushes. A second later, two helmeted heads popped up like jack-in-the-boxes, ready to give chase in a dramatically changed atmosphere. Anger became a primary factor. I was suddenly aware of the new dimension and turned to run at top speed. I also resorted to leaping across crevasses instead of going round them. Small bushes presented no problems in jumping over, nor were open spaces avoided where swiftness could be gained. I kept going without looking back until it felt safe to slow down. The forest engulfed me safely into its bosom. Gasping for air with sweat covering my body I slowed down. Relaxation took over from anxiety after a feeling of that day's adventure having ended.

Much later I ventured out and cautiously headed to where my satchel and belt were hidden. With the kit retrieved, I returned to my campsite for a cigarette.

Late that afternoon the clear summer skies clouded over whilst previously crisp dry air became oppressively sultry. It felt and looked as though a late summer storm was developing. A scattering of old buildings in the valley was considered for shelter. The so-called old haunted house was nearest, so I made for it. Of all the buildings available, it was the very one that should have been avoided for a night's stopover. Numerous tales of ghosts living within its crumbling walls founded its reputation as a haunted abode. Darkness closed in during my approach to that enormous ramshackle structure. While entering the doorless opening, large spots of rain splattered onto sunbaked dry ground and against my denim jacket. "At least it'll be warm and dry in here," I thought reassuringly while peering into the dimly lit strange smelling interior before moving cautiously through the doorway looking left and right.

As with all abandoned buildings, it had an air of mystery surrounding its interior atmosphere. That sensation was generated by stories and reasons as to why it became abandoned. In the first place the building had a reputation of being haunted, which didn't reduce a powerful sense of foreboding. My belief in ghosts and spirits was intensely solid, partly due to some ghostly experiences while living in Egypt. The Catholic Church also promotes a signing of the cross over one's chest with the express words, "In the name of the Father, Son and Holy Ghost." Father Sullivan's vivid descriptions of hell's eternal fires and stories I heard about the farmhouse would make curly hair go straight before turning grey.

In the extensive front room I looked about for the headless farmer who used to live there before his accident. While pausing in that room's doorway, my eyes pierced a gloomy interior to see bales of yellow straw piled at one end. A sense of relief pervaded my being; there was nothing there but animal feed and bedding. I inhaled the welcome aroma of baled hay. It provided a feeling of well-being. A sudden gust of wind hissed past the back of my head and splattered a shower of rain noisily against the wall. My heart skipped a beat. Hairs on my neck stood on end. I spun round half-expecting to see the fabled headless farmer with his head tucked underneath an arm. Any composure gained in the past ten seconds evaporated in a flash. Renewed fear took a firm grip on shattered emotions. Both bladder and bowels were heeding a call from nature but it was impossible to run with pants wrapped around one's ankles. A strenuous mental and physical effort ensured nature did not have its way. My pants were up, they remained clean and dry, except both legs were trembling like jelly on a plate and threatened to buckle at the knees.

That old farmhouse had been built in a very isolated part of the valley. Its prime condition had deteriorated; it stood without doors or windows, with a partially collapsed roof. Another aspect that didn't help was it being surrounded on three sides by encroaching trees. The crumbling monolith stood in a perfect place for ghosts to happily haunt it without being disturbed. The expression, "If a tree fell in the forest and there was no one there, would it make a sound?" came to mind. It was supplemented by a new interpretation. "If a ghost rattled its chains and there was no human there to listen, would it make a sound?" That thought was set aside very quickly.

Several deep breaths were taken whilst reminding myself not to be stupid by saying, "Nothing in here, nothing to fear. Nothing that wasn't here during daylight," and repeated it several times. A sudden clap of thunder destroyed any self-assurance and firm resolve. That sound wasn't rattling chains, yet it still made me jump out my skin and restarted a calm heart into its mad rush to explode. Those feelings weren't made any easier by an increase in wind velocity creating a moaning sound to float through the building. It also splattered rain noisily against exterior and interior walls. Everything was happening at the same time and increased a sensation of impending doom in rapidly gathering darkness.

I climbed a creaking, rickety old staircase to three bedrooms and a bathroom. With each step the floorboards groaned under my weight. Wind started howling through openings devoid of window frames. My own shadow jolted an increased apprehension that grew by the second. The only comfort I had was a small bore shotgun held tightly in both hands. It was loaded with the safety off and its barrel pointing straight ahead. I was ready to blow away any ghouls or ghosts who would at any moment jump out and grab me. Although not feeling in the least bit cold, my teeth were chattering hard enough to break. If that previous occupier wanted to stop me climbing those stairs, he or whatever it was would have a barrel full of buckshot before I bolted.

I moved cautiously through each room, peering into every recess and corner. I even looked up each chimney for anything that shouldn't be there. More thunder boomed. It was much closer and sounded a lot louder. I gripped the gun tighter while backing up to a wall. My eyes narrowed, teeth were clenched to

Nights in the Forest

stop them chattering while I desperately fought for control. A full minute must have passed before I could move. All the rooms were cleared, the terrible fear inside subsided, a calm confidence returned.

Whilst standing at a gaping hole that used to hold a window frame, several deep breaths were taken as I stared into darkness. The air smelled fresh and wet. A powerful wind howled and thrashed sheets of rain against one side of the building. Elongated branches on a nearby tree waved and thrashed heaven's teardrops off its leaves. I imagined forest animals and birds taking cover in crevasses or holes in the ground. An enormous rumble of thunder followed a bolt of crackling lightning that pierced pitch darkness. It split the heavens in two and looked very impressive. Frankly, I would have preferred being in bed at home. Although not the best of times to wander about in a forest, let alone stand inside a dark, draughty, haunted house during a thunderstorm, that was where I was. Count Dracula may have felt at home under the same conditions. It certainly didn't suit me one little bit.

A clap of thunder occurred directly overhead. Not only did it shake the building, it shook me as well and disintegrated whatever vestige of security I had managed to build up. Although dry, a fear of the unknown made me feel very cold. I curled up in a corner. Torrential rain splashed onto the ground outside. Dry baked earth soaked up the heavy downpour like a sponge until it became waterlogged. When that happened, hard ground was converted into a soft quagmire that splattered against the building. Meanwhile I cradled the gun for comfort. My eyes closed, I counted to ten before opening them to stare at the darkness outside. "It's just dark, just dark. There's nothing to be afraid of, it's just dark," I muttered to myself and repeated those words over and over. A howling wind continued blowing rain onto the house like shotgun pellets. Background sheet lightning lit a blackened sky and silhouetted a distant treeline. Several bolts of lightning split darkened heavens in numerous places before spearing into earth with uncompromising brightness.

I pulled out Uncle's tin of tobacco and rolled a cigarette. My hands were shaking while fingers folded damp cigarette paper.

Nonetheless, I managed to make a pretty awful-looking roll-up. After taking a long draw, a level of calmness returned. Pale blue wisps of smoke disappeared with each gush of wind whistling through that opening in the wall until I finished smoking and found it impossible to fall asleep. The noise of thunder continued unabated as storm clouds passed slowly overhead. They looked so low, there were no doubts in my mind, by standing on the roof, I could touch them. Apart from that, there was no intention of going to sleep only to wake up from a tap on the shoulder by a headless ghost. Fear, the noisy crash of thunder and a profound sense of survival kept me awake. I managed to remain that way until the noise became a distant murmur, which encouraged a drowsy, tired mind to finally switch off. The second cigarette had gone out and remained dangling from lips as this chin of mine sank onto my chest. I felt a cold but comforting .410 stock against my forehead. My finger caressed the trigger guard. My mind resorted to a firm declaration. "Nothing can touch me, I am armed and alert."

Sleep finally embraced me with a silence that enveloped an exhausted being. It carried me down that tunnel of oblivion much deeper than usual. Under normal circumstances the dawn chorus would have woken me. However, on that fresh sundrenched morning my sleep was disturbed by human voices.

My eyes flicked open to look on two upturned faces. An old couple had set out for an early morning walk and happened to look up at the opening. I stood up quickly with the gun inadvertently pointing at them. They were obviously startled because the old woman began pulling at her man's sleeve, urging him to move on quickly. "Come on Harry, come on, let's get out of here," she muttered.

They shuffled off in one direction while I made a hurried exit through the back door. That couple would head for home, ring the police and further enhance my already deteriorating reputation. They would report to the authorities on the whereabouts of a dishevelled, wild-looking young man who pointed a gun at them. Would the police listen to my side of the story? After the previous day's episode, I doubted it.

Nights in the Forest

Despite such a poor start, it was a beautiful morning and fresh from an evening's rain. I had all the time in the world to enjoy it. First things first, breakfast, then that long awaited, much-needed wash.

Anthony Corbyn

Chapter Three

Caught by an Act of Treason

I returned to the campsite near Penny Pool, a short distance from the haunted house. One night in that building was enough for anybody. My tiny campsite just inside the forest had been selected as an excellent spot for a number of reasons. It remained well hidden but with a clear view of the surrounding hills and particularly the track leading down to the river.

Another fire was lit in the small hole dug the previous day. Within a few minutes an open tin of beans was being heated. They were enjoyed with a few slices of stale bread. Once the morning ritual of breakfast was completed, I stripped off and had an all-over wash. It felt good being clean and I celebrated by rolling my first cigarette of the day and leaned against a tree. My mind wandered over potential hunting grounds that would provide food for my diminished larder. Those reminiscing thoughts meandered toward a brief period in the Army Cadets. I figured the next war would need lots of seasoned recruits who knew how to shoot. That thought prompted me to join the Army Cadets. Not long after learning to march in step and just before being taken to a rifle range, the sergeant stuttered out a question. "H ha how old are yo yo you?"

If I learned nothing else that day, one thing was certain. I knew why he was in charge of Army Cadets and not front line troops. "Sixteen," was my reply because if I were any younger they wouldn't let me have a go. We went on a rifle shooting exercise at the Royal Navy rifle range where the newly formed Army Cadet platoon were handed old .303 Lee-Enfield rifles and five bullets to shoot. It was great fun lying in the dirt and blasting away at stationary targets. They were only 25 yards away and couldn't be missed. The rifles made more noise than a shotgun and gave a good firm kick on the shoulder. My own scores were good enough for the sergeant to promote me to marksman, despite only firing five bullets. The character next to me was short and very skinny. Every time he fired, the recoil pushed him down the bank. He had to crawl forward to fire each successive shot. I recall the sergeant muttering something that sounded like "B blithering idiot." His pre-emptive word to those two started with "F f f" but he never managed to get the rest out. At that stage I understood why he was running an Army Cadet platoon. Just imagine what our Army Cadet Sergeant would have been like under active service with bullets flying in all directions. "E, e, enemy to yo, yo your front. Open f f f ..."

John Pilchard never liked anyone having more fun than him. When he learned about the Army Cadets and what it was like, he wanted to join up. Despite his protests, John's mother enrolled him into the Air Force Cadets. According to her, they were more appropriate to her son's station in life. Apparently the upper echelons of society, even ones living on National Assistance, didn't grovel about in mud shooting each other; they directed lower classes from behind desks or flew planes and bombed the living shit out of everyone below. John was issued with a nice, second-hand Air Force shirt, which became the sum total of his uniform. Needless to say, "upper classes receiving National Assistance" couldn't afford trousers, shoes and a beret as well. John could march proudly up and down but he never got dirty, never crawled over wet grass or through mud and never fired a real rifle, so he couldn't possibly have had as much fun as those of us in the Army Cadets.

Those reminiscing thoughts made me smile as my mind returned to a current problem of refurbishing my diminishing larder. Hunting with the shotgun was all well and good but it did attract the local gamekeeper. It meant resorting to a silent approach. Catching pheasants was not too difficult. All one had to do was dig a narrow trench about two feet long and a foot deep. The start of the trench would be level with the ground and slowly descend until it was a foot deep. That was the easy bit, unfortunately, I didn't have any corn. A trickle of those seeds would exit the trench and form a wide circle. Any pheasant encountering that circle would follow it by gobbling down a free feed. As a natural course of events, the bird would end up going down the trench. Even the most cautious bird would pick up one grain at a time and slowly descent into the earth. Once inside there was no escape. It couldn't back out or take off with its only exit avenue by someone grabbing hold of its head and pulling. No corn, no pheasant. Rabbits, on the other hand, could be trapped by a variety of methods, the primary one was with several nets covering a number of holes in their warren. Starting a small fire and fanning smoke into another hole usually prompted them to scamper out. Providing one covered their exit holes, rabbit was on the menu. Unfortunately, as with not having any corn to bait pheasants, there were no nets for catching rabbits. On the other hand, I did have a bow with arrows and there was no hurry.

Late morning sun dried any open ground leaving the forest floor damp and musty. I remained relaxed, at peace with the world and smoking when the sound of my name being called filtered through trees. I sat up, listened for a few seconds, then decided to play it safe by dousing the fire in the usual way before backing under cover to watch and wait.

Five people were making their way down the track, which passed close to where I had been a few minutes before. Two of them were my friends, John from Boxfields and Dave from next door. Close behind were three girls I couldn't recall seeing before. They must have taken time off from school or been sent by the authorities to find me. Whilst they may have been friends, I remained out of sight watching that narrow trail behind them. Most of that track could not be seen with much of it threading between trees, hidden by bushes or through long grass. If any police or adults were following, they wouldn't be spotted until they reached open ground, so I remained out of sight, just in case. The boys and girls were chattering like a bunch of monkeys with intermittent calls of my name. Their noisy shouts must have scared off game for miles around. That annoyed me, since it meant going deeper into the forest to carry out any successful hunting. However, it had been two days and nights since actually talking to anyone, so I focused on finding out what was happening back home.

I continued watching until they crossed that small bridge by the waterfall just in front of my hiding place. The group was bunched up, throwing stones into the pool. All of them were talking at the same time, so I couldn't make out what anyone was saying. Every now and then, one would call my name. After moving a little closer, their conversation became clear enough to identify. I took the opportunity to make my presence known by stepping out of hiding. "What do you want?" I asked. The clear sharp tone was deliberately intimidating and clearly indicated my annoyance at the amount of disturbance they were creating.

All five spun round to see me standing close by. My feet were apart with the gun cradled in my arm and dressed for the hunt in denim green, hanging from a broad leather belt were a pair of knives. One was a stiletto for throwing and a Bowie for slicing and cutting. Included in my armoury was a small hatchet hung in a separate press-studded sheath. That multi-purpose instrument had a screwdriver at one end of the handle with a hatchet and hammer at the other. My appearance must have impressed the girls who stepped back in surprise, if not in a little amazement.

John spoke first and as usual, he asked a question. "Where in heaven's name have you been? Everyone's lookin' for you."

"Why?" I asked.

"I don't know, word is you shot your mum," he replied and took a step closer. Both eyes were squinting in what appeared a determined effort to confirm what he saw. Just to make sure, his eyesight hadn't failed, a hand reached out and touched my shoulder. The temptation to shout "Boo" at him was suppressed.

I thought it odd how a single shot into the air two days ago had been converted into a story about shooting my mother. However, it represented an opportunity too good to miss. Enhancing a disreputable reputation before one's peers doesn't come very often, besides I was anxious to impress the girls. "Is she dead?" I asked with as deadpan a face that could be mustered while suppressing an urge to burst out laughing.

"No, I seen 'er this morning," Dave responded. His heavy West Country accent sounded homely and very welcome. Whilst he may have sounded simple, it would be a mistake to think Dave was a country yokel without a functioning brain. That would be judging a book by its cover. My next-door neighbour may have sounded like a simpleton but he acquired more qualifications and passed more exams than John and I put together. Perhaps that means that I'm dafter than I appear. There were no doubts about proving how stupid John was, even though he was my best mate.

"I 'eard you shot a copper as well," John queried.

The same comments referring to Dave could be said about John at this point. However, if one can't say something nice about somebody, it's best to say nothing at all, so I won't add to that derogatory comment just made. Quite obviously, John wasn't sure of his facts. Like most things, particularly a half-truth or misinformation, it's always far more interesting than reality. Being honest at that stage would not embellish the story, so I drew myself to maximum height before saying, "I shot two of 'em," with a confident air while maintaining a deadpan expression.

Gasps of amazement sounded from the girls who were staring in open-eyed wonder and admiration. All three moved closer to touch the gun, sheath knives and small hatchet. Meantime I acted like a macho male by staying cool and not moving while becoming aware of their feminine presence stirring a feeling deep inside. I breathed in deeply to inhale their body scent and enjoyed the effect it had on my emotions. Girls smell different to boys.

One girl stood directly in front. "Where did you sleep last night during the storm?" she asked while the other two continued staring while waiting for an answer. I provided them with a little drama by turning slowly and pointing the gun barrel. "In there." All eyes turned toward the haunted house. A predictable, unbelieving silence fell. Everyone was aware of bets being laid on anyone able to spend one night in that notorious building on their own. Till that day, no one had. The girls came closer with wide admiring eyes. The one closest looked directly into mine while whispering a rhetorical question. "You stayed there on your own last night?"

It sounded more like a statement. Yet her voice had a soft, murmuring tone that sounded incredulous. I studied curly red hair and a freckled face with extra large lips. To anyone, especially me at that moment, she was very, very pretty. The second our eyes met, a tingling current passed between us. A sensation percolating into my loins made me nervous and I shifted from side to side in a sure sign she disturbed me.

John broke the spell by asking another question. "Have you had anything to eat?" My well-built, ginger-headed friend could be guaranteed to bring up the subject of food during any alternative topic of conversation.

"Yeah," I replied slowly before adding with more than a little relish, "A nice big rat." A series of gasps erupted from the girls. As one, they and my mates refused to believe me. I dismissed their disbelief with a nonchalant wave of my hand. With centre stage mine, there wasn't any way it would be given up to anyone. "Rats in that house," I continued with a nod in the direction of the building, "are as big as this." I demonstrated an exaggerated size with my hands. "They're so fat! You can knock 'em on the head with a stick cos they can't run fast enough to escape."

"You never ate a rat. You never did!" John exclaimed ardently. From the look of his face, he was about to throw up.

"They don't taste much different to pigeon, John," I responded. That simple statement convinced him I was telling the truth. He witnessed me eating a pigeon and had even been party to the event on one occasion. From what John knew about me, eating pigeon after cooking it over an open fire was normal.

"How'd you eat it?"

"I cooked it over an open fire of course."

"What, fur an' all?"

"No but the guts were good." That comment had as much truth in it as the rat story but John's eyes bugged out. Whatever I said made no difference because he had reached the believing anything stage. This made any incredulous story worth telling. Bullshit always sounds good, so long as you believe it. Eating rats' guts not only sounded bad, I imagine it would taste worse.

"Er yuk, you never did." The flexibility of Johns eyelids were given free reign. They were squinting again and his mouth looked as though he just sucked a lemon.

"They're the best bits," I stated before wiping a sleeve over my mouth and smacking lips. I thought John was going to throw up again as someone moving closer distracted me.

"Liar!" Dave exclaimed in my face.

Naturally, he was absolutely right but that exclamation simply presented me with a challenge. That's something no one has ever seen me walk away from. Standing my ground and bluffing is an art form, so I replied with a succinct "Am not."

"Prove it."

"Right then, next rat I catch, I'll share it with you," I challenged and looked him straight in the eye. That shut him up.

"What are you going to do now?" the ginger-headed girl asked softly as she looked at me with bright, encouraging eyes.

I had no idea if she believed the story but my eyes were staring straight ahead. They do say that one's eyes are the windows of your soul. If she looked into mine, perhaps she would see a liar. "I'm going for a swim," I answered and pushed through my visitors toward the rippling pool of water. Naturally, with an audience on hand, my walk was slow, deliberate, self-assured, even cocky. "Anyone want to join me?" I called without turning. Their initial objections resting on not having swimming costumes soon disappeared as they watched me strip naked and jump into an icy cool pool. I dived deep and stayed under for as long as possible before coming up and gasping, "It's beautiful, come on in."

Two of the girls were first to respond to my open invitation. They stripped down to their bra and panties in no time at all and started paddling or playfully splashing about in the shallows. Both were shouting and squealing while throwing water at each other. Meantime Dave removed all his clothing, while John's preconditioned inhibitions stopped him short of becoming totally naked. He decided to splash about in his Y-fronts.

After the girls got themselves wet, they started enjoying the event and wanted to swim. They were shouting encouragement to each other but none were willing to take the lead. I shouted to Ginger to come in while the other girls continued persuading her. She started laughing as more peer pressure was added with her friends yelling, "Go on then."

Anthony Corbyn

It wasn't until the situation turned into a dare, Ginger decided on doing it. With hands on hips, she turned and threw their dare back at them. "I'll do it but I bet you two don't," she challenged. Having said that, she removed her bra and her panties in a flourish and discarded them unceremoniously onto the riverbank, then quickly disappeared below the surface. Moments later two girls turned away, pulled their bras and panties off, threw them onto the riverbank and dived in with Ginger.

Before long all three were splashing and laughing at the sheer pleasure and delight of swimming naked with boys. After all, it was something considered very naughty and they'd never done it before. The latest movie about a nudist colony off the south coast of France called "The Isle of Levant" proved very interesting and provided an opportunity for teenagers to see naked adults and make snickering remarks. During the film, when the first full frontal male nudist came on, Vladimir, my friend from Czechoslovakia, couldn't help making a comment. His exclamation of "Cor! Look at them hairs!" was loud enough to get him thrown out.

However, we were not in a cinema but naked teenagers in a swimming pond in the middle of the Wiltshire countryside. John and Dave joined in the fun of diving under the cold water or splashing the girls. From a personal point, my underwater expeditions were prompted by the prospect of a better view. On more than one occasion I nearly drowned in those ice-cold, crystal clear waters of Penny Pool. Ginger was a well-formed teenager and well aware of her physical attributes. Once the necessity of encouraging her passed, she became more than willing to flirt by showing off her naked body under water.

After a while, ice-cold water cooled us to such an extent we wasted no time getting out to lie in the sun and dry off. John sat in his wet underpants, Dave with his back to the girls, while I sat next to Ginger, unabashed and admiring the obvious differences between us. An amazing change of attitude came over the girls who were very shy to begin with. After fresh cold water and sunshine warmed their exposed bodies, they became openly friendly to the point of flirting and almost touched us boys. At our age it must have been curiosity. Or it may have included rampaging delinquent hormones that needed little if any encouragement. As a certified juvenile delinquent, there was no reason to suppose my hormones were any different. There is little that can be said about Dave but John's flexible eyelids were squinting again. They were attempting to cover the clandestine operation his eyes were performing. Personally, I think the eyelids were restraining his eyes from popping out.

Within a minute Ginger unfolded her arms to lean on elbows. This allowed a full frontal exposure of her breasts. She had good reason to be proud of them, since they already consisted of a good handful. It became increasingly difficult not to look away from two dark pink nipples. Ginger must have noticed my admiring glances but didn't seem to mind. Eventually her chin went up and her eyes probed into mine. "What are you staring at?" came a soft question on smiling lips.

I felt blood rush to my face and quickly recovered some composure before answering in a voice low enough for her to hear but none of the others. "You're very pretty and quite sexy to look at." My flirtatious remark made her smile. It seemed to confirm that flaunting herself had the desired effect because Ginger raised her body to lean on hands, thus allowing everyone to have a good look. At that stage Dave, John and I were openly staring. Hells bells, there wasn't anything better to look at. Suddenly and without warning, Ginger turned round to sit up. In doing so, she briefly spread her legs and therein lay the greatest secret revealed to all. Although only the briefest of glimpses, that V-shaped patch between her legs was definitely ginger.

My heart skipped a beat. Those juvenile hormones suddenly galloped away in my blood stream, thereby evaporating any ability to control the effect they had on my body. My female-sensitive system began announcing its presence by becoming stiff. At any moment everyone would see my dick growing larger. There was only one thing for it. I took a deep breath, pushed my hands between my legs and shouted, "I'm going for another swim," then turned my back on Ginger and jumped into ice-cold water, which had the desired effect on such overheated emotions.

The others didn't take up another chance of leaping into the pool but watched from the bank. John and Dave became more interested in looking at the girls getting dressed while I waited for my embarrassing condition to recede before climbing out and pulling some clothing on.

Once everyone was dressed we began walking up the track, although I fell behind with my newfound friend. We became at ease in each other's company with a tinge of excitement at being almost alone. "Are you coming back with us?" she asked softly.

I shook my head while saying, "No, I expect the police will be waiting for me," before stopping to face her.

"When am I going to see you again?" she whispered. Her eyes flicked across to our friends walking ahead before staring into mine.

I felt excited! My heart started pounding, which wasn't the first time that day. A girl asking a boy for a date just didn't happen, at least I never heard of it. But then, it had been an extraordinary day. We stood silently facing each other. An afternoon sun filtered through the shaded pathway highlighting a mass of damp red hair tumbling over her shoulders. It cast a shadow on her face, yet allowed bright emerald eyes to shine. Ginger wasn't just pretty anymore. She was the most beautiful thing I ever saw. Fortunately, my trousers were on, otherwise there wouldn't be anywhere to hide my erection. I forced myself to answer her question despite being disturbed. "I don't know," I muttered, once my brain engaged the mouth and forced a tied tongue to work. That was the extent of any dialogue from me. My mouth dried up, it was difficult to swallow, one emotion piled on top of another. We walked on in silence to the wide track that formed a crossroads. I still couldn't give her a straight answer. I wanted to see her again but there was no way of knowing when it would be possible.

John, Dave and the other two girls stood waiting for us. It seemed as though that moment represented a turning point in my life. Something deep down kept telling me no, while Ginger stood there with a pleading look. John needed to get going because there was one thing he didn't want, and that was getting into

Nights in the Forest

trouble with his mother for being late. She never liked him being out after dark, late for dinner and certainly not playing with me.

"If you don't want to go 'ome, you'm welcom' to stay in my 'ouse," Dave suggested in a slow West Country drawl.

I hesitated. His offer needed some consideration, since it provided a good opportunity to see Ginger sooner rather than later.

"You cun climb in through me bedroom winder tonight, a'ter dark," he continued before concluding with, "I won't tell any'un, bis can trust I."

Those fatalistic last words held a hint of irony and retained a danger signal in my instincts ever since. I looked at Ginger who was nodding encouragement. My thoughts were, "It will give us a chance to meet again because she lives in the same street." Although I couldn't recall seeing her before, she smiled at the look in my eyes. Without turning away I answered, "Might see you tonight, maybe sometime tomorrow." I couldn't be sure if my friend knew the comment had been directed at him or the girl standing in front of me because I never looked at him. Nevertheless he answered. "Okay mate, me mum sends me to bed at 'alf past nine. I'll see ye then."

We made some hurried arrangements on what we should do at his bedroom window, where he would be waiting. With arrangements made I turned to face the others waiting for our whispered conversation to end. Ginger reached out and touched me on the shoulder, static electricity powered down to my toes. Both knees threatened to buckle. My subdued erection was suddenly restored. An imaginary soul went off like a firework rocket. We hesitated for a moment as our faces came close enough to kiss. With a heart pounding fit to burst, legs all a tremble and eyes staring into hers, I pouted my lips. Her eyes widened and a pair of large lips pouted in expectation of meeting mine. My bravado suddenly evaporated, I turned and ran back to the campsite.

The day was spent wandering through the forest in a daze with my mind fixed on images of a beautiful, naked, ginger-headed girl. How could a chance meeting with someone have such a profound effect on anyone's thoughts? My original plan to carry out some hunting altered dramatically because any ability to concentrate had been disrupted. As darkness fell, I moved along the track toward town and waited at the edge of Top Wood. When it was completely dark, I moved on. Being close to houses made me nervous, although darkness provided a sense of security. Although I didn't possess a watch, it wasn't difficult to work out what the time was by the level of traffic and people moving about. One clear indication of time was the jingling hand bell of a fish and chip van. He always appeared at around suppertime when those who could afford a ready prepared, take away meal would queue up to pay for it. Naturally his takings would be greatly enhanced on a Friday when the Catholic population on the estate outnumbered the Protestants in the line. Those of us in the Catholic faith weren't supposed to eat meat on a Friday, only fish. Although not a Friday, even from such a distance, the aroma of freshly fried fish and chips smothered in salt and vinegar, wrapped in newspaper, made my mouth water. It was a potent reminder of how hungry I was. On moving closer to Dave's house, I made myself comfortable and smoked a cigarette while watching from a vantage point until it felt close to our meeting time. I moved into his back garden and hid behind old bean sticks that still had some wrinkled foliage attached. My friend's bedroom window couldn't be mistaken because Dave made periodic glances out of it. However, I wouldn't cross that garden while light from his room shone like a searchlight across a wide open vegetable patch.

Dave's mother commanded her son to turn off the light. Seconds later, bedroom and garden were plunged into darkness. I waited several minutes before slipping silently between potato mounds. Short sprouts were probing through soft piles of earth. In a few weeks, those green shoots would be two feet high and covered in a variety of coloured blossoms. Dave's family would have potatoes with every meal for months. On reaching my benefactor's bedroom window, I waited until my breathing was under control. One hand touched earth clinging to my shoes, the other felt a hard stone wall. Both ears and senses remained alert to any sounds that might indicate danger. With no voices or movement detected, I reached up and tapped the windowpane. When it opened a second later, Dave's face appeared close to mine and we

Nights in the Forest

both said, "Shush." After handing over my gear, I climbed in and sat on his bed while we carried out a whispered conversation.

"Be you 'ungry?" he asked.

"A bit," I replied. No hunting had been carried out because most of the day was spent wandering through the forest eating nuts and berries. The exotic aroma of fish and chips hadn't helped either. My stomach rumbled to remind me what it required.

"I'll get 'ee somethin' to eat," Dave said and slid off the bed.

"No!" I exclaimed quickly. That reaction indicated how loudly my instincts were shouting their warning about being careful. Any sense of danger and my inner voice kept saying, "be on the lookout for trouble."

"Will yer take it easy," Dave responded to my hissed outburst, "I'll be no mor'n a minute, it'll be all right."

I watched apprehensively as he left the room. Although reassuring myself that Dave was a good friend, the fear inside continued growing as minutes ticked by. Internal alarm bells were ringing quite loudly at that stage. I pulled on my green denim jacket. The knife belt was buckled up with the bow and quiver placed on the bed in preparation of throwing them out the window. I picked up the gun, checked the breech and made ready to make a hasty departure just as Dave returned and asked me what I was doing.

"Getting out," I replied hastily.

"But I 'as a sandwich fur 'ee," Dave said with a bewildered look on his face.

Very slowly, with a wary feeling, I climbed off the bed. Hunger has always been a powerful enemy against instinct. Whilst alarm bells were still ringing, an appetite and Dave's innocent voice saying, "Relax, you cun trust I," dulled them.

After placing my kit under the bed, I set about satisfying those hunger pangs by eating that delicious sandwich with the window left off its latch. Dave's mother made strawberry jam and baked her own bread. There are few things in life that are irresistible and I had two of them in my hands. Some time later I curled up under the bedclothes feeling content and secure. Those irritating alarm bells were faint tinkles in the distance yet remained a clear reminder that instinct remains with us all the time and should only be ignored at our peril.

Strange places have always taken me time to get used to and when sleep came under those circumstances, it was always light. Voices in my head contained a dreamlike quality before reality forced its way through. The voice belonged to Dave's mother saying, "He's in there with my son, officer."

"All right, Missus, you can leave it to us now," a masculine voice replied.

The light tinkling turned to sirens that encouraged me to spring out of bed, pull on my trousers and throw the window open. Before Dave opened his eyes, I leaped into the darkness outside. Whilst in midair, a massive pair of hands plucked me from the sky and a set of muscular arms wrapped themselves around my body. Hard as I tried, escape was a futile endeavour. A deep voice with a heavy Welsh accent penetrated my panic-stricken mind. "Be still, boyo, I'm takin' you 'ome. No amount of fightin's going to 'elp you now."

A rage, fired by frustration and a feeling of betrayal, pushed me to greater effort, which resulted in no change to the situation. The big Welshman was our local bobby whom I met on numerous occasions. The policeman anticipated my escape avenue and plucked me out of the air in mid-flight. I continued squirming under his arm while being carried over the fence to mother next door. During the short journey I managed to land several good punches onto a massive bulk restraining me. A shiny police button was also ripped off except it made no difference. Moments later we were sitting in mother's kitchen with any attempt at escape restricted by a huge hand pressing onto my shoulder. It prevented me from moving, never mind making a run for it. Mother started fussing around, putting the kettle on for tea as she incessantly chattered away. Uncle nonchalantly made himself a cigarette and offered one to me. We sat smoking in silence while the big man in blue explained to everyone what would happen next.

The idea that her only son might be taken away really upset mother. She couldn't understand what all the fuss was about.

After all, it wasn't the first time I ran away. Perhaps she forgot the broken window, discharging a shotgun in a built-up area with intent to cause grievous bodily harm, shooting at two policemen while they were trying to apprehend me, causing alarm and despondency, provoking authority with rude gestures etc. The list seemed endless and it would be a total waste of time explaining it to mother. Saying, it wasn't my fault, wouldn't make any difference for reasons that have already been explained.

It turned into an early night for me with frustration fuelling tears of anger to stream down my face while lying in bed. A friend's betrayal resulted in being captured like a fool. That was the last time instincts were ignored and the last time I ever believed anyone who muttered those fateful words, "You can trust me."

I contemplated leaving soon after our infamous policeman left but without my confiscated hunting gear there was little point. The anger at such a misfortune prompted several promises to myself with the first one being, next time, be more careful and secondly never ignore the one thing that could have saved me. Always listen to those warning bells called instinct. As my thoughts eased into the next plan, I relaxed, wiped the tears away and gazed out the window onto pitch darkness. I smiled a little while muttering, "Dib, dib, dib. Dob, dob, dob."

Anthony Corbyn

Chapter Four

Life at School – or playing Truant

Corsham Secondary Modern School classes had my undivided attention. And for some time there were what one might describe as normal goings on. Despite the adult pessimistic predictions, end of term exam results showed I managed to come third out of a class of forty students. That only goes to prove that when this rebel puts his mind to a task, there is nothing he can't accomplish.

End of term became a trying time for everyone with friendships being put under severe pressure. This prompted an anticipated amount of increased fighting in the school yard. On one particular occasion, the reason for the argument which resulted in a challenge has been lost in the mists of time, so it couldn't have been that important. Nevertheless, I provided my opponent with enough provocation to finally make him crack. He pulled out a knife.

The schoolyard monitor saw a knife being pulled although he couldn't have been unaware of the circumstances. What happened next, altered the fixed, biased opinions of several people, who were convinced I was a troublemaker in a unique category. The confrontation needs describing in detail so as to apportion blame appropriately.

After the knife was drawn, my adversary lunged. The troublemaker, me, sidestepped to deflect the small pocket-knife. I then threw a punch with my free fist. It was a punch one dreams of making, a short sharp uppercut landing on a rapidly advancing chin. My attacker took the full force of that uppercut on the point of his chin and its impact made him stagger back into a teacher. My claim to fame is in having felled one pupil and a teacher with a single punch, since both ended up on the ground. The story became inflated and taken out of context. Nevertheless, it provided added weight to my exaggerated reputation of being a fighter. I've always been quick to take advantage of any situation so felt obliged to leap forward and stamp on the hand still clasping a knife. My subsequent attack was prompted by nothing more than a desire to accomplish one objective, to break a few bones. As luck would have it for my opponent, I failed.

Within seconds, we were bundled off by the scruff of the neck to the headmaster for punishment. As usual, a number of offences seemed to have been committed including being in possession of an offensive weapon along with intent to inflict bodily harm. Although those allegations sounded familiar, they were being directed toward my opponent. My offence was assault and battery with the intention of causing as much damage with my foot as possible. Despite strenuous denials everyone, especially me, knew it was the truth.

With a well-earned reputation as troublemaker, the headmaster naturally assumed, I was the culprit who started the fight. He was right. However, there's no way I was going to confess because the teacher who witnessed the incident rallied to my defence. Apart from which I had already established my nature as being a sneaky coward.

One can only imagine how difficult it must have been for the head to comprehend that turn of events. Despite my adversary's protestations that he wasn't at fault, and it was me who instigated the fight, the teacher remained adamant in what he saw. He expressed an opinion that punishment for any knife-wielding student should be very stiff. The headmaster agreed with the teacher and needless to say, so did I.

That event sparked a rethink of our benevolent headmaster's point of view. Up till that moment, he had been able to determine, I was nothing but a troublemaker who earned the reputation of being appropriately labelled "a bloody hooligan". "You do seem to have more than your fair share of fights, don't you?" he stated once we were alone.

"Yes Sir," I replied making an effort to look guilty while holding back the tears. I discovered that squeezing the bridge of one's nose hard made the eyes water, so I could make tears appear at will. "It's the other lads, Sir. They pick on me because I'm from a broken home." I sniffed noisily, blinked several times then wiped my sleeve across a runny nose. Even if I say it myself, the performance deserved an Oscar.

"Yes well, so it would seem," the headmaster said. He began looking for the right words to express his regrets at having misjudged me. "I er must say, er that was my impression of you up till now, it has been well, er what can I er say, ahem, been misconstrued, ahem, I apologize." The final frog in the headmaster's throat must have been a big one because a very long "ahem" erupted while he looked at the ceiling. It sounded as though he was being throttled but my prayer wasn't answered.

A huge pang of guilt was buried under a glow of victory. It felt great because God was having a joke. It had certainly been my fault, yet for once the cards were showing a different picture and made me even more intent on taking full advantage of the situation. I believed that tears provoke sympathy and can play a dominant role in altering people's perception of what they think they saw. For the time being, things were going my way.

On the last day of term another argument with an old friend erupted in the schoolyard. By that stage I established a reputation among the teachers as being a goody-two-shoes whose difficulties came about because of my parents' separation and being picked on by my peers. That impression, however precarious, needed protecting. I had to put the fight off. "I'll sort you out after school," I growled thus avoiding a schoolyard fight that would draw attention to myself and spoil the new image.

Once again the reason for that argument became lost during heightened emotions. Although, when it came to having a schoolyard fight, who the hell needed a reason?

Actually Steven Pryce was an okay guy. He came from a large poor family with as many if not more problems than my own. Physically, Steve represented a very well built youth with a stocky, solid frame. He was also exceptionally strong and not the sort of person anyone could push around. Hercules might but there were none fitting that personification around. Even the teachers were prone to leaving him well alone whenever he objected to doing what they wanted him to.

As a tribute, I'll relate one incident between Steve and a P.T.I. also known as a Physical Training Instructor. At a physical training period, Steve turned up at the gym without a pair of shorts. Our trainer had a reputation of demanding consistency in dress when performing in "his" gym. Steve's parents couldn't afford the required uniform, so Steve entered the competition in his jeans. The verbal confrontation went something like this.

"Pryce! Where's your shorts?"

"Haven't got any, Sir."

"Put a towel round your waist. You're not going to play football dressed like that."

"Will not."

"What!"

"Will not, Sir."

"Do as you're told."

"Won't!"

"Yes, you bloody will. Now, take those damn jeans off and put a towel round your waist."

"No!"

"If you don't do as you're told, I'll send you to the headmaster's office."

"I know where it is, Sir." That said, Steve pulled on his jumper and headed for the office. The teacher didn't stop him but sidestepped and allowed his rebellious pupil free passage while he stormed head down toward the door. It wasn't just Steve's natural physical strength; he also had a very stubborn streak. Whenever he decided not to do something, nothing was going to make him change his mind. If one wanted a tough cookie to fight on their side, Steve was the one you chose. Idiots like me are the ones who decide to confront him with fisticuffs.

After school, Steve and I stood facing up to each other with our mutual friend holding both jackets. John was Steve's friend and mine, so could not make up his mind which one he should be a second for. To avoid any misunderstanding of the issue, he decided to sit on the fence and act as second to both parties. That was John.

Nights in the Forest

I was not anxious to indulge in fisticuffs with an oversized teenager who already had his shirtsleeves rolled up. Clenched fists were raised in a classic boxing stance. He was ready to fight. It left little option but to indulge my friend. I began bouncing around on spring-loaded feet with fists held high and not at all sure if it was such a good idea. I actually liked Steve. Apart from which the original reason for the fight could not be remembered and my anger had long since abated. "Come on then Steve, let's be having you," I shouted while jabbing at the air between us.

Steve didn't move. He remained rooted to the spot like an uncompromising boulder with fists the size of large rocks. "You go first," he responded.

"No mate, you go first," I replied firmly and followed through with a quick left jab, a weave, several more quick jabs complemented with a few incredible bounces and a right-handed haymaker. My idea was to impress him with speed and how futile it would be to engage in combat with such a superior boxer. A few seconds of demonstrating superior skills succeeded in getting me puffed out before I warmed up. More exercise had just been completed in those thirty seconds than I managed to accomplish in the previous month.

"You started it, you got to go first," Steve said while remaining rooted to the spot.

"Come on, what's the matter. Scared are you?" I taunted.

"No."

"Come on then," I reiterated.

"No."

Further verbal provocation was aimed at getting the fight started before exhausting myself prior to the actual contest beginning. For all my bravado, no anger had come to the surface and the situation deteriorated into a comical standoff. Meantime, John stood stoically to one side with a jacket over each arm and a confused look on his pink face.

"Get on with it, man. Come and get a good thrashing," I shouted after catching what little breath remained in my lungs.

"Won't," was the stubborn response.

"Scared cat." That remark must have prompted Steve into taking the initiative because he suddenly lumbered forward to throw a punch I managed to deflect with my arm. The tingling sensation produced by that impact reached my finger tips. A bruise erupted in less than a second and remained for two weeks. I sidestepped and threw a good strong right, it being my best counter punch when at close quarters. Getting into a fight with Steve meant only the very best punches would provide a slim chance of seeing me though. He made an attempt at ducking, which resulted in my fist bouncing off the top of his head. The jarring rattled all the bones in my hand and up the forearm before seeming to dislocate my elbow and shoulder. That pain gave a clear insight into what it felt like to have an arm torn off. God only knew what it would be like receiving a headbutt from my opponent.

Steve blinked in pained surprise, and then snorted like a bull, before making a determined charge.

It became blatantly obvious that putting a lot more effort into delivering a blow to his mid-section was needed to take the wind out of his sails. When my fist landed it felt as though I punched a rubber tyre and bounced off Steve's belly. A steel-reinforced arm caught me across the chest and I suddenly found myself lying flat on the ground unable to breathe. Steve generated so much momentum during his attack that he stumbled over my prone body. He couldn't maintain his footing so ended up on the ground beside me. We scrambled to our feet with Steve managing it first although he held his stomach. I'd hurt him. But was it enough? I scored two good hits but then, so had he. We were even. I got up in time to sidestep another charge. Things began getting serious because although my best punches were delivered, they bounced off the target continuing to advance on me.

Steve's arms were held out like the horns of a bull. They were a constant reminder that if they ever wrapped themselves around me, it would all be over.

I remained nimble enough to keep sidestepping and heaved in belly shots one after the other. Every punch drained my strength, hurt my hand and made my arm ache but didn't slow his advance.

Steve had me back-pedalling while he advanced like a tank fitted with rotating gun barrels. I threw out left after left with unfaltering repetition. My only defence system was working overtime. Almost every punch in ten landed on target. Despite such accuracy, the "tank" simply blinked before advancing with its gun barrels swinging like scythes.

"I must box him," I kept muttering to myself whilst maintaining a tactical withdrawal and defence posture. That's all very well, although nobody informed me how to stop a powerful tank twice my size while running out of breath. A resounding thud reverberated through my body as a fist landed on my shoulder, which threw me off balance. The shock wave buckled my knees. I staggered in an attempt to regain my balance. Steve saw his advantage and pressed home the attack. With arms outspread he closed in with no chance of my avoiding him. The only hope remaining was to regain that lost balance. I stood firm and put everything into one final belly shot, delivered as the encircling arms folded about me. Steve's mouth was close to my ear. I heard air whistle out his lungs. We fell to the ground with my left arm free and my right trapped tightly between our bodies in a steel trap that got tighter by the second.

I pounded Steve's right ear. Each time my fist made contact he winced yet the steel band encircling my body remained unfaltering. Both eyes felt as though they would pop out their sockets and began watering. I had a hard time breathing. With my mouth next to his left ear I resisted the temptation to bite it, instead ground my teeth and hissed, "You had enough yet?"

"Yeah. You had enough?"

I answered Steve's question with a simple "Yes." It was all, the remaining air in a pair of squeezed lungs could manage.

He released the bear hug and that allowed me to roll away gasping in some much-needed air. A few seconds later we sat facing each other with Steve holding his right ear and wiping some blood from his nose. I gulped in sufficient air to say, "Gee, Steve but you're as hard as nails."

"Ah maybe so, but you 'as a wicked right. That last un in the belly really got me," he replied.

"Look at my hand," I said holding it out for him to see the bruised knuckles. "A damn rock for a head, that's what you've got mate."

We were grinning at each other like a pair of Cheshire cats before standing up to shake hands. Steve, John and I walked toward Corsham train station chattering about the fight. We stood on the bridge across the railway line that passed through our town and connected the city of Bath to London. A steam train passed and drowned our conversation with noise, as we disappeared into billowing steam and smoke. We looked at each other and waited till the noise died away before recommencing a discussion

"You're a good fighter, Steve, a real tough guy."

"Thanks, you lived up to your reputation. I still fought you though didn't I?" he replied, holding his damaged ear whilst I rubbed the bruise on my arm. "Not scared of you, was I?" he added with a little pride.

"No mate. You're not scared of anybody, we all know that." I turned to John and fired a playful punch at his shoulder. "Me and you next time, eh? What do you say, old buddy?"

"No thanks, I've seen the way you fight. If you thought you were going to lose, you'd fight dirty," he declared.

"Too damn right," I replied, after all, who enjoys loosing.

It had been a private fight. Nobody except the three of us would ever talk about it and we were smiling as we went our separate ways in peace. I've always been unsure about that fight, never fully able to decide who won it. On the one hand, neither of us lost and I concluded that a draw with Steve was as close as anyone was likely to get, so I left it at that – a draw.

I continued attending school for weeks and abandoned the forest whilst the circumstances evolved to my advantage. Although teachers still considered me as something of a rebel who continued having a bad influence on others, they started calling me by my first name. Now that I had apparently reformed, they gave me the benefit of the doubt including the responsibility of being milk monitor in charge of the tuck shop. That gave me good reason for suspicion and I wondered if it was a crude attempt at reverse psychology. Despite my reputation for being a truant, I actually read a lot and anything that created an interest always motivated me into studying. The subject of reverse psychology was one that required a considerable amount of surreptitious reading yet provided some enviable knowledge on how the idea worked.

Give the most hardened renegade in any sphere of life some responsibility and he almost always settles down. In my case, they probably hoped I'd become an ardent student. Had it been anyone else, someone who didn't have a suspicious mind with doubts about the motive, it may have worked. If that had been their intention, it was wasted, since I saw it as a golden opportunity to provide my family with some of the good things in life we couldn't afford.

My scheme worked something like this: Before handing out any free milk that came in one-third-of-a-pint bottles, I drank as much of the stuff as my stomach could hold. There were also several large trays of hot jam doughnuts, fresh from the bakery. Those sugar-coated, jam-filled, puffed-up balls of dough were provided for the milk monitor to sell in the tuck shop. In theory it was a non-profit making enterprise. I found it difficult to understand how a non-profit business could survive. No capitalist could.

I decided other students could subsidize my hunger for jam doughnuts because I had never been able to afford them. My desire in acquiring a few opened my mind on how to achieve that goal. In defence it must be said that my motives were not entirely selfish.

Having established how the system would operate, I set about using two methods to secure sufficient funds to pay for my treats. In the first place, many students were short-changed at every opportunity. If anyone discovered my ploy and protested, I simply apologised before giving back the shortage. Most students, however, were not inclined to check their change, especially if there was a long eager queue. My second method to make up funds came about as a direct result of reading about industrial production systems in relation to supply and demand. It's really very simple. A product being manufactured and deliberately kept in short supply, automatically generated a high demand, therefore it could be sold for a higher price. There remained a risk of a competitor producing the same product, except in my case I held a monopoly. Which any businessman will confirm is the best position to be in.

That theory was put to the test. One day a long queue began forming and I reduced the number of doughnuts on display. Naturally, according to previous lessons learned about supply and demand, the price was raised. While many students objected to paying the hiked up price, there were more than enough who were able to afford the increase. From that small test of the tuck shop I began running it as a business with the profits being ploughed into an alternative project requiring revenue, namely, supplying nutrients to my household.

Some complaints reached the teachers who should have replaced me straight away. The headmaster should have caned me or at the very least waved an index finger for ripping off the unfortunate, also known as idiots. However, people in charge of moulding young minds and developing responsible attitudes, honesty and character were in favour of keeping me in charge of the tuck shop. They encouraged my illicit activity by accepting doughnuts from the tuck shop at below cost price. Bribery became part of my business empire. I had no respect for the teachers involved, only a great deal of contempt for them and felt it was a good time to take advantage of the situation. It became the best schooling in life ever dished out to a rebel.

Fresh doughnuts and bottles of milk kept turning up on the kitchen table at home each afternoon. They were a godsend. Mother's suspicious nature required answers to her questions. "Where did they come from? How much did they cost?" were two that kept cropping up. When I told her they were leftover goodies that would be thrown away, she needed no further encouragement. A quick sign of the cross before grace and she enjoyed the bounty provided. It made me feel good to see mother and Uncle enjoying themselves at someone else's expense.

Nights in the Forest

Life seemed on the up. The police warning with its threat about putting me away turned into an adult restraint on my juvenile desire to cause trouble. The authorities informed mother that if her son continued to behave, their threat to put him away would be suspended. That news called for a small celebration that was held in the kitchen. With Laura working, Freddy in hospital and my two younger sisters being looked after by an aunt there were just three of us left to discuss what to do.

"You be good boy now, eh," Uncle said.

"I'm always a good boy, Uncle."

"Yeah, yeah, but now you are being better, eh?"

"Do as Uncle tells you, son," mother said, before stuffing the remains of a doughnut into her mouth then washing it down with a one-third pint bottle of milk. The sound of happy gulping ended with a satisfied sigh followed by a belch and an "Oops, pardon me."

"Have another one, Mum," I said pushing the plate across the table.

"I drink a toast for being good boy," Uncle said, before licking smeared jam off one side of his mouth. A long pink tongue pushed strawberry jam over a wider space. This was wiped away with the back of a hand. Crossed eyes stared at the red smear through heavy glass lenses before a smile developed and that tongue reappeared between nicotine-coloured false teeth. Mother and I raised our glasses of homemade alcohol to drink to that proposal.

Despite being surrounded by a loving family providing a calming atmosphere, a call of the forest invaded my mind. It made me think about hunting, fishing, swimming and wandering, although the best part was a sense of freedom. I had been a prisoner of society's restrictions long enough and proved whatever the elders wanted of me. The time came to do my own thing again.

A school bus picked up a group of school children from the estate close to Bottom Wood, a narrow strip of woodland running parallel to the Bradford road. While hiding in a leafy, ivy-encrusted tree close to the bus stop, I called down to John Pilchard passing by. His mother had given my friend strict instructions not to associate with me because of the antisocial influence I had on him. John found it difficult to obey those instructions, particularly since he had a yen for being rebellious himself. Whilst that hankering was never allowed to show itself in public, if the opportunity ever presented itself, he did it sneakily. This only goes to prove there were a lot more sneaky people around than they were given credit for. Just because one was a mummy's boy didn't disqualify you from being a sneak. Actually that imposition made being sneaky of paramount importance.

John leaned against the tree, knowing he mustn't look up. "What do you want?" he asked in a low voice. A small group of juveniles waited for the bus close by. They could see John leaning against the tree but not me on a branch horizontally above him.

"Do you want to go fishing?" I asked.

"No, I'm not allowed to play with you," he hissed back.

"Yes I know that." I took a deep breath and looked down on John's neatly combed dark ginger hair before continuing. The nickname Kipper suited him but I never used it. "Look at the sky, mate. It's going to be a fantastic day."

"So what," he responded in his usual very negative way to my pointing out the beauty unfolding around him.

"The fish will be on the bite," I continued in a dreamy voice before adding in deeper earnest, "What would you rather do John? Run free through the forest then go fishing or sit in a stuffy classroom wondering how much fun I'm having and how many fish I've caught, eh?"

John shuffled then stuffed his hands deeper into those neat, grey school trouser pockets. His head turned to look up and down the road. "If my mum found out, I'd be in real trouble. You know that."

His comments were perfectly correct except they contained a wistful longing tone. John wanted something he shouldn't have and was scared of the consequences if anyone found out. "How's your mum going to find out?" I asked and became exasperated at my friend persistently refusing to carry out what he would really enjoy doing.

Nights in the Forest

A long pause followed while John thought about my proposition. He needed to make his mind up soon because the bus was due any minute. We both knew it. "The teachers will tell her." John began to weaken despite continuing to make feeble excuses while waiting for me to overcome his objections.

I could tell he was about to give in because the fidgeting became more pronounced. The time for a good excuse not to go fishing and have some fun with me had almost run out. "Don't be daft. Just go over to your friend, tell him you're not feeling well and you're going back home. Simple!"

"My mum will find out," he repeated while his fidgeting became more agitated.

I maintained pressure by insisting that since his mother went to work, she couldn't find out. Besides, he would be home before her.

"I don't know about this," he started muttering to himself with obvious signs of his resistance cracking.

He obviously needed one more little push. "We can go skinny dipping in Penny Pool," I whispered.

That short statement brought John's shuffling to a standstill. The thought of swimming naked without the embarrassing presence of girls would have brought his mother's hand to her mouth. She considered that sort of thing very naughty, rude, even primitive. It was the sort of things people of lower classes did, people like his hooligan friend he was told not to play with. The sound of a diesel engine chugging noisily over the hill ended John's hesitation. He strode toward the group waiting close by and made his excuses. Although I didn't hear what he said, a few seconds later John walked under my hideout whispering one word, "Okay."

"I'll meet you at the other end of Lovers' Lane in an hour. You better bring some grub with you." I remained in the tree watching the bus belching noxious diesel exhaust until both black smoke and bus disappeared from view. At that stage John's figure started walking faster in the opposite direction. I smiled at how easy it had been to influence my friend and was pleased to know we were going to have some fun together.

I stuffed some bread with a block of Echo margarine into a satchel along with a tin of Old Holborn tobacco and a box of matches. The belt with knives and hatchet was slung around my waist before I climbed out my bedroom window. What my mother didn't see wouldn't worry her.

After arriving at the meeting place, I waited till John could be seen making his way across the fields overlooking the village of Box. At that stage I slipped over the wall into thick undergrowth where he couldn't see me. My friend looked lost. He clambered onto the wall and waited. His head flicked from side to side searching the road by glancing up and down for several minutes. I smiled because if I didn't show myself soon, John would leave or my suppressed laughter would burst out. Like a phoenix rising out the ashes, although in my case it was from behind a wall, I raised my head just behind a nervous John. "Were you followed?" I hissed. My question startled him into leaping off the wall.

"You idiot!" he exclaimed, "How long have you been there?"

"Just long enough to make sure you weren't followed," I replied before jumping down beside him and shouting, "Come on, let's go."

We ran most of the way to Wyvern Valley and passed through a meadow we called Buffalo Field. It consisted of open pasture covered in ants' nests that created mounds of earth, which became overgrown with grass. Little imagination was required to call them buffalo humps. We spent many hours practicing our spear throwing and firing arrows at the tufts. The pair of us would gallop past on imaginary horses the way we saw American Indians doing it in the movies. John and I looked at each other with a temptation to proceed as before, except that stage in our lives had passed some time ago.

At my secret campsite the fishing poles were retrieved from their hiding place before I lit a small fire. With those minor projects completed, we settled down to carry out the primary reason of our absenteeism, some serious fishing. More than an hour passed, during which our conversation covered a variety of subjects including a number of questions from John about the red-headed girl.

Nights in the Forest

"What's her name?"
"I thought you knew her."
"No, I don't. What's her name?"
"Anne," I replied but didn't wish to pursue the subject.
"Anne who?"
"Anne Downs, why?"
"Oh, I was just wondering where she came from."
"Ireland, I think. Why?
"Ireland, eh."
"Wondering about her, were you? Fancy her, do you?"
"No! I just wondered what happened to her."

"I think she moved away," I stated firmly as a final comment on a passing phase of my life. I couldn't help speculating on what might have happened between us if Dave and his mother hadn't betrayed me. Time passed. The fishing lines continued hanging limply in the water. Crystal clear waters of the stream continued flowing. Ripples carried dried upturned leaves like tiny canoes at a gentle meandering speed. My eyes peered through a glinting surface in an attempt to catch sight of any fish. It seemed they were not on the bite after all.

By about mid-morning I settled back to roll myself a cigarette while my friend watched. As usual, he hadn't brought any cigarettes. In due course he finally managed to screw up the nerve to ask me to make one for him. I ignored his request and smoked what I wanted from the one already alight. The butt was handed over for John to finish. "Stay here, mate. Have a smoke and watch my line. I'll be back," I said while moving into nearby trees.

Previous experience was enough to let me know the fish weren't about to surrender themselves to dead worms on rusty hooks. Therefore, my only nourishment for the day would be bread and margarine. That kind of food wasn't really good enough for a seasoned young hunter. It meant putting a little work into the day to provide a quantity of alternative nourishment. I recalled seeing several pigeon nests in some low branches not far from the campsite, so it was worth a second look. My habit of noting where potential food for future needs might be was put to the test. Whilst moving quickly between trees the clap of a pigeon's wings attracted my attention. My eyes searched a multitude of tangled branches until they spotted a dark patch amongst thick foliage. Close-knit twigs indicated a nest. A wood pigeon leaving a nest provided evidence of either eggs or young and it was therefore worth investigating.

A low set tree with heavy, almost impenetrable growth obstructed any clear passage to the nest. Nevertheless, with my multi-purpose hatchet, the foliage was smashed through until I reached the nest and peered over the edge. An unusual sight of three young pigeons in residence confronted me. The birds were plump with some wing feathers already developing. I estimated their departure from home as being about one week with one member about to leave prematurely. I reached in, grabbed the nearest startled bird and stuffed it into my shirt. A warm dark place calmed its instincts to escape while I climbed down.

On my arrival at the campsite, the young pigeon had been plucked clean. My friend watched me draw out the entrails before holding them under his nose. "Makes really good fishing bait, does that," I said.

John's curious gaze altered to one of disgust. He saw me do that sort of thing before and said it always made him wonder how anyone could do such a thing. The cleaned-out carcass was washed in the river before being skewered onto a stick and propped over the fire. With slow cooking and constant turning the skin started crackling and an aroma of cooking meat over an open fire pervaded the atmosphere to make the whole day worthwhile. I looked at John's wide eyes watching the skin crinkle as it ran with fat that dripped onto the fire sending up little spurts of smoke. There is an essence of beauty in the pungent smell of burning fat blended with wood smoke. It made my mouth water.

"It'll be ready for lunch. Do you want some?"

John stared at the almost ready-to-eat bird roasting over flickering flames. He shook his head. "Err, no thanks."

"You did bring some grub with you, didn't you?" I asked.

"Yeah, got some in my bag here," he replied while tapping the bag beside him.

Nights in the Forest

I couldn't think of anything better to eat than roast pigeon and asked John what he'd brought.

"Jam sandwiches," he replied.

I sighed. Anything except one of John's jam sandwiches. I had to have one. My friend had numerous advantages not fully appreciated by himself. In the first place he had a mother who could cook and secondly, a father who worked on a farm. Whilst his mother made jam from all sorts of fruit, his father had access to freshly made butter along with free range eggs as well as milk straight from the cow. Apart from that, if John had a gun, he could go shooting whenever he liked. Although John's parents were separated, unlike mine, his were still in touch and remained friends.

I pondered the dilemma on how to separate John from one of those jam sandwiches that always impressed me whenever I was invited to his house. That was some time ago, certainly not since my reputation developed into its destructive mode. The unjustified standing given to me ruined any chance of being invited to John's house ever again. It was the only place known to man where jam sandwiches were available in abundance. My reminiscing thoughts returned to the task in hand. Some dry bread smothered with margarine was wiped over a roasting carcass. A flame leaped out and crackled as it licked melting margarine. Greasy yellow smells great when it's burning. However, my intention was to catch the droplets of melted margarine impregnated with pigeon fat onto my bread.

When the pigeon was ready, John pulled out his sandwiches. I watched him take a huge bite and lick any jam that oozed out. What the gutsy sod had done amounted to a declaration of war. I made a great show of pulling soft tender meat apart. A lot of exaggerated slurping noises were made while licking fingers and saying things like, "Ah yummy, this is soooo good," every time I swallowed.

John remained hunched over the fishing pole trying not to look, although his eyeballs were hard over to the corners watching me.

"You sure you don't want some?"

"No thanks," he replied but couldn't resist asking, "What's it like?"

"Well, you've had it before. It's absolutely delicious, like beef, tender young beef roasted over an open fire with a hint of smoky flavour added to it." Which, as far as I was concerned, was perfectly correct.

"Beef!" John exclaimed.

"Oh yeah. Roast beef, do you want some?"

"Alright then, I'll try a little bit."

"Swap you some for a jam sandwich."

John looked at those thick, chunky, crusty bread sandwiches then at the tiny roasted pigeon leg being offered. "I'll give you half."

The cunning devil had obviously learned some of my negotiating habits. It only took a moment for me to agree. After all, half of something was much better than half of nothing. My friend pulled that overloaded with strawberry jam sandwich apart. He measured the two halves against each other, licked a blob of bright red oozing temptingly out the smallest one. John then held it out to me. I almost bit a piece out that pigeon leg just to make things even. We made the swap in top speed and just before a second strawberry managed to escape. John tentatively munched on soft pigeon meat while nodding and muttering his approval. Meantime, I was back in heaven's arms allowing strawberry jam flavour mingled with fresh homemade butter on crusty farmhouse bread to caress my taste buds. Roast young pigeon with jam sandwiches for pudding was an à la carte menu fit for any king; the world was indeed a wonderful place. Every bone was sucked dry, every smidgen of jam was licked from any finger. After lunch we gave up fishing to recline in the afternoon sunshine for a while before going for a swim. A short while after our swim we sat on the riverbank drying off. I rolled a couple of cigarettes so we could both have a smoke while chatting about the great day we were having. John and I reminisced what it had been like last time, when the girls had been there. Both of us expressed numerous licentious comments about their naked bodies and what we would do if they ever came swimming in the nude again. I thought it best not to tell my friend about those underwater expeditions and how I nearly drowned. After all, there are some things heroic reprobates do not tell their friends.

John brought up the subject of fishing and our lack of success in catching anything. I felt obliged to make up whatever reasons came to mind, wrong bait, wrong time of day, too hot, too cold. My list of excuses was cut short by John interrupting. "Have you ever caught any fish in this river?" he finally asked in an exasperated voice.

"Hundreds," I replied indignantly. Apparently, using an old fisherman's adage has always been okay as long as you have a person who is willing to listen and believe every exaggerated lie you tell them.

"Are you sure?"

"Yes."

"Why aren't they biting today then?"

"Could be they're not hungry."

"Fish are always hungry."

"Maybe it's too cold."

"It's not cold."

"Maybe it's too warm. There are lots of reasons."

"Yeah, well name one," John challenged.

"I just have."

"Rubbish!"

"Could be the wrong time of day, in case you didn't know, fish have a different time scale to humans." My attempt at pacifying his constant questions worked. For a while tranquillity pervaded the atmosphere. A soft breeze was barely enough to wave long weeds surrounding us. It felt good to have peace and quiet without those persistent irrelevant questions disturbing my thoughts. We had been fishing. I had carried out a successful hunt. We had eaten a feast fit for a king. Enjoyed an afternoon swim and relaxed in the sun while having a smoke. That final thought prompted me to consider rolling another cigarette but John finally broke the long silence with another question. "Anyway, what time do you reckon it is?"

Anthony Corbyn

I put the tobacco tin aside and sat up. I took a deep breath before looking at a clear blue sky. Not a single cloud was visible. The sun was still well above the forest treeline. A song thrush fluttered by and disturbed a red admiral butterfly. I put on my wisest face, thereby giving John an impression of my knowing about such things without any need for a watch. A noisily sucked index finger was raised to gauge wind direction. My eyes traversed the skyline to collect unknown information that could be interpreted for John's benefit. Nothing but trees and undulating deserted pastureland could be seen. "Mmm," I murmured in the best knowing murmur known to man, "according to the sun's position, colour of sky and direction the birds are flying …" I hesitated, took another deep breath and opened the tin of tobacco. "From my undisputed calculations, it's about four o'clock." Having delivered my unchallenged interpretation of time I began rolling a fresh cigarette.

A stunned silence followed before John leaped to his feet. "Four o'clock!" he yelled and began scrambling around like a man possessed, hopping on one foot trying to get his pants on. At the same time one arm managed to find a shirt sleeve and one foot slipped into the wrong shoe. More haste, less speed were the thoughts that came to mind as he careered and stumbled in panic.

The last thing seen of him that day was his pink bum contrasting sharply with the lush green fields. I hoped John managed to pull those pants up before he reached the main road. After lighting up and lying back to relax, I pondered on his dilemma. In my case, there wasn't a need to panic or make a mad dash for home. A long, slow drag on the cigarette made its tip glow brightly. With air so still it allowed smoke to hang lazily about my face as it slowly drifted out my open mouth. "It's closer to three, John," I said softly.

Chapter Five

A Variety of Pets

Most if not all children want a pet of some kind and there's a vast selection available, be they dogs, cats, birds, fish, mice, rats, snakes or lizards. I was no exception to the rule where wanting a pet was concerned. However, my idea was to acquire one of the unusual kind. Some people, including mother, could not understand my preferences for anything unusual. On the other hand, Uncle was always supportive of any pet I managed to obtain. In fact, he was directly responsible for providing instructions on how to obtain my first pet, which was a jackdaw. As a natural course of events, I discovered that such a black flying object came from the crow family and was related to ravens. Uncle Willy told me, when he was my age and living in Poland, he took a young jackdaw from its nest to raise as a pet. He eventually managed to teach it to talk and come to his command.

During our discussion of keeping a wild bird, I pulled out a packet of Domino cigarettes that Dave found in his mother's secret hiding place. Dave managed to nick a full packet of five and gave them to me because, although being untrustworthy, he had a generous nature and did not smoke. They weren't bad, especially when one considers the pack came for free, which was just as well because Dominos were not designed to last long. There were only five in a pack and three hard sucks usually finished one off. On the other hand, one afternoon on my return from school, I purchased a five-pack of Joysticks. Now those things were total opposites of Domino. Five Dominos end to end were barely equal to one Joystick. Anyone attempting to finish one of those things off in three hard sucks would need lungs equal to a vacuum pump. Although Joysticks were expensive, they represented a full half hour of smoking. However, whenever I managed to get some, they remained in my secret place, especially when one took into consideration that I was not the only smoker at home.

Uncle looked at the Domino and rolled it in his fingers before lighting mine and his own. A short silence followed before he shrugged. He was not impressed and made no comment on the smouldering object rapidly disappearing with fragments of ash dropping onto the table. He continued the dialogue on his youth with, "Zis bird he is comen ven I say, eh eh."

"The bird came when you called, eh?" I asked. It was an unfortunate turn of events, whenever talking to Uncle I began copying his inadvertent expressions.

"Tak tak to jest so."

I couldn't understand how a bird could speak Polish, in English yes, but Polish. Never! Nonetheless, after our discussion it would come down to putting some effort into a search because, according to Uncle, the time of year was just about right. At Top Wood the trees were infested with a huge rookery with young rooks stretching their wings to strengthen their flight muscles as they walked along the branches. By leaving the sanctuary of their nests, they made easy targets for a bow and arrow, slingshot or air rifle. Meat was a rare commodity in our household and an overfed young rook was always welcome on rather than at the dinner table. In amongst the lower branches and smaller trees of the rookery, there were some perfect nesting places for jackdaws

During our discussion, mother came into the kitchen to make tea and sat with us. Uncle offered her one of the Dominos. That was unusual because he knew mother never smoked, although it didn't stop Uncle persuading her. He told her every sophisticated woman in the world smoked. Well, mother's attempted new venture into the world of sophistication worked for a few seconds. Her eyes became crossed as a tiny Domino cigarette between her lips was fired up. She puffed and produced a whiff of smoke. The sight filled her with joy – she could smoke!

"Do this Mum," I said and released twin plumes of smoke out my nostrils.

"Look, look!" mother exclaimed excitedly, "He is making smoke come from his nose." Mother had always been a keen competitor but never a smoker. Her attempt at copying my little trick resulted in a disastrous failure with lots of spluttering, coughing and gasping for air. She decided that smoking was a dangerous filthy habit and swore never to try it again. Mum was absolutely correct, it is and will always be a dirty habit. The three of us settled back to drink our tea while Uncle and I completed our smoke. Mother's cigarette was nipped out and tucked behind my ear. Adults do it all the time while saying "waste not want not" and it therefore seemed appropriate to follow their advice. The discussion between Uncle and me went on for some time with more advice coming from him than a United Nations committee could contend with, but it's amazing how much one needs to know in order to catch a jackdaw.

The hunt for a young jackdaw began at Top Wood but continued into the forest where I spent a considerable amount of time rather than going to school. On one particular occasion, there was plenty of that elusive wildlife on hand and my camouflage was good enough to observe their goings on without disturbing it. I remained quite still while curled under a bush. A pair of squirrels played close by and their acrobatic agility was so impressive it became an absorbing and mesmerising pleasure to watch. I often contemplated killing those animals for food because they're good to eat, almost as good as young rooks who ventured out beyond the safety of their nest. On that particular day though, my search remained restricted and focused on finding a pet and not engaged in hunting for food. I relaxed and began rolling a cigarette when a blackbird fluttered past to land close by. Its sudden appearance stilled me. My fingers holding the half-rolled cigarette stopped moving. As long as I remained perfectly still, the bird, less than a few feet away, ignored me while providing a song sweeter than anything any human could sing. A full minute went by before my movement prompted the bird to take off giving its traditional warning cries that echoed throughout the forest.

With the cigarette lit, I sat back to watch smoke drifting on a breeze toward some birds in the branches. It's surprising how much food becomes visible when one remains quite still and knows where to look. However, that was not the purpose of being there. The search for an occupied jackdaw's nest continued until one was discovered with three youngsters at home protesting loudly at my intrusion.

Before the search began, Uncle advised what size of bird I needed for the best chance of its survival after making a premature departure from home. He leaned forward to whisper the most important secret information, "You must be vaiting til ze feathers start to forming on ze vings. The fluffy stuff, she is become black. You understanding vat I mean."

I nodded and took his advice on board and could see the birds in that nest were not ready. They were plump well-fed balls of dark premature feathers. Their condition required to delay the need to take one for a pet. During the following days, I made secret journeys to feed the youngsters with titbits until they became accustomed to my visits. Like all wild animals they were happy to take food from anything prepared to stuff it into their wide open beaks. They became accustomed to an alternative diet of bread, bits of Uncle's Polish salami, worms and insects. It never seemed to make any difference how much they ate, they were always hungry and it was quite surprising how quickly the day came when a choice had to be made. I climbed the tree and peered into the nest. All three looked very fit and certainly made a lot of squawking noises whenever my head poked over the edge of their home. By that stage, fear did not prompt their cawing but a natural desire to compete for food. Well, on that day I had nothing to give them and reached in to pick one up. That experience provoked a new kind of screeching from what I now considered my pet. The terrible shrieking continued for a few moments until the bird became enclosed within the warmth and darkness between my jumper and body. Its wriggling to escape the entrapment tickled for a few moments but quickly settled into a tremble from fear.

Back at the house Uncle was full of extensive useful and useless information, apart from advice with constant recollections of his youth about what he did with his pet. There remained little doubt that Uncle was getting a great deal of pleasure from my venture. He was enjoying the entire experience as much, if not more than me. Part of Jack's training consisted of calling out the word "Jaaak" every time I passed his perch. Whenever the bird responded, it was rewarded with a titbit. Jack would eat just about anything, although he retained a strong preference to meat or bugs. Although he didn't know it, the meat came from shot animals, although there were plenty of garden bugs to supplement his diet. Wild animals grow up very quickly, that's a fact, because their very survival depends on it. Those aspects of wildlife are obvious to any hunter. Apart from that, it says so in the book called "Animals in the Wild" at the Corsham public library.

The first part of my pet's training didn't last long before Uncle taught Jack to jump onto my shoulder whenever its name was called. We spent a lot of time together with the fledgling being thrown onto my shoulder each time I called him. As the days went by, the distance between Uncle and me became greater as Jack's wings grew stronger. By the end of the first week, Jack was flying to my shoulder without being thrown at me. All he needed for a prompt was to call his name. There's something magically satisfying when one has the trust of a wild animal that comes to your call. I certainly felt pride swell to bursting the first time Jack landed on my shoulder. He was able to fly some distance at that stage and could at any time have flown away.

The ultimate test came one day after returning from school. I spotted Jack perched on the roof and called him in the usual way. With a resounding screech he flew down to land on my shoulder.

We quickly became the talk of Rudloe Estate, especially while walking up the road with him on my shoulder. We were a popular sideshow but at no time did I ever put a restraint on my pet, nor was he ever placed inside a cage. That bird remained free to come and go whenever it pleased him. Those were the very specific conditions Uncle insisted on, and I was more than happy to comply with.

Several weeks went by since my pet first came down from the roof because Jack was always there waiting for my return from school. One day, although I called several times, he never appeared. By late afternoon it became a real cause for concern because something felt wrong. I kept reminding myself that as a wild bird, Jack would only be doing what came naturally and gone off to do his own thing. After all, who would know better, that's exactly what I did all the time.

Uncle gave me an idea of what might have happened by saying, "Maybe he finding himself a girlfriend, eh, eh." He winked while nudging my ribs with his elbow and added, "He young and good looking, maybe starting a family, eh, eh."

"I just hope he'll come back eh," I responded hesitantly.

"Tak tak, but you must not be surprised if he is not, eh, eh."

The disjointed comment in a heavy Polish accent only served to remind me what we had talked about, along with the possibility of Jack leaving. Those fears were pushed to the back of my mind. It was a subject I had no intentions of thinking about. We heroic delinquents are very good at putting vital information aside if we are not happy with it.

For several days my calls continued without a response. As the days passed, any expectations of Jack's return faded. I finally resigned myself into accepting the time we shared together had been brief but good. It seemed as though my pet had returned to where he really belonged but the memory of our time together would stay with me forever.

Three weeks after Jack's disappearance and during a return from a hunting trip in the forest, I changed my normal route back home. The pride I felt in accomplishing a successful hunt was supported by a school satchel full of rabbits, pigeons and a rook. They would be placed on the kitchen table in front of mother and Uncle to see their eyes light up. I moved toward the far side of Rudloe Estate that backed onto open fields and an area that was normally avoided because there was nothing of interest there. While walking close to some houses, the squawk of a jackdaw attracted my attention. That strangely familiar noise raised a haunting memory and provided a deeper awareness that something was amiss, which quickly turned into powerful curiosity. I felt obliged to check it out and moved toward those noisy calls to investigate.

At a high wooden fence I searched for a gap in the panels to peer through and saw piles of old wooden boxes with a small wire cage on top. The black shiny form of a jackdaw huddled inside the restrictive enclosure as it perched on a swing. The sight was so horrifying it prompted me to call, "Jaaack." That caged bird went into a frantic frenzy and immediately began screeching in a familiar tone. I had finally found my missing pet and my shock at seeing it trapped inside a cage hardly big enough for a budgie prompted me to run home at top speed. I burst in on Uncle working in the shed and panted out my discovery to him.

"You are being sure of zis?"

"Yes, it's Jack I know it's him. It's him!" I exclaimed excitedly.

"I go vis you now," he said calmly putting down his tools. "Ve go see zis person und get Jack back, eh, eh."

"Make him let Jack go, set him free. Make the man set him free," I begged.

We quick marched along the road and arrived at the house where I saw Jack was imprisoned a few minutes later. Big band marching music pounded the air with a volume that vibrated the door Uncle knocked on. A dog immediately started barking, snarling, scratching and jumping against it. Fortunately for us it couldn't eat its way through dark blue painted wood. "The person living here has no regard for animals Uncle," I said just before the door inched open. A powerful smell of sweat and stale air reached my nose. It turned my stomach and made me wonder how anyone could live in such putrid stench.

An ugly, very large, unshaven face with bulging eyes glared at us through the gap. "Wadya want?" The question erupted in an angry tone above the volume of music. A waft of warm air pouring out included the putrefied smell of stale beer and cigarette smoke. Intermingled with the stench was the unmistakable smell of animals that farted a lot and had wet hair.

The man's reaction and the smells permeating the atmosphere left me with no doubt, we were confronting a subhuman species. Meantime that vicious looking mongrel dog barked and snarled at Uncle and me. However, the subhuman made no attempt to keep the animal quiet, nor turn the radio down so we could be heard.

"I am vant to talking vith you about ze bird you haf in ze garden," Uncle said. But he had not raised his voice above the noise coming from the radio and dog. I could hear Uncle but it was obvious the man couldn't.

"Whaat!" the subhuman shouted.

"You are having a bird in a cage, it belongs to ze boy here," Uncle responded in a voice several octaves higher while pointing at me. Some foul language followed before Uncle and I were told to "piss off". Until that moment I had been unaware of such humans infecting our society with so much antagonism, bad attitude and contempt for other people's feelings. It looked as though their life evolved round a total lack of consideration for anything or anyone but themselves.

"Ze bird it belonging to ze boy, you must let it go," Uncle shouted. His raised voice prompted that mongrel dog into becoming berserk. Snarling jaws with dripping saliva were the only parts protruding through the gap, which was just as well. From where we stood, it looked like a killer beast ready to devour anything, dead or alive.

"Get lost dickhead!" That instruction was followed by more foul language before the door slammed in our faces.

From the stunned look on Uncle's face, he had a hard time holding back a store of temper. He obviously knew it would be useless against such ignorance.

"Call the police," I said firmly.

"Yeah, yeah, zis ve are doing," Uncle replied before raising his chin to present a dignified undefeated profile. Then issued the single word of command, "Come." The pair of us turned and quick marched to the nearest phone box. Uncle Willy shoved pennies into the box, dialled the number, pressed button A and used the best English I ever heard from him. He explained what happened before a long pause was followed by a "thank you". A few minutes later we marched off in triumph to wait for the man in blue.

Later in the day a policeman arrived on his pushbike and the three of us set off to the subhuman's house. The dog had been put in the back garden by the time we arrived, except it continued barking while the owner stood in the doorway. He retained a defiant look with his arms folded across a dirty vest. No amount of

Nights in the Forest

reasoning by the policeman could move him. From a subhuman's point of view it had done nothing illegal and nobody could prove the bird in the cage was Jack. The policeman could do nothing and a door slamming on our backs as we walked away concluded our attempt to free Jack.

That evening Uncle, mother and I sat round the kitchen table discussing our options. I wanted to climb over the fence and set Jack free of that stupid little cage but Uncle and mother were dead set against that avenue of thinking. Being on a suspended sentence meant, if I was caught breaking into someone's garden for any reason, it meant more trouble. From my point it would have been worth it. Then Uncle reminded me about that vicious dog and its purpose. Uncle and the police attempted to reason with Jack's abductor but neither adult seemed able to come up with a solution. That left only one option, coming up with my own.

My dreams that night pictured a tortured Jack calling for help with his cries falling on deaf ears. He attempted to prize the bars apart and squeeze through the gap. I saw a ferocious dog waiting to pounce on anyone attempting to assist. My subconscious visualised that subhuman pacing the house with an angry look on his face and smoke billowing out his ears. The property was surrounded by a high wooden fence and guarded by two fierce animals, with my pet destined to remain a prisoner forever. I endured a very restless night's sleep. By breakfast I came to a difficult decision on what needed doing and with my mind made up, nothing was going to stop me. It never had in the past but this time it was for someone else's benefit.

After telling Uncle my plan to resolve the issue, he placed a hand on my shoulder and said softly, "It vill be taking much courage boy."

I put a cigarette between my lips and looked him in the eye. "So, tell me. As a man with courage, who fought both the Germans and their enemies, what would you do in my place?"

Uncle lit his cigarette and the one hanging from my mouth. He inhaled deeply, blew a long plume of smoke, he nodded slowly and said, "The same."

Anthony Corbyn

A glimmer of sunlight topped the horizon as I peered through a gap in the tall wooden fence and spotted an oversized mongrel stretched out below the cage. The bird remained stationary while I studied it. There was no mistaking it, Jack's wing feathers had been clipped right back so he had no chance to fly even if he wanted to. He was sealed inside a wire cage and guarded by a dog. Had Jack managed to escape, my pet would have been at the mercy of that animal. Angry tears blurred my vision. They were wiped away. I took several deep breaths. The rage inside grew to bursting and made my body shake while I took a few moments to calm down until, like the bird in the cage, I became absolutely still. My .22 BSA Airsporter rifle was eased through a gap and I took very careful aim. The dog twitched at the sound. A second later the quivering body of Jack lay on the bottom of the cage. His release from captivity relied on a painless death. My aim remained true, Jack was free.

My depression lasted several days with Uncle's understanding and reassurances being of little consolation or help in pulling me out of it. The idea of hunting to take my mind off the subject did not seem appropriate. There was one thing I could not do during those depressing days, it was to kill something else.

I persuaded John to play truant and join me in an adventurous expedition. As usual, his resistance to absconding from school and enjoying himself was supported by the fear of his mother discovering he had played truant. Worse than that, her loving son had been out with me. I never felt like being on my own that day and compromised the day off school by suggesting we only have half a day. John considered my proposal by rubbing his chin and frowning the way he always did before nodding.

We wasted no time setting off to Lord Methuen's private estate. John and I passed through heavy wrought iron gates at the main entrance. The long carriageway leading to the manor house was lined with huge chestnut trees. We stood in silence for a few moments while John's guilt complex rose to the surface about taking the morning off from school in the first place. Intruding on his Lordship's private property could be tantamount to asking for a prison sentence being handed down. According to John, it was a well-known fact that Lord Methuen was a justice of the peace. I simply stated that our intrusion onto his Lordship's property was not to cause damage or carry out any poaching. "Anyway," I whispered, "it makes it all the more exciting and if we're really careful we won't get caught." That said, I quickly moved behind the first tree, waved at John to follow, and started running. We suddenly became two fugitives nipping from one tree to the next. Being a dishonourable hero, or reprobate according to John's mother, I led the dash. On one or two occasions I dived for cover into tangled undergrowth. Johns red face, wide starring eyes and panting made me smile as we headed toward the lake.

Rumour had it that a large pike lived in that small lake at the far end of his Lordship's grounds. Apparently, the fish was monstrous. And I wanted to find out if it really existed. There was only one way to make that kind of discovery and it was simply to have a look. I led my friend through a narrow strip of trees that masked the high drystone wall surrounding those extensive grounds. John constantly demanded to know how much further this supposed lake was. Like any good political leader I kept assuring him with terms of "not far now". We eventually broke cover and sat down beside still waters with several water lilies floating around the edges.

"Not very big is it," John declared in a whisper.

"Big enough to house a man-eating shark," I replied and threw a pebble at a white water lily. The pebble missed and bounced across the water. Expanding rings were set in motion across green murky waters. We sat in silence watching with bated breath for a few moments. My suggestion that we go for a swim was swiftly rejected by John. The entire purpose of our enterprise was to confirm the rumour of a pike living in that lake. However, seeing it presented a problem because, as everyone knows, fish live under water. I began wishing for my fishing poles hidden beside a tree in Wyvern Valley. There were no doubts that pike would be easy to catch. All I needed was the right bait, an extra large hook, some really strong fishing line and my best fishing pole. I began working out where the materials could be acquired from when John interrupted my thoughts.

"How long are we going to wait?"

"As long as it takes John," I answered quietly and foraged through my pockets for the tin of Uncle's tobacco. Satisfying my curiosity and confirming the truth about something could take quite a long time. On the other hand, a shoe and sock on my right foot were removed and the naked foot eased gently into the water. John's eyes widened in surprise and he wanted to know why I was tempting fate. My reasoning was simple. If the pike was going to make an appearance, it needed something to tempt it out of hiding. I wiggled my foot and caused a few ripples but no splashes. Tempting fate may have been one thing, giving a ferocious man-eating pike a free feed of one's foot was something else.

"You're flipping mad."

"Yes, I know that but unless you are prepared to make an offer, this is the only way to get that fish's attention." I looked at John and wiggled my foot harder when my caution had been inadvertently thrown aside. The splash sent ripples across the still waters. So did the next and the next. The water lilies waved and encouraged me to continue, other than their response, nothing happened.

"You're flipping mad," John repeated before gasping out, "I heard that fish is big as this." He demonstrated by stretching both hands as far apart as they would reach while adding, "And it's got really sharp teeth."

Despite feeling a tremor of fear run down my spine, I felt duty-bound to remain calm by saying, "Of course it has sharp teeth John, all pikes have them."

John was obviously determined to undermine my heroism because the next thing that came out of his mouth was a whispered, "I heard that a cow came down to drink at this lake one day and got attacked by that pike."

I thought about that for a moment. It was another unfounded rumour based on hearsay. However, if true, it made perfect sense. After all, this lake was that pike's domain. A cow dipping its nose in those waters for a drink could be considered as an invasion of privacy. Defending its property by taking a bite out of that cow's nose seemed like the right thing. I took a drag on my cigarette and smiled. At the same time, that foot on the end of my leg had a good idea. Without any instructions from me, it slipped quietly out the water. John and I chatted for ages and he smoked one of my cigarettes before we decided to make the effort of attending school. We arrived just in time to line up for lunch. If we played our cards right and said nothing, there was a good chance we would not have been missed. I never did see that pike. Conversely, we had fish cakes for lunch and it made me wonder if God was rewarding me for some reason or other.

That same afternoon Uncle, mother and I sat round the table drinking tea and talking about pets. Mother's idea that another pet should be found did nothing to help because there was no alternative to Jack. Nevertheless, she suggested I go down the road and see some people who had a bitch with a litter of pups, and they would all need a good home.

With some reluctance, which included a sceptical mind, I went to the neighbour's house and knocked on their door. I can tell a lot about people from conditions surrounding their house and those living in the house I called on were definitely townies. They built a fence surrounding their property, their ground, their possessions, with each small piece having a price on it. A large black Rover Seventy-Five stood in the street opposite their gate. There were no garages attached to houses on that estate and anyone fortunate enough to own a car parked it outside. These were people who would brag about how much they paid for this or that and calculate the cost of everything. They even expected to get paid for anything they did, even though it was supposed to be a favour. Those were conclusions I drew up while standing on their doorstep. In my opinion that kind of human lived on the wrong planet. They were about to come unstuck because between myself and their doorstep I had just about enough money to buy a can of pet food.

When the door finally opened, the first thing that hit me was a powerful smell. Cool evenings made them turn up the central heating and shut all windows and doors to keep warm with every human and animal smell trapped inside. The smell reminded me of a recent encounter and it didn't help to put me in a good negotiating mood toward the occupiers. Basically, a very succinct conversation erupted between one juvenile and an adult.

"Yes." The sound was a socially acceptable version of "Wadya want?"

"I heard you have some pups."

"Yes."

"I heard you want to get rid of them."

"Yes."

"I may be interested."

"Why?"

"I may want one."

"Come in," the woman said the second we established why I was there.

I knew they could not possibly be aware of the stench they were living in, since no normal human could have put up with it. Once inside I spotted six very lively pups running around in helter-skelter fashion between table legs and those of humans sitting at it. Animals are disinclined to put up their paws when nature calls and are apt to just answering the call wherever they are. I felt certain the deep pile carpet must have been saturated in dog piss. Whilst dog poo could be seen and picked up, any carpet will soak up piss like a sponge.

The woman invited me to sit on the settee where a mass of dog hairs clung to its once pristine fabric. I pinched my nose, although the smell did not seem to affect any other human resident. Three children sat at the table. They were very pink and clean. Their father sat at one end with mother at the other. Each one looked like cloned humans, since each child bore a striking resemblance to their parents. The low volume of music from a radio made it audible enough to make out Buddy Holly singing his latest hit "That'll Be the Day".

A sizeable dog basket stood in a corner with an even larger bitch overfilling it. She was either pregnant again or very overweight. To my way of thinking, any animal needs lots of exercise.

Townies don't have a clue, their ability to come to terms with country life or know how to treat animals does not exist. I wanted to take one pup for no other reason than to give it some reality and living space. Dogs have fur coats and four legs, which is nature's design. They're made for living outdoors or open shelter. Four legs need twice as much exercise as two. Nonetheless, we two-legged animals dictate how much exercise the four-legged ones got.

The pups were running amok with one squatting in a corner for a piss while the family continued chattering and eating their dinner. The mother of three instructed me to select a pup and wait until the family finished eating their bangers and mash before she attended to me. Therein lay another clue to her ignorance. One does not choose an animal, it chooses you, since their instincts are far more advanced than any human could hope to acquire.

I watched the antics going on until a pup scampered across the room to stand at my feet. Big brown eyes looked at me for a few moments with its head cocked to one side and one ear flopped over. It snarled then attacked my shoe before pulling at the laces. The animal also bit my hand when I reached down to pick up the small bundle of hyperactive, multicoloured fur. The bite was not of a savage animal but a friendly one and a bond was instantly established. I lifted it up by the scruff of its neck to check if it was a dog or bitch as we continued looking into each other's eyes. The pup, which was a bitch, uttered a soft yelp. I placed it on my lap and patted the tiny body gently to calm her as we waited until the humans finished eating their dinner. Children and parents persisted in feeding animals with bits of food from the table. I believe that's a dirty habit and never understood it, which left me drawing the only conclusion available – that's what townies did.

With their meal over, the children scattered while the father went into another room to read a newspaper. The woman towered over me wearing a flowery ankle-length skirt and not very elegant fashionable high heel shoes. She wore the latest beehive hairdo, which made her rotund stature look taller than she really was. The sleeves on her red buttoned-up blouse were rolled up to reveal pale pink flabby arms. With her face painted in a multitude of colours she looked like a prize fighter coming out for the last round. Maybe this time her face won't get hit by the world champion winning on points. Conversely, the woman could have been a low-class prostitute procuring the services of her first customer. This was particularly obvious when she asked how much money I wanted to pay.

"None," I replied.

"Well!" she puffed in exasperation. Both hands immediately rested on broad hips as she leaned forward. "Don't you think the dog's worth, anything?" Her voice could only be considered as being a raised condescending tone, particularly on the word "anything". A note of sarcasm was detected in the moral pressure she began applying to obtain some cash. Adults do that to each other. It also works exceptionally well on most of us younger generation.

I wanted to correct that description by informing her, the dog was actually a bitch, but my reluctance to being offensive stopped me. I have never been prepared to put a price on any animal's head and responded by saying, "My friend said you were giving them away. In any case, I don't have any money."

From the look of her eyes and open mouth, she obviously had never encountered that tactic before. With hands remaining on childbearing hips, a pair of frustrated eyes glowered down on me. "Well, you'll have to give me something for the dog. Nothing in this world's for free, you know."

"I know that Missis but I don't have any money," I reiterated my lack of finances in some faint hope the message would eventually get through.

"Well. What are you going to give me for the dog, little boy?"

That kind of attitude some adults have toward children got up my nose. Once again, I bit my tongue to the reply bursting to come out, "Well, keep the animal. It's a mongrel bitch not a damn dog. It's not worth a penny anyway." However, a new element entered the game in the form of a little warm bundle of fur that had fallen asleep on my lap and we just became attached. "I'll give her a good home."

Nights in the Forest

"Well yes of course you will," the woman said while patting me on the head. I seriously considered biting her hand but the patronizing statement concluded with, "What do we get for letting you take the dog?"

I came close to reaching the limit of my patience and took a deep breath before answering. "You get one less pup to feed and look after," I muttered between clenched teeth while wondering if my hostess could tell the difference between a snarl and a smile. I doubted it.

"Well!" There was that exasperated expression erupting again. It seemed a prelude for everything she wanted to say. "Everyone around here expects something for nothing."

At that stage my simple juvenile analysis of those people was confirmed. They needed some tangible evidence that provided them with proof of greater wealth. My family managed with the bare necessities of life, yet we possessed a wealth those people would have no idea how to begin counting. I left with a new friend under my arm and walked into clean fresh air outside. A great sense of relief overcame me at having made good my escape and in rescuing a helpless animal from a life inside. I was unable to understand why those people didn't realize how much their house stank. During my walk back, the pup was put down and I walked away from her. She yapped before following for a few yards. Four tiny legs were loaded with springs as she bounced toward me, and then promptly sat down. After calling to her while slapping the side of my leg, the pup leaped up and scampered toward me. I turned and continued walking and before going far I turned to see her sitting down again. Her persistence in sitting down every few yards happened several times until she point-blank refused to budge. No amount of calling and leg slapping would move her. The animal had a real attitude problem concerning the need to walk as opposed to being carried. There were no intentions on my part of allowing her to be boss and carried wherever I decided to go. Uncle once told me, the difference between man and animals was man's will, it is stronger and the reason why we were the dominant species. Ha! Someone needed to inform Uncle about a new breed of animal. My newfound friend and I became locked in a battle of wills, her reluctance to obey left little option but to begin walking backwards calling to her while slapping my leg. My nerve had almost given out when the pup yelped and bounced after me on little furry feet. It seems Uncle had been right, although it sure as hell was a close-run thing.

Animals, particularly pets, need a name. At that time, the only one which came to mind was Lassie. That popular name came about because of a well-known story of a Collie with the same name. Not only were books written about her, a number of films were made as well. "Lassie" and "Lassie Come Home" are two that spring to mind.

Mother wasn't sure if her idea had been a good one until I handed the little bundle of fur over for a closer look. One lick on her face was enough to dispel any doubts and for the next couple of days all of mum's attention was diverted to the pup. From the attention being doted on it, Lassie could have been a newborn child and I believe Uncle became jealous of coming in second.

On the third night, Lassie was put into Uncle's shed. I made up a soft bed for her inside a cardboard box to keep warm and snug. That idea did not make her happy and she whined for most of the night. By the second night in the shed it became clear she would remain outside for keeps so the whimpering finally stopped. In the meantime Uncle set about building a kennel. By the second week, Lassie had her own home, which stood on the front lawn and things began settling into a routine. Everyone, including Lassie, seemed happy and content. During dinner one evening Uncle, mother and I were discussing the cost of feeding my new pet, although I could not understand mother's concern, after all, it was her idea.

"It won't cost anything, Mum, we'll just feed Lassie with food scraps off the table."

"Ha! There is hardly enough to feed the family never mind that dog."

Mother had a point. However, the subject needed setting aside while I tucked into an oversized faggot made by Loves, the local butcher. Faggots and peas with mashed potato was rare expensive fare on our dinner table. They were also my favourite food, next to rabbit, pigeon or rook pie.

"You must going hunting for food, maybe you feeding zis dog und us, eh, eh." Uncle had spoken, yet it sounded like a declaration.

"I'll need to take more time off school Uncle, I can't go hunting otherwise." My attempt at getting Uncle to see my point regarding hunting as opposed to school reflected my ambition.

However, his opposition to it remained adamant. "Zis you vill not do."

Things got pretty tough at that stage because not only did I have to attend school but hunting could only be made in free time. That only occurred during very early morning, early evenings in summer months, on weekends or during school holidays. In fact, hardly any time at all. Responsibilities needed attending to and these included educating myself, providing food for Lassie and everyone else living at 123 Rudloe Estate, Hawthorn. Growing up was not easy when one's time is absorbed by providing for others. Things would have to change. They did, but not to my advantage.

A Rhode Island Red is a fair-sized chicken and mother's original idea for purchasing it was to have an egg-laying bird on hand to save money. Naturally, the stall holder at the Saturday market never told mother the chicken had long passed its egg-laying days. Even a useful chicken passes its shelf life date. What mother purchased turned into an enormous, aggressive bird that quickly established a territorial area. It spent hours on top of Lassie's kennel preening a mass of motley brown feathers. The kennel, built by Uncle and the home of Lassie, became an entrance to a den and will be described in detail later. It became a hazardous affair for anyone attempting to approach Lassie's home while a big, rusty red, oversized, bad-tempered chicken was roosting on it. She, the chicken, would attack anything trying to pass close by. The only passage to our front door was a pathway with a dog kennel standing nearby. Our admirable chicken's disruptive and belligerent attitude earned her the name Guardian.

Each morning mother inspected the kennel looking for any eggs Guardian may have laid. However, there were several problems with mother's persistent pilgrimages. In the first place Guardian was far too old to lay eggs, secondly, the chicken's vindictive nature prompted her to attack anything or anyone, including mother, approaching the kennel, thirdly, Lassie shared that abode with Guardian and according to mother, "that dog has an appetite for eggs." That declaration was issued after every unsuccessful egg collecting expedition to the kennel.

"What makes you say that Mum?"

"That chicken eats everything. She's been here a week already and not a single egg. Ha! You know why, that stupid dog eats all the eggs." Anyone would have a hard time trying to convince mother otherwise with that kind of logic.

"Ach, the chicken she is needing more time to settle," Uncle assured her.

Uncle and I knew it would take more than time. A blessing from God and a miracle might do it, more than likely a trip to a local grocery shop. Uncle burst out laughing when I asked what the chances were of Guardian actually laying any eggs in the near future. Our discussion resulted in a surreptitious trip to a shop as the only way to keep mother happy. With no alternative, Uncle gave me some money to go shopping. The list was very short, actually only one item appeared on it – "six eggs". "If mother wants eggs then eggs are what mother will have," I said as the pack was hidden in the garden shed for safe keeping.

Next morning mother stormed into the kitchen in an excited fit while holding up an egg. My lovely mum wanted to share the egg but Uncle and I insisted she should have the first fresh egg for breakfast herself. By the time breakfast was over, mother claimed it as the best egg she ever tasted. Fortunately for her devoted male companions, mother was short-sighted enough not to see the image of a lion stamped on it. Now that would have taken some creative imagination to explain away.

The remaining eggs were placed in the kennel each successive morning. Uncle and I watched as mother's pride came close to bursting while pooh-poohing our previous claims about old hens.

Nights in the Forest

Mother's confidence grew to announcing she would be going into the market again and buying another chicken. Uncle and I grinned, what else could we do? Without any options we were committed to buying more eggs. Although seriously considered, the idea of another chicken never got off the ground. When no more eggs appeared, mother became concerned that Guardian had been disturbed and wanted to know if either of us had done anything to upset her. "I bet it's that damn dog," she hissed. The gleam in her eyes proved she found the answer.

Uncle did not want to reveal what really happened and convinced mother the chicken's egg-laying days were over. "She is out of seazen," he said softly with a hand on her shoulder. It was uttered in his most sincere voice as he pulled mum closer. He kissed her on the forehead and muttered reassuringly, "Chicken she lay eggs like having babies, eh, eh. Even ve humans must having a rest eh, until next year anyvay."

That settled mother for a while. The days passed quickly as autumn passed into winter. It was late December by the time winter really set in. Biting cold nipped at finger tips and ears. Hunting had not been good even though my confiscated small bore shotgun was returned under specific instructions. Any move by me, from what was considered normal by adults in authority, carried escalating levels of punishment. That threat seemed fair enough but there was a strong sense of being imprisoned with constraints imposed by adult rules. There were times when I considered breaking away. Except my resistance against such wilful urges remained strong and held me in place.

On Christmas Eve, I was lying in bed watching millions of snowflakes floating down to earth. They were big, bigger than I had ever seen and clearly going to settle. The sky was chock-full of them swirling in the wind. Within a short time everything outside became covered in a white blanket several inches deep. While gazing at the white wonder cascading down, I came up with an idea and got dressed in warm clothing before stepping out into cold night air. The heavy falls had diminished to a few flakes. Nevertheless, there was more than enough snow on the ground to complete the project in mind. It would take time but however much time was spent would be worth every second.

The early hours of Christmas morning saw my task completed. Snowflakes had stopped falling altogether by then, leaving an empty, almost black velvet sky sprinkled with stars. Below that vast empty expanse, our front garden contained a massive monument to my endeavours, it was the biggest snowman ever built and stood at least ten feet tall. Most of the snow on our front garden and adjacent roadside contributed to the construction of my monolith. Although soaking wet and very cold, I took time out to inspect my night's work before going into mother's bedroom. I smiled at the sleeping forms of mum and Uncle competing on who could snore louder. The first thing that needed doing was to stoke up the pot-bellied stove and put a kettle on it before waking the happy couple when the tea was ready. I recalled Uncle saying he couldn't function properly before a cup of tea and a cigarette.

I shook mother awake to stare into an upturned face with bleary eyes surrounded by puffed lids and bags under them. We were almost nose to nose when I whispered, "Your Christmas present is waiting outside by the gate. It won't fit in through the door."

Mother's eyes began blinking rapidly before they lit up. "Too big to bring into the house?" she queried.

"I can't get it through the door Mum."

Her mouth fell open as she made a huge effort to get out of bed and woke Uncle while doing so. They both followed me into the front garden where mother craned her neck in open-mouthed wonder at my white monolith towering above her. "It's for you, mum," I said putting an arm around her and concluding with, "Merry Christmas."

Mum burst into tears while Uncle burst out laughing as we held hands and danced around the white monster. We were shouting and singing carols at the top of our voices. Lights came on and neighbours appeared at their windows, wide-eyed, open-mouthed and unable to believe that the crazies were up at five in the morning dancing and singing round a giant snowman.

Nights in the Forest

Christmas would never be the same again. I did my best with whatever materials were on hand, which cost me nothing. Time was the only thing available but I was more than happy to give it to mother. My work created happiness beyond price and much later the same day, I sat on a chair outside cleaning my small bore shotgun with a kit Uncle gave me for Christmas. The sun shone down from a clear blue sky. A huge snowman stood like a monumental sentinel at the entrance to our house. Not only peace and tranquillity filled the air but God was in his heaven and everything was right with the world. During the festive season there was always a feeling of goodwill.

A cleaning cloth had just been pulled through the barrel for the third time. I watched a long-haired German Shepherd wander past my snow sentry into the garden. The dog started sniffing whilst advancing cautiously toward Guardian sitting atop the kennel. As it closed on the structure, the more agitated one very large antagonistic Rhode Island Red became. A large comb on Guardian's head flopped over one eye; to see anything making a direct approach meant cocking her head to one side. That physical attitude presented the world with a sharp beady yellow and red eyeball with a definite glint of danger. Unfortunately, one ignorant animal, namely a dog, couldn't detect it. As the oversized long-haired German Shepherd moved closer, Guardian's feathers became fluffed out to give the impression of growing bigger.

The dog had almost reached the kennel when a wild screech rent the air. One very large angry chicken leaped onto one petrified dog's back as it turned to flee. A very surprised, bewildered and totally disorientated animal charged down the garden path howling before running blindly. In the meantime, a furious chicken dug its claws into flesh and clung to its back while pecking away for all it was worth.

My laughter was still echoing through our house when Guardian came strutting through the gate clucking to herself, the way chickens do. She fluttered onto where she belonged and commenced preening herself. Occasionally she cocked her head to one side, peered from that beady eye then clucked contentedly at a job well done.

By February, temperatures dropped to record lows and it was no surprise to find Guardian belly up stiff as a post. I thought it must have been old age but exposure may have been a contributing factor to her demise. She was ceremoniously placed on the kitchen table while a family meeting was held to decide what we should do with the corpse.

"What do you think she died of, Uncle?"

"Probably ze cold, her age, maybe something else," he replied. Whenever Uncle didn't know the answer to a question he ensured no loss of face by providing a multi-selection of possibilities, any of which could be correct.

"Best thing is to bury her then," I suggested.

We watched mother prodding a frozen bony breast. She obviously had other potential uses for a dead chicken. This was reflected when she said, "There's not much meat on it but I think it should be good to eat." Her words were as much to herself as to Uncle and me staring at her in amazement.

Guardian had been a pet that now represented meat, food and nourishment, so a vote unanimously decided to put the carcass to good use. That decision came after we convinced each other, it hadn't died of plague, some other unmentionable transmittable disease and it's what the chicken would have wanted. To this day I remain convinced our pet died of a very old age. Guardian was much too tough a bird to have been killed by a mere minus fifteen degrees of freezing cold.

Several hours of constant boiling produced a strong-flavoured chicken soup, which everyone claimed as the most delicious they ever tasted. The flesh, what there was of it, didn't improve one iota, nor did it become tender no matter what mother did. Bits of meat the texture of hemp rope were being pulled from between my teeth for days after.

Chapter Six

Dangerous Visits to the Underworld

Our front garden was extensive and well laid out because Uncle devoted a lot of time and effort into producing a flat grassy lawn that fronted the road. He also planted a colourful flower border around the edges. Pansies were his favourite, so naturally an abundance of them surrounded well maintained home turf. Intermittent, various coloured rose bushes and wallflowers filled in the gaps. Red, yellow and white provided a beautiful sight to any passer-by.

Lassie's kennel was set aside near the house where she spent most of her time waiting for my return from school. We would set off to the forest and hunt, fish or expand our horizons by exploring new pastures. Those expeditions were always a relief for her because on several occasions Lassie had been alone for some time. With nothing better to do, she would charge the fence and bark at people passing by. However, a real dislike developed for anyone on a pushbike. There appeared no logic behind her reasoning, although it may have been something to do with legs seemingly rotating in midair. Whatever the motivation was, it remains one of life's great mysteries.

A chain linked fence surrounding our garden was strengthened to ensure Lassie didn't escape again. Her reputation of being a vicious attacking beast grew daily. I personally couldn't understand how that character trait came about but there was some concern that one day she'd get herself into real trouble. For the most part, my bitch's actions were simply playful, although it became difficult to distinguish where she drew the line between playfulness and aggression.

On one occasion she chased an old man on his bike and I have to admit, at the time, she was being playful. Most dogs love chasing anything on the move. However, the old man's attempt at kicking Lassie promptly superseded her playful attitude with anger taking its place. After all, nobody likes being kicked, particularly dogs. That little escapade sentenced her to being secured within the garden. Restricting any animal's movements wasn't something that came naturally to me, nor, for that matter, to Lassie.

My idea to build a den, with its design inspired by a movie, was quickly transferred onto a page of notepaper into a rough outline of what it would look like. The only question remaining unanswered was where to build it? A decision on where the digging should start came quickly and by the time mother returned from work, she couldn't believe her eyes.

A huge square hole at least ten feet by ten feet had appeared right in the middle of Uncle's front lawn. My explanation to mother seemed simple enough. All the turf had been carefully removed, the topsoil had been put aside and all the excess diggings would be carried away, when the den was finished. By the time it was completed there wouldn't be a trace of the current mess. Mother remained sceptical and unconvinced. She almost wept with despair as she ran inside.

Lofty and John were summoned to the cause, although whenever a proposed new venture and task needed working on, John never appeared on time. He turned up much later when the hole in the middle of that famously manicured front lawn was almost two feet deep. My friend appeared in spotlessly clean clothes with shoes polished to parade ground standard. He stood beside the fence standing at ease watching Lofty and me digging. After a few minutes I stopped to look at him. "Why don't you come over and give us a hand?"

"I'll get dirty, me mum wouldn't like that," he replied in a quiet voice and nice friendly smile.

I climbed out the hole and confronted my friend supervising from the other side of the fence. "You're supposed to be helping us dig this hole," I muttered through clenched teeth and leaning over to look the late arrival up and down. "You turn up two hours late, and look at you. You're all dressed up for Sunday school."

"Yeah well, me mum doesn't like me going out unless I'm clean and tidy," John replied. He had good reason to shuffle nervously while squaring those dropped shoulders and looking away from my angry glare.

"So. Does that mean you're not going to help?" I demanded.

"Can't," was his short reply.

"Well!" Lofty exclaimed from where he stood in the hole, "If you're not going to help, I'm not going to dig while you watch." That said, he threw the shovel down and sat on the edge of the hole. John had only been there for a few minutes and a labour dispute and strike was the result. To be fair, it was nothing less than one could expect. After all, he was John!

I stood close enough to smell aftershave on his face and wondered why he went to so much trouble and how soon he would actually start shaving. Fair-haired people, even ginger-headed ones, always started shaving much later than we dark-haired people. That's a well-known fact of life. I rubbed my smooth chin and said, "Okay, if you don't help us you can't come into the den when it's ready."

John took my ultimatum as an affront. He couldn't understand why I became upset just because he arrived two hours late and unable to work. My friend obviously put himself through a lot of trouble getting ready to make an appearance, only to have his presence of just standing and watching rejected. He stood there with an aftershave splashed face going red and his mouth open.

I turned and jumped into the hole. It was pointless attempting to persuade John into changing his mind because he simply didn't understand. Let's be honest, understanding his dilemma was easy. He couldn't very well tell his mother he intended seeing me and had therefore obeyed the rules laid down whenever venturing out. Had he told the truth, his mum would have prevented him leaving. Talk about being caught in a cleft stick. "Ignore him, Lofty. When the den's ready he'll be the first wanting to come down and he'll be the first refused."

Lofty's face lit up. His lips broke into a grin. He looked at John then me standing in the hole. "Yeah, yeah, that's a great idea," he stuttered and started laughing as he dropped in beside me and picked up the shovel.

John remained outside the fence watching until the silence got to him and he felt obliged to say something. As usual, whenever John spoke it inevitably meant asking a question. "How deep are you going to dig it?" Neither Lofty nor I looked up nor answered. A few minutes of digging followed before he spoke again. "Where's the entrance?"

Those of us digging continued ignoring him, until the sound of an ice cream van sounded on the tense atmosphere. It was playing Green Sleeves with tinkling bells and distracted my attention from digging. I watched a colourfully painted vehicle stop close by with its continuous tinny tune playing. I delved into deep pockets to salvage any coins and came up with a few halfpennies. John and Lofty watched in avid anticipation of there being sufficient funds for more than one ice cream cornet. Unfortunately, one of them would be disappointed. I scrambled out the hole and ran to that ice cream vendor and purchased one small two-penny ice cream cornet. That little treat left me broke. By the time my slow walk took me back to the front lawn, only one thing remained – the soggy remains of a cone. A small dribble of white vanilla flavoured ice cream coloured the sides. Both my mates looked expectantly at the edible wafer.

"Good was it?" John asked.

"Delicious."

"What flavour was it?" Lofty asked.

"Gorgeous vanilla I think."

"Didn't last long, did it?" John retorted.

"No it didn't."

"Not a lot left is there," John stated half-expectantly.

I looked at the remains of melted ice cream surrounding wet wafer and seriously considered finishing it off in front of them. Three pairs of eyes were transfixed on the object in my hand. One pair brightened considerably when I handed the misshapen soggy cone with melted ice cream to Lofty.

"Cor, thanks," were the only words escaping his mouth before a wide open tooth-encircled cavity encapsulated that wafer. The entire remains disappeared in a second. I have never seen eyes close in rapture before, not the way his did that day. Lofty and I recommenced digging. After about an hour with none of John's persistent questions answered, we sat down to have a long cool refreshing drink of milk.

The white nectar, cow juice as we called it, was delivered to household doorsteps every morning in pint bottles, whatever the weather. Having a refrigerator to keep things cool was something prosperous people could afford. Those on a subsistence allowance ventured to keep things cool by storing them overnight in a pale of cold water. The only option was to consume perishables before they went off. Bread went stale, margarine melted, milk curdled and any fresh meat became putrid very quickly. Meat was one item of food that never became a problem. Most of the time, we never had any, unless my hunting in the forest had been successful. Milk was consumed on a daily basis, whilst remnants of stale bread were used to mop up soups, casseroles and used to make bread and butter pudding. In our case the butter was substituted for the ever adaptable Echo margarine. Bread and whatever was available pudding with a sprinkling of sultanas became a rare favourite.

John moved inside the garden and stood between us in his gleaming brown leather shoes purchased from St Vincent De Paul's. He crouched down dangerously close to the dirt. "Can I have a drink?" he asked.

"You haven't earned it," I replied handing whatever remained to my other friend sitting beside me. He wore a torn shirt, frayed shorts, no socks with mud encrusted shoes, covered in dirt and sweat.

Lofty wasn't going to miss such a good opportunity to teach John a lesson and promptly emptied the remaining milk noisily down his throat. The steady glug, glug, glug, sounded like water going down a drain. It didn't take long to hear a satisfied sigh, a belch, then a smirk appear on his happy face. That action ensured his fair share and denied John any reward.

"It's not my fault I've got me best gear on," John whined.

"Come on mate let's get on with it." I tapped Lofty on the shoulder and we dropped into the hole.

Suddenly! John jumped down beside us demanding the shovel. Lofty pulled it out of reach. "Give me that shovel, I'll do some digging," John hissed while holding out his hand.

Lofty had been in possession of that shovel for hours and wasn't about to give it up to anyone. He held onto it very tightly and kept it out of Johns reach.

"If you want to use the pick, Lofty will do the shovelling," I said breaking the antagonistic silence while holding the pick out to John.

I quickly became impressed with John's endeavour to make up for his failings. Once the shine left his shoes and dirt worked its way onto his shirt and trousers, an amazing transformation developed. He actually began enjoying the physical effort and worked like a man possessed. The pick came dangerously close to killing two other occupants of that overcrowded hole. Dirt and stone fragments began flying in all directions and mounting up. Grim determination showed on his red face as sweat formed and wetted the armpits of such a pristine white shirt.

I took the shovel from Lofty to give him a break and began digging a long trench toward Lassie's kennel. An idea was about to unfold and it represented a master stroke of lateral thinking. My pet's kennel would be our secret entrance to the underground den and I intended digging a tunnel that would connect the two. By the end of our first day we sat on the edge of an enormous cavity produced in the middle of Uncle's front lawn. A large pile of earth and stone made a conspicuous mound on one side while the hole dominated what remained of the garden. My mother made numerous visits to watch our progress before leaving in a wailing fit of despair.

Any reassurances continued falling on deaf ears so I decided on enlisting more help to finish the job as quickly as possible. There was only one way to put mother out of her misery and concerns. We, the gang, had to complete my project in record time. The thought of Uncle's imminent return prompted me to complete the den and fully restore the garden to its former glory. My project was placed in the top priority bracket. Most of the garden remained undamaged, in which case I saw no reason for mother's prophetic warnings of dire repercussions about to descend on everyone via Uncle.

More friends were requested to assist in a search for timber and sheets of corrugated iron to place over the hole. I could then put every cut turf back into place. Then, all I had to do, was get rid of several tons of stone, rubble, rocks and earth. The only difference would be a periscope protruding from one corner disguised with a few re-planted bunches of flowers.

Two more days passed but after a lot of searching and hard work donated by the gang, with some arguments thrown in, I looked at what could be seen of the finished den. A large pile of debris and earth remained. But I promised mother it would be removed soon. Right then, only one important thing remained – we had to try it out.

Those involved with the den's construction became automatic members of my gang and we dropped into its entrance inside Lassie's kennel. Then we crawled along that cunningly constructed tunnel to the den. Once inside our tomb-like environment with a candle, everyone wanted to look through the periscope. We shuffled round taking turns at peering through the periscope on an uninterrupted view of the outside world. The area we could see included the entire garden and big wet nose of Lassie sniffing at our funny object moving in the corner.

During the gang's first meeting we formed a committee to decide what rules to impose and who would have permission to come into our inner sanctum. It was my gang, in my den, in my garden, so naturally I assumed command. John was considered the intellectual; actually everyone knew he was a teacher's pet, so he became responsible for recording every regulation. Our decisions were written on paper so there could be no arguments. The rules were applicable to every member without exception. That decision came about because I insisted on forming a democratic gang who lived by the rules the majority made. Apart from all that mumbo jumbo, I demanded it.

Rule one. No girls. Lofty held our solitary candle close to the paper while John began scribbling and smiling to himself. The candle cast a shadow over his face and highlighted a prominent nose. He looked even more grotesque than usual.

Rule two. No farting. A one-week ban will be imposed on any perpetrator of this offence. John began nodding vigorously and scrawling pencil marks in shadowy candlelight. Other members were murmuring their approval while a hushed discussion went on for the next rule.

Rule three. Alcohol and girly magazines are permitted. No one could figure out where any alcohol was going to come from but girly magazines presented no problem. Everyone knew, their fathers, in my case Uncle, had some securely locked away in their secret places. On the other hand, John had a curious frown rippling a freckled forehead.

Rule Four. No animals with the exception of Lassie. I demanded a concession by explaining it was her home being invaded every time we came to the den. Lofty wanted his two pennyworth to be put in by insisting my dog was not allowed in the den. "She can come down but must remain in the tunnel. She smells!" he concluded amongst whispered approval from the others.

One Saturday afternoon, the gang assembled to discuss what we should do for the rest of that day. Everyone was chattering away, minding their own business and putting forward various venues for consideration. Suddenly! And for reasons I wasn't sure of, my unpredictable mother insisted that all my friends should go home. Mother got down on all fours, stuck her head inside Lassie's kennel and shouted her demands down the tunnel. "Hey! You kids down there. You come out of this hole right now and go home."

I pushed my way to the periscope. Only one thing could be seen, it was a big brown eye staring back at me. Frankly, I've never been able to understand why mother didn't like having half a dozen kids under the front lawn. Her objection to their presence was demonstrated by jumping up and down on the roof. Those actions created considerable panic below as dirt and stone immediately began tumbling onto us. I shouted for everyone to stand up and support the roof. Their response was instantaneous.

Nights in the Forest

As one, we stood within the confines of our potential tomb and pressed our shoulders against what can only be described as fragile timbers. Meanwhile mother continued her ravings in an apparent attempt to bury her son and all his friends alive. The screaming above and below didn't last long. It suddenly went quiet. I peered through the periscope to see mother disappearing into the house.

"She's going back inside," I whispered in a voice hardly audible above the heavy breathing and whining. My scream of "Scramble!" couldn't be mistaken for anything else.

Lofty had the good fortune of being nearest the exit. He dived into that bolt-hole and crawled in double time along the tunnel while I remained at the periscope. Mother reappeared. She was staggering along holding a bowl of what looked like dirty washing-up water slopping over the sides. My warning call of "Lofty, look out," came too late.

One eager young escapee managed to reach Lassie's kennel and was about to make good his escape. As luck or good fortune would have it, he arrived at the same moment as mother. She promptly emptied a bowl full of dirty, soapy water over his head. Lofty let out a yell of surprise, scrambled to his feet and made a run for it. In the meantime, mother began having a laughing fit that buckled her legs. She went down onto hands and knees. With a body trembling from a laughing convulsion she crawled back to the kitchen to get more water.

I knew what my duty was and remained staunchly at my post beside the periscope watching the funny sight of Lassie's kennel disgorging one gang member after another. Moments later, mother came staggering out with another bowl of water slopping everywhere. Her cackling laughter echoed into the confines of the den where I watched through the periscope. The last escapee made it before she had time to drench another rascal. Nonetheless, that didn't stop her throwing water down the hole anyway. Mother caught her breath and stopped giggling before she bent down to yell into the tunnel, "Is there anyone left down there?"

There was no reply from me looking at her buttocks in the air, her head in the kennel and her voice booming down the shaft. I jammed a fist in my mouth to stop any laughter erupting. I turned the periscope toward the playing field and saw every gang member waiting for me to emerge. I'm not stupid and waited till mother went back into the house before chancing my own escape.

From that day we used the den with caution. Everyone considered it dangerous to attempt an entry of our sanctuary while mother was at large. Although six gang members were able to chase Lassie off, she became accustomed to following the last man down. However, mother presented a different problem altogether.

"It's not such a big problem," I said with an assuring wave of my hand to those sitting in a circle. "All we have to do is wait till my mum goes shopping." My simple logic brought smiles to their faces.

By the time the den was well established, regular meetings were held in its dim, dank, muddy cavity. This muddy surface was a direct result of rainwater seeping in from high ground. Science lessons at school revealed that water always finds its own level. Unfortunately for us, our den was below ground level and all raindrops fell on the surface. Apart from that, normal gang life for those involved began to look good. Our meetings involved smoking, looking at any girly magazines that could be "borrowed" and cracking dirty jokes. There were a lot of knock-knock jokes that were quite stupid but funny at the time.

> Knock knock.
> Who's there?
> Mandy.
> Mandy who?
> Man de lifeboats we'em sinking.

Uncle returned to find his beloved garden and lawn the site of a ferocious terrorist battle. Although, after a few weeks, he also settled down to accepting things the way they were.

Lassie was almost full-grown and ranked highly as one of the scraggiest looking dogs ever born. She also became rebellious for some reason and her normally playful nature turned aggressive with barking and snapping without good reason. A local policeman came round to warn me that time was not on her side if she continued behaving badly. I took her with me on fishing trips and hunting expeditions to the forest, which at that time of year never happened very often. As dogs go, Lassie could not be considered a pretty sight. A black patch over one eye gave her a very close resemblance to a buccaneer. Adding to her piratical appearance was a ragged pair of ears, with one flopping down while the other did its best to stay erect. The deceptive smile served as a disguise for her shocking mood swings. Black, brown and white in various shades of imperfection would best describe her colour scheme. As to her physical dimensions, it would have been anyone's guess which part belonged to any particular breed. She was called a Heinz fifty-seven variety, which I thought was a bit unfair. Whatever her lineage, it was of no consequence to me because Lassie remained a faithful inseparable companion.

A particularly exciting adventure we shared was embarking on a caving expedition. Although one must confess to them not really being caves but old mines where sandstone blocks were cut out and used as building material for local towns and the city of Bath. The mines at Boxfields had long since closed down with every shaft entrance either sealed off or notices in big red lettering put up to deter anyone from entering. Notices with the words "Mine do not enter", "Danger do not Enter" and "Trespassers will be prosecuted" were of little deterrent to mischievous hooligans and juvenile delinquents. I learned from an early age that satisfaction came from achieving objectives by one's own means, particularly when it came to being dangerous or forbidden.

Early one morning a group of youths from nine to fifteen stood in front of the entrance to a forbidden mine. We came prepared and some were better equipped than others. Candles and pieces of Perspex were standard lighting equipment and as an ex-Cub Scout my own preparations for the expedition were made well in advance. This included making sure I had two candles, some matches, several ready-made cigarettes, a pile of sandwiches and a bottle of milk to drink. All these items were stowed securely in my school satchel. The stone mines at Boxfields were a long way from home and I had every intention staying out all day. Apart from that, whenever Lassie accompanied me she remained perpetually hungry. I never knew an animal could consume so much food and still stay as skinny as she did.

When looking at the motley bunch of kids standing around, it made me wonder on the reasons why such a varied selection of idiots wanted to congregate. We were about to undertake an extraordinary endeavour, actually it was downright dangerous. Apart from that, it was forbidden, which happened to be the primary reason John decided not to come. Lassie and I stood beside the group's self-proclaimed leader called Tom who wasn't only the eldest but taller than anyone else with ginger hair, blue eyes and buck teeth. He also had a torch, which made him rich and therefore in command. Even at that early stage my dislike for Tom grew beyond reasonable proportions. Then came Mike who was much smaller, with dark hair cut short and a perpetual smile on his face. He couldn't do anything about it, that feature was given to him by God before he came into the world. Then there was David, also known as De De on account of his initials, who was a foreign import from Italy. With a name like David d'Angelino it was hardly surprising. He presented a sombre moody person who came from a broken home and poor family. It clearly showed in his clothing that cried out for repair. He had a pale face topped off with an unruly mop of fair hair and must have taken after his mother. Everyone knows Italians are dark-haired and olive-skinned. Lastly there was another David, the youngest member of our adventurous party and the roundest. Being a bit on the short rotund side naturally earned him the nickname of Stumpy.

We were a bunch of misfits about to partake in the challenge of going underground to find a small part of real life in a place that remained forbidden to the likes of us.

"Follow me," Tom called out with a distinct air of superiority as he waved his arm in a forward motion. He began striding toward a dark opening in the ground. At that moment, my decision not to like the nerd exceeded all boundaries, despite not knowing, nor ever having met him before. On reflection, my aversion toward him becomes simple enough to explain. In the first place, Tom was bigger than me and assumed command. From my point of view anyone in command represented someone in authority, unless it was me. Since all my problems came from that category of people, it seemed reasonable enough to evoke a distrust and dislike. His self-assuring physical posture and condescending tone of voice didn't help either. Add to that a total distrust for anyone taller than me and one can imagine my scepticism extended to almost everyone. I had a diminutive stature compared to most children my age.

We motley bunch of degenerates followed our leader into the entrance of that forbidden zone and within minutes were swallowed up by darkness. It became very quiet. We started whispering as a small torch in Tom's hands lit the way.

Lassie wagged her tail vigorously. This was a new adventure for her and she was happy to tag along. As we progressed deeper into the underworld, water constantly dripped to ensure the path everyone walked on remained wet and slippery. Although we had only been going for a few minutes, some idiot yelled, "Bats!"

By identifying such creatures under those particular circumstances, whoever the idiotic person was, he created a considerable amount of panic and tested the ability of some of us to persevere with such a foolhardy venture. His scream of fear vibrated round claustrophobic surroundings, which prompted Lassie to start barking. Naturally, all the sounds echoed back and forth, multiplying as they bounced off sheer walls along deep, endlessly long tunnels of darkness.

Bats, as anyone knows, get in your hair and suck your blood. This knowledge prompted our diverse bunch of numbnuts to put their hands on their heads. Being very dark and deep underground made everyone nervous and jumpy. Someone shouting "Bats!" did nothing to calm things down.

The movie "Dracula" was showing at the Corsham cinema and everyone scrambling about in the dark knew, bats were related to him. When our hysteria finally subsided, Tom's commanding voice had been reduced to a nervous whisper. "Come on, f, f, follow me, k, k, keep the noise down." Our strong leader had spoken, yet I detected a distinct tremor in his stutter. We closed up for moral support and followed our gallant fearless guide ever deeper under the Wiltshire countryside.

There were numerous stories about those mines at Boxfields. They were put about by adults to frighten children into not going down the darkest of depths. I wondered if those parents remember scaring their little darlings by jumping out and shouting "Boo!" or throwing them into the air to thrill them with fear. Surely they could recall how those things made their children scream with glee. Their offspring enjoyed the charade, they still did, even in dark underground mines. One story about the particular stone mine we were going down referred to a group of children, just like us. They'd gone down several years ago and became lost in the labyrinth of tunnels never to be seen again. Apparently, and according to an adult, the group formed into a cannibalistic tribe to survive. They lived in the mines and ate any children who ventured within.

I puzzled at the logic of that account for some time before coming to the conclusion it could not possibly be true. If a tribe of teenagers managed to get in the mine, I saw no reason why they were unable to get out.

Several candles and pieces of Perspex were lit as we continued exploring. Except our lights weren't so much to see where we were going but to keep those pesky bats away. Flickering flames made our shadows dance and gave the impression we were being followed. The passages during some early stages were wide and high, so it was easy to stay close and communicate to each other in whispers. Word filtered down our meandering line that Tom the dork was going to take us to "The Cathedral". That news created a surge of excitement, since everyone heard about that mysterious place but few had ever seen it. The Cathedral was the biggest mined out area of all time but hidden deep within the mine system. I personally felt that if we ever saw that fabled place, the horrors we were experiencing getting there would have been worthwhile.

Nights in the Forest

We continued moving downward for some time. I didn't know if anyone else noticed that in some places the roof was much lower than it had been. I could see it just above my head, whereas a few minutes ago it had been out of sight and this newfound knowledge was passed on to De De. We stopped for a moment to hold our candles high. Sure enough the ceiling could clearly be seen. David gave a small grunt, it may have been a gulp, it may have been a muted whimper, but it sounded like a single-worded prayer. We looked at each other over yellow candlelight exchanging nervous smiles. De De looked particularly frightening with the candlelight casting shadows across his face. In fact, I felt certain Dracula himself would have turned away as I did before moving quickly to catch up with the others.

We reached a section called "The Steps", a narrow stairwell cut into stone descending steeply into a void beyond torchlight. The nerd called a halt. "You 'ave to be careful," he whispered. His words evaporated into thin clouds of vapour as we clustered around to hear his final instructions. Our leader had acquired a habit of raising his hand before saying, "Follow me."

Everyone stood back to watch him descend and disappear into the darkness. My dislike for him grew and I still had no idea why. Lassie and I remained close behind as we stumbled down slippery steps that were rounded from years of use and erosion. At the bottom, our seemingly fearless leader squeezed through an opening obviously made after the entrance had been sealed off. Those who came before must have removed sufficient stone and rubble to open a gap large enough to allow a small person through. Fortunately for adventurers like us, the grown-ups never knew about that hole, besides, they had more sense than to think about descending into such a dangerous place. They were responsible oldies who put up notices outside the entrance which read "Danger Keep Out". This naturally encouraged juvenile delinquents like me to challenge the notice and go where no man had gone before.

Lassie was pushed ahead as we followed a dim beam of light continuing to descend. Apprehension added to the fear setting in on everyone. The excitement of adventure had passed some time ago with nothing but peer pressure holding us together. No one wanted to admit they would rather turn around and go back to the surface. We could have a sandwich and drink of milk in sunlight before going home. Up there blue skies with abundant open fresh air scented with the aroma of flowering shrubs, overhanging foliage and a soft carpet of ground cover waited to welcome us. It was also dry, warm and clean.

The ceiling continued getting lower until we were walking like old men with bad backs. It didn't take long before we were on hands and knees with Lassie the only one on her feet. I looked at the huge flat rock above my head with chisel marks clearly visible in sallow candlelight. Obviously, at the time those chisel marks were made, the mine had plenty of stone left. That thought set my imagination working overtime. This mine must have been abandoned because the roof fell in. From the way I saw things at that moment, we were nothing but ants under a giant's foot waiting to squash us flatter than a sheet of paper. I blinked, and then shook my head in a desperate bid to get that mental picture out of it. Something else caused me to feel some concern. In the past few minutes, nobody whispered a word as fear tightened its grip on minds and voices.

The last few feet were so narrow we were on our bellies squeezing through a small gap with the pair of shoes in front of me barely able to fit through. Nevertheless, I was determined not to display my fear by backing out and pressed on regardless toward the dim light by pulling and pushing myself along with arms, fingers or toes until I was through and able to stand. I breathed a sigh of relief, stretched my arms and rubbed my knees before looking around. The Cathedral was suitably impressive. Despite holding my candle up high, the ceiling remained out of sight. Tom flashed his torch up and down massive square columns of stone left to support the roof. The dim yellowish beam lanced through darkness as one after the other, the members of our expedition party slipped through the hole and into cavernous darkness.

"No talking," Tom said softly as we gathered round.

Nights in the Forest

I was about to ask why not when a frightened voice squealed, "I'm stuck."

The only torch available shone onto a small round face and one arm protruding from the entry hole. The top half of Stumpy managed to get through but the wider bottom end hadn't made it. Willing hands pulled at his arm and shirt resulting in Stumpy crying out in pain as a lump of stone dug into his hips and the shirtsleeve started ripping off at the shoulder.

"We have to move him further this way," Tom instructed before adding, "Clear away any stones under him and let's make the hole bigger."

Those instructions were easy to give, although not so easy to carry out in the dark by a bunch of scared kids. We did what we could while chattering quietly and giving our rotund friend assurances that he would be okay. Tom hissed a loud shush. Everyone stopped what they were doing. "You have to be quiet, if you make too much noise, vibrations will bring the roof down on us," our heroic leader whispered.

"Well, that stupid remark has just made everybody even more scared," I retorted softly, although most dorks are reputed to being stone-deaf, so Tom didn't seem to hear me. There was nothing I could do to help pull Stumpy out the hole so moved off slapping my leg for Lassie to follow. We sat down some distance away from the problem where my mind could dwell on the situation. My thoughts put everything together as I saw it in simple terms that could be understood by a fool. We were deep inside Mother Earth's bowels. Our only escape route was blocked by Stumpy who got himself jammed in the hole as tight as a cork in a bottle. No one on the surface knew we were in the mine and it would be impossible to reach us anyway because Stumpy blocked the way. Nobody could get out and nobody could get in. Those problems were simple enough, although a dilemma was in the making when we tried to escape from our self-imposed prison.

If we ever managed to get that little fat guy in, it was going to be much harder getting him back out. I figured that one out because for the time being, he was on a smooth downward sloping surface. It would be relatively easy pulling him through. Going back would be uphill against the edge of that hole. From the amount of fat he carried my calculations put it at about a week before he would be thin enough to pop through. I opened my satchel to check its contents and began working out how long my limited food supply would last. One thing was certain, from the amount of water dripping on us we would not be dying of thirst.

Lassie rested her head on my lap. I patted her gently while giving a little reassurance by saying, "You and me gal, we have no problem. Food rations for a week." She licked her lips at the word food but whimpered softly after realizing her next meal would be some time ahead.

I concluded we would be stuck underground for some time and it seemed reasonable to take the opportunity of having a look around. After all, everyone had gone to a lot of trouble getting down to where we were and this chance wasn't likely to happen again.

The Cathedral had been suitably named. It was a very big impressive chamber. Not only did it have an extremely high ceiling, corridors leading to it extended for miles. Whilst Lassie and I meandered over piles of stone the more interesting it became until we eventually came across a small room carved into solid rock. A large block stood in the centre serving as a table and I placed my candle in the middle before sitting down. Lassie wasted no time sniffing out every corner before squatting for a pee. The walls in that underground chamber were covered with names of men who worked the mine many years before. The room presented a perfect occasion to spend some time studying them before adding my own and Lassie's. The next ten minutes were occupied with carving both names in stone to join those immortals. Having completed that undertaking, Lassie and I made our way back to find out if the boys managed to release Stumpy. He'd been freed all right yet persisted in tearfully muttering something about his mother and wanting to go home. During the time Stumpy was recovering from such a traumatic ordeal, his rescuers spread out to explore the place they risked their lives to see.

Our escape route had been opened so I celebrated by sharing a sandwich with Lassie. She had her head on my lap while my

Nights in the Forest

thoughts pondered on the one talent my pet developed. Lassie chased her own tail. My fingers scratched her head while recalling the kids having a good laugh as she spun in circles snapping at the strange appendage. She must have believed it belonged to another dog because whenever she managed to catch up with herself she hung on for a while and ended up spitting hairs. All those watching would clap their hands and cheer the bizarre event while Lassie wagged what was left of her tail.

The performance could not have been hurting her, since she would always respond to my shout of "Tail!" With a bark, my mad animal commenced the chase by spinning on the spot until she caught it. She ended up with a tail resembling a hairless finger. Despite being a lovable rogue, Lassie's days were numbered because, as with her owner, a suspended sentence hung over my pet's head and ready to fall at her next offence. There were no doubts about it, we were two of a kind and suitably matched.

I moved behind a giant pillar with the intention of playing a joke on the intrepid bunch of school children by scaring the living hell out of them. My hands were cupped together to make a soft owl hoot, which echoed along the corridors and chambers. The whispering group fell silent.

"What was that?" someone asked.

"Sounded like an owl."

"Don't be stupid," Tom's distinctive broken voice responded.

A long silence ensued while they listened intently. My imitation of an owl must have been good because it held everyone's undivided attention. Another softer hoot was given.

"There!" the second voice exclaimed, "It is an owl."

A solitary torch beam began flashing in all directions, extra candles and pieces of Perspex were lit in a bid to catch a glimpse of the creature. I wanted to give another hoot but my hand was stuffed inside my mouth to prevent laughter erupting. The single beam continued flashing back and forth while dim candlelight or flaming Perspex spluttered and sparked. The group spent several minutes searching for the elusive owl while Lassie and I remained hidden.

That owl hoot turned into a short distraction before the group reassembled at the exit hole to discuss who should go through it first.

"Stumpy should go first," I said to Tom.

"You shuddup," he hissed while pointing an accusing finger at me. "I'll go first," was Tom's response to my suggestion.

I thought it was typical of his kind of bravery and attempted to put logic up for consideration. "Well what if he gets stuck again?" I questioned firmly after convincing myself it had a very good chance of happening. That kind of question was looked on as a direct challenge to Tom the dork who considered any decision made by him as the definitive one and could not be argued with.

That index finger pointed directly at me again. Through torchlight I saw a grubby fingernail close enough to scratch my face and I was tempted to bite it when he hissed, "You're going to shut your gob or I'll bash you." Our illustrious leader was obviously feeling challenged but not up to displaying any qualities of conflict resolution other than by brute force.

That didn't bother me too much. I remained unperturbed with my next verbal response, which was more direct as a hand reached down to pick up a lump of stone. "You just try it and see what happens," I hissed back softly. With one arm behind and knees bent in readiness to strike, my thoughts were racing while seriously considering that if he came any closer I might bash his scull in. We would really be in trouble then.

Our illustrious dork brain advanced with a scowl on his face and menace in his voice. "You asked for it," he muttered.

"You come one step closer and I'll scream." My threat stopped Tom in his tracks. He saw me looking up into the darkness with a wide open mouth. My reasoning was based on what I heard him saying earlier. If he really believed in his own fear about vibrations and the roof caving in, my ruse might work. Just in case it did not work, my arm was held back with a stone clenched tightly in a fist. We stood still for a moment gazing at the darkness above. It was a Mexican standoff. The dork finally turned away muttering something about getting the hell out of there.

Nights in the Forest

My hand opened and a stone dropped with a plop onto the ground behind me and I sat down. My heart was thumping at a pace fit to burst. It had been a bluff too close for comfort. I wondered how much damage the rock would have done to his head. While lighting a cigarette I watched what turned into an interesting scenario of how we were going to escape. Tom wanted to go first with Stumpy directed to follow. That would give those left behind the problem of getting him through the hole, leaving our leader an ability to seek help should we fail to push out little fat friend through. It even sounded like a good idea but before long we discovered Stumpy had become jammed even tighter in his bottleneck. Any amount of pushing and shoving just seemed to get him in firmer. There was no alternative but to pull him back out.

"Take his clothes off and smother him in butter," De De suggested, except he had no idea where the butter was coming from. My sandwiches were covered in margarine, so his suggestion ruled them out. Besides they were for eating not smothering over some fat kid who was at that moment whimpering for his mum and holding everyone up.

Stumpy removed his clothes except for a pair of baggy Y-front underpants, before being pushed back into the hole. On the other side Tom instructed Stumpy to, "Pull on my feet." By pulling on Tom's feet and while being pushed from behind, our little fat friend slowly disappeared into the hole. His helpers wasted no time following and scrambled over each other to get out.

Minutes later the final pair of feet vanished and The Cathedral became very quiet. Lassie and I were alone staring at the blackness. I took one last draw on my cigarette, blew out an invisible plume of smoke then flicked the butt across the darkness. A small red glow tumbled over and over until it landed in a shower of sparks and disappeared. I felt my way toward the exit, looked at a faint flickering light in the shadows ahead, lifted Lassie and pushed her through the opening, then followed. Our ascent to fresh air and freedom had begun. It didn't take long to reach the surface where the group emphasized their relief at being alive before splitting up to make their way home. I raced Lassie across a meadow that bordered Lovers' Lane before making for Rudloe Estate.

A week later, on a Saturday afternoon, Lassie was poking about in the garden next to a heap of overgrown soil and rubble from the den's diggings still waiting to be removed.

An old man approached on his bike. I recognized him as the same person who complained about Lassie in the past. My pet also spotted him and instantly went on the alert. Her crouch and stiff twitching tail indicated her readiness to attack. The old man may have passed his sell by date but he saw the danger and peddled by quickly while giving Lassie a very provocative wide-eyed stare. Even I didn't like the look he gave my dog, so I was not the least bit surprised when Lassie took umbrage. She had never been inclined to obey my command to "Stay!" and like her rebellious owner did whatever she wanted. Her charge up that pile of rubble could not be measured in miles per hour because flashes happen in a second and it was used as a ramp to clear the fence in a single bound. Seeing the dog's intention, the cyclist changed gear and peddled faster. It made little difference because, although Lassie wasn't very big, she had four legs and could outrun anyone on a pushbike. Within seconds she managed to acquire a very firm grip on a flapping trouser leg and hung on until the cyclist crashed to the ground. I raced across while shouting at her, except my pet had already achieved what she wanted and skulked off.

The old man wasn't seriously hurt but a lot of problems regarding Lassie's behaviour were brought to the surface. When the policeman arrived he gave a final warning. His words echoed those remarked by the old man when he swore vengeance by vowing to have that vicious animal put down. I guess what he said was fair enough, although one could not lay the entire blame on Lassie. After all, the vindictive look that old man gave my pet had been more than enough to set her off.

Chapter Seven

Sinking the Battle Fleet

The latest war movie was on in Chippenham and Uncle gave me sixpence to see it. Alec Guinness played the star role in "The Bridge on the River Kwai". We were told it was a true story and therefore a good enough reason to see it. War films were a common feature at the time but this one did not exploit the war about the Germans getting beaten by the English. It was about English prisoners of war building a bridge for the Japanese. The movie emphasized how prisoners were forced to build that bridge and how Alec Guinness became a hero by providing stiff upper lip non-violent resistance. However, after its construction a bunch of English commandos blew it up. The explosion was timed to coincide with a Japanese troop and munitions train crossing it. Naturally, Alec gets killed, which was only to be expected of a hero.

War stories had a powerful influence on young males whose brave fathers, mothers, brothers, sisters, aunties, uncles, and any relatives who were able, fought the enemy on land, sea and air. It is all well documented the history books which tell about great ships of the time from German and English navies, including many other nations, whose ships were sunk in some of the most memorable battles on the high seas. There was always a great loss of life, valour and glory along with monumental disasters on each side.

Those history books, according to my records, are all wrong. Graf Spee, Hood, Achilles, the aircraft carrier Ark Royal along with many others went down in the swirling ice-cold waters of Penny Pool. I know that's a fact because I sank them!

That battle fleet was assembled from plastic replica models requiring an inordinate amount of time and patience to stick all the bits together. It was never my intention to just construct those models; they had to float as well. To accomplish that criterion, an amount of sand ballast was introduced at an early stage prior to the ship being tested for stability in a bowl of water. Once satisfied with its performance, the finished ship was added to my growing fleet. More building funds were always needed and these were acquired by doing odd jobs for anyone willing to pay.

At the end of six months I had a battle group worthy of any warmongering nation. The fleet consisted of two aircraft carriers, five battleships along with a whole flotilla of frigates and cruisers. I could not help thinking what a wonderful idea it would have been if those navies had joined forces the way they did on that particular day. They would have enjoyed world domination with the victorious nations sharing power instead of fighting over it.

The entire fleet stood proudly on my bedside table. There were several planes famous in their day to provide aerial cover for ships at sea. These included British, German, American and even Japanese planes, although I felt the Spitfires, Hurricanes and Messerschmitts had far greater significance in battles than American Mustangs or Japanese Zeros. The aircraft were an addition to my fleet and not the main purpose of my plan, which was to put the fleet to sea, have one glorious battle and sink every single ship.

My preoccupation with war and destruction coincided with the impending celebration of Guy Fawkes Night on November the fifth. That man continues to be celebrated with bonfires while an effigy of such an infamous person is placed on top of an enormous pile of accumulated rubbish. Someone then sets the heap alight and while it burns, the entire scenario is accompanied by a firework display. Everyone cheers and has a good time eating and drinking. My primary recollections were of the best being left till last. After the fire burned down to a pile of hot ashes, potatoes were placed in amongst them. When the skin turned black, the potato inside was cooked to perfection and eaten with dollops of Anchor butter if one could afford it or Echo margarine if one was on National Assistance. Echo margarine had a significant influence on my life and since the subject has already been covered, I rest my case.

Guy Fawkes, although fighting for the Spanish, was a rebel of his time and a heroic intruder against authority. It's a great shame

Nights in the Forest

he failed in his bid to destroy the Houses of Parliament. Nevertheless, England keeps his memory alive by celebrating his failure. I am led to believe he was betrayed, almost certainly by someone who said, "You can trust me."

The ongoing turn of events were destined to becoming a very busy episode for me because my time would be consumed on several fronts. Not the least of which was caused by Auntie Mary and Uncle Jim from Harrogate in Yorkshire. They sent down a small black and white television as a present for mum. This unprecedented event came about because our rich cousins gave us the opportunity of being the first ones on our estate to have a television.

Mother, Uncle and I gathered round that new electronic device on a table to stare at. I had never seen one before and was not particularly impressed. For the most part it was a lumpy brown, plastic, square-shaped, inanimate object. The screen must have been all of twelve inches across and a short length of electric cable hung out the back. I noted three coloured wires sticking out so it never even had a plug. We gazed at it in silence for several moments until mother and I looked at Uncle for guidance. He was the full-grown man of the house and one who knew every answer to any question. Uncle had a shed full of tools and was always fiddling around with something and making it work, so why not this new piece of electronic equipment? It looked almost the same as our radio, and he made that work.

Uncle watched us staring at him. Mother and I waited in anticipation of him performing a minor miracle. He breathed in deeply, took a drag on his cigarette and scratched a scull growing wispy strands of grey hair before smiling. The glasses were pushed up his nose closer to a pair of bulging eyeballs. It did nothing for his comical appearance except exaggerate their size. Our wonder man looked like a professor about to solve the mysteries of life. He shrugged his shoulders and shook his head while saying, "Zis vill not be vorking." That short statement summed it up for me and when mother asked why, Uncle lifted the cable and made a second profound statement. "She is having no plug." He was absolutely right about that, even I could tell there was no plug connecting those loose wires together. We were advancing in leaps and bounds, two insurmountable problems had been solved in less than a minute. I wanted to shout, "Go on Uncle, show us what you can do now," but kept quiet.

There were few if any spares of anything in the house and our search for a plug resulted in removing one attached to the radio. That proved Uncle's intellect, because the consensus of opinion was, if it worked on the radio it must work on the television. Two hours after its arrival the switch of our new piece of electronics was turned on. Mother had already placed her favourite chair in front of "the box" as we called it, had her arms folded and waited patiently for a picture to appear. It didn't. Naturally, she was extremely disappointed and complained about the screen displaying a blurry dark grey picture while hissing menacingly at her like an angry snake. Uncle did his best by turning every dial and pressing every button. He even moved it to the other side of the room before switching the thing off, then back on. It was all to no avail. Despite his best endeavours, I knew the future had finally caught up with Uncle and it had left him behind. After more than an hour of flickering dark grey, various levels of hissing, no picture could be seen not even the sound of voices heard. I could not understand it. After all, the plug came from the radio and that had voices coming out of it. Uncle finally threw a wobbly and switched the television off. Uttered some very loud incantations in Polish and stormed off to hide in his shed. There were many things Uncle had an infinite amount of patience with; however, it seemed that television was not one of them.

He set about discussing the reasons why mother's sister had disposed of that piece of junk by sending it to us. Mother naturally defended her sister's motives and the discussion quickly degenerated into a heated debate. Mum started talking rapidly in Maltese while Uncle made equally rapid responses in Polish. The mayhem and shouting continued unabated without either party understanding a single word. Any visitor would have thought they had arrived at the local lunatic asylum.

In the meantime I foraged through piles of packaging scattered across the living room floor until a letter from Auntie Mary was found. This vital piece of information had been discarded for no better reason than, neither mother nor Uncle could read. After reading it carefully, I raised my voice to acquire some attention by declaring, "It needs an aerial," above the multilingual argument. When the foreign chattering, that none of us understood, stopped, mother and Uncle looked at me.

"Vat?"

"It says in the letter, you need to put a plug on and install an aerial to make it work," I said before reading the appropriate passage aloud. The letter ended with the usual blessings of God on the family and hopes that we would all live happily ever after. That prompted mum to make the sign of the cross and Uncle to look at the ceiling in despair. Well they would, after all, both were devout Catholics.

By all accounts our happiness would be complete if only we had a television aerial. However, my vision of the future did not include an inanimate electronic device that never worked and drove people nuts. I had never even seen a television so had no idea what all the fuss was about. Besides, there were far more important issues than watching a box that hissed and displayed fuzzy grey stripes.

Whilst the battle fleet was being built, more time, money and effort was directed at providing firepower in one form or another. Most of my pocket money had already been spent on gunpowder in the form of bangers and rockets. Blowing things up was a primary source of pleasure, which I acquired from fireworks. I invested a lot of time constructing a cannon with the solitary purpose of using it to destroy the fleet at sea. A steel tube was mounted onto a wooden frame. One end of the tube had been sealed off and a small hole drilled at that end to hold a banger fuse, which, when lit, would ignite the gunpowder. The finished project resembled an old cannon aboard a sailing ship. Although quite pleased with the visual result of the completed work, I needed a test site and my bedroom seemed the obvious place. With my vision focused toward the end, all that remained was the means to justify it.

The idea was simplicity itself. I would load the cannon, then fire it at the bedroom door. At least that would provide sufficient information on the level of penetration it was capable of and reveal whether my idea actually worked.

Testing the cannon inside our house could prove hazardous so I set about taking extra precautions. Any knowledge of explosive powder was limited to grinding off brown match heads. They were brown because red heads have a tendency to self-ignite while being scraped off the stick. I discovered that on the third red match. A box of brown matches with all their heads ground into a powder generated enough power for the purpose in hand. That idea was used during my first test.

My solitary cannon was loaded carefully and set up with its barrel pointing at the bedroom door. The ground match heads had been carefully pressed into the barrel with a wad of cotton wool. It was followed by a nine millimetre spent bullet collected from the local military firing range at HMS Royal Arthur, a navy training station at Neston. I knew the idea would be dangerous and it prompted the preparation of a safety barrier consisting of the mattress and pillows off my bed.

With some trepidation I reached out and lit the blue touch-paper. It started glowing. Then, as soon as it began fizzing, I ducked behind the barricades. A few seconds later a muffled boom filled the room with smoke and a nine millimetre hole appeared in the door. A feeling of elation overwhelmed me. The initial test confirmed it – a box of matches contained enough power to drive a bullet through a half-inch piece of timber from three yards. I would explain about that hole in the door to mother if she brought the subject up.

Gunpowder, on the other hand, would be something else. The range would certainly be greater, since it was bound to give additional power. I had no idea how much but the question intrigued me. The first test was so successful that a second cannon needed building. With a template already in existence, it only took two days before another was ready for testing.

The next move was to transport the fleet and both cannon to Penny Pool where a grand finale would be set up. On a beautiful

Nights in the Forest

late autumn day befitting the event, I set off and arrived well prepared with both cannon loaded and ready to fire. A fleet of magnificent ships were in my school satchel, with my trusty BSA Airsporter rifle slung over my shoulder to ensure victory. Some considerations were given to inviting John in joining me but it was a school day. He would be studying hard in a stuffy classroom while I enjoyed a very special day at Penny Pool deep in the forest.

Both cannon were primed before being placed on a strategic mound pointing up a stream of slow moving water. I wanted as many favourable conditions as possible so the cannon were loaded with shot from a shotgun cartridge. The ships were placed into an area where the water swirled outward in a gentle motion. Logic suggested it would have an effect of pulling the cluster of ships away one at a time. That was critical to my plan. I didn't want a mass escape then have to blast away at the whole fleet with only two cannon. Once the ships were launched, I moved to the cannon and waited for the targets to come within range. What a magnificent sight they made. An armada of the greatest battle ships ever assembled. I watched in agitated anticipation as they began peeling off one at a time. The Achilles broke away first. Being small and close to the edge of swirling water, she was pulled out by the eddy. I judged the distance carefully. When the range closed to about fifteen yards, Achilles sat in the middle of slow flowing water. I lit the fuse and stood back to watch the effect.

When the first cannon roared it spewed a bunch of grapeshot across the water. The splash of shot was masked in a cloud of gunsmoke. Achilles was hit several times and showered in a deluge of water. The salvo spread right across her with pieces of ship being blown away before dropping into the water. She heeled hard over, righted herself, then continued moving down the river. That ship was a lot tougher than she looked. A full barrage of shot had shaken it but she maintained her way downstream. The distance closed, the second cannon was lined up, the fuse lit and once more I stood back to watch what a close range discharge of grapeshot would do. A second boom produced the anticipated cloud of billowing grey smoke, which dispersed into a quickening breeze. A shower of shot smashed the ship's side and tore great gaps in her hull in a volcanic spray of water. Moments later Achilles began wallowing as water poured into her damaged hull. I stood to attention and saluted as she sank.

Both cannon had been fired and proved very effective but in terms of damage to the fleet, only one ship, and the smallest one at that, had been sunk. I looked at the puddle where that valiant ship had gone down. Outgoing ripples were the only evidence of her sinking.

There were nine ships left but no time to reload either cannon. It was, however, something I had taken into account. With no time to waste, I ran to the bridge overlooking the fleet to load my air rifle and took careful aim. It wasn't very sporting but then, it was war. From my position, what remained of Achilles could be seen belly up just below the surface. The time had come to finish the job so three shots were fired at her upturned hull. Plastic shattered under an impacting pellet, the bow came up for a second in a last farewell gesture before disappearing. More ships began breaking out and making a run for faster flowing water. It suddenly became a question of load, fire, reload, fire, as the entire fleet began moving as one. Some shots were aimed across the bow into the water to create the illusion of realism. After all, how many movies of battleships fighting it out have been made where a salvo falls short or long? One needed near misses to give those water spouts and close calls of impending danger. That scenario added to the overall picture of tension and apprehension, it also increased the fun.

Some ships proved much easier to sink than others. The Hood went down after four direct hits, while the aircraft carrier Ark Royal took so many hits, I lost count. The most impressive ship afloat on that day was Tirpitz. She simply refused to go down. I started by shooting away her flag on the bow before taking out the turrets one by one. The ship shuddered and heeled from every hit but regained her way before continuing to defy the odds.

As Tirpitz moved further downstream at full speed, she became more difficult to hit. Her profile quickly diminished and once round the bend, she was out of effective range. I continued dropping shots onto the battle grey structure but she simply absorbed the punishment and continued moving away. For a while, my fire concentrated on her stern, which took out a large section. Water seeped into the hull and although the ship was going down, she remained in trim.

Other ships were coming on line as the current took hold. I became hard pressed in attempting to stop them. There wasn't any spare time to shoot across a bow or time for falling shot to produce water spouts. To achieve a successful mission by sinking the whole fleet, I had to make every shot count. I began taking slow deliberate aim. As each ship came into line my shots mercilessly pounded the hull, until its destiny was confirmed at the bottom of the river.

Most of the fleet was eliminated but two managed to escape until they were out of range some distance down the river. I bombarded them with drop shots but they had little effect at the extreme range of my air rifle, whatever shots were landing on target, simply bounced off.

A more glorious end was devised for the remains of Bismarck and Graf Spee. Both ships were of typical German design but included my masterful construction. Some satisfaction was felt in knowing they were difficult to sink. I took some time out to think of an appropriate way those mighty ships should meet their end. While sitting on the river bank having a break, trailing cigarette smoke inspired an idea. "Fire!" I exclaimed.

A fire was lit aboard each ship before casting them adrift. Now they really did look realistic. Battle scarred with shattered decks, destroyed gun turrets, ablaze from stem to stern and shot pouring down from above. They sustained several more hits before being doomed to the inevitable. As a magnificent ending to the battle, they sank together, as they should. In those last moments of glory I left them alone to sink in peace. A hiss of steam became their final defiant gesture before disappearing.

Suddenly, an anticlimax enveloped me. The joy of such a celebrated victory was short-lived. I achieved my objective but at what price.

Later that afternoon, while walking home through the forest deep in thought, my mind wasn't on hunting, although my eyes continued glancing from side to side catching fleeting glimpses of game. I made slow progress along a familiar narrow pathway. Overhanging foliage brushed my head with slithers of sunlight spearing through gaps. Bright gold flickered in a hypnotic dance as it came and went in monotonous regularity. Despite my mind working on another idea, the positions of animals and birds were being monitored by my subconscious. That information would be stored and recalled at a later time when it was needed.

Sunlight poured down with uninterrupted glory. I was out the forest crossing open fields, but I still hadn't been able to summon up what my destructive powers could accomplish next. It had to be greater than sinking a mighty battle fleet single-handed. Suddenly, an idea came to me like thunder from a cannon packed in my satchel. The vapour trail of a plane passing overhead provided me with an inspiration. Air Power! My sadness at losing a battle fleet evaporated as urgent thoughts began racing through my head. Ideas began pouring in like water cascading into smashed hulls. Those thoughts, however, were not about sinking; they were overtaken by a new idea – flying!

My idea wasn't just influenced by that plane. A coming event about to be celebrated on a national scale also contributed to my inspiration. It was Guy Fawkes Night or, as the rest of the world knew it, November fifth.

A considerable amount of thought went into how improvements could be made to fireworks available over the counter. For example, most bangers never made much noise and cheap rockets were merely a whoosh without much else. At the prices I could afford they did not provide a spectacle. There was no wow, no joy of satisfaction with the expression of, "Oh boy, look at that." Something was needed to improve Standard Fireworks.

A small collection of rockets were purchased with Uncle encouraging me to pursue any experiments by providing much-needed funds. Due to the strict security precautions I imposed, my bedroom door remained closed at all times.

Nights in the Forest

I set about constructing three sets of wings that were designed to be attached to the rockets. Each pair had different dimensions, and once glued on, were left to dry before taking those three trial rockets onto the roof. I judged the rooftop angle of our house as just about perfect and at the correct height to give my experimental trials the best chance of success. It made a perfect launch pad for rockets. While on the roof, I noted a contraption Uncle claimed was our new television aerial. From the way it had been constructed, there was little option but to conclude, we would be short of wire coat hangers for the duration of my childhood. According to Uncle, we would be having a night of television as soon as the programs came on. He'd already been to Corsham and picked up a newspaper that contained a list of BBC programs. It looked as though we would be having an entertaining evening, always assuming we could find that place Uncle called the BBC.

I fixed a milk bottle into place on the roof with the opening pointing heavenward at about forty-five degrees with a rocket loaded into its muzzle. According to my calculations, that angle of trajectory would provide excellent results. The wings were levelled until everything looked just the way it should. That blue touchpaper was lit. When it started glowing I rolled away. This was to ensure a safe distance between myself and the rocket's exhaust.

Suddenly! The fuse started fizzing and my eyes remained focused on what was happening. The subsequent results were as spectacular as anyone could imagine. However, the rocket's flight path bore no relationship to the carefully calculated and proposed trajectory. The wings tore off, and the rocket somersaulted amidst a shower of sparks and swirling smoke. A sickening thud sounded as a termination to its aerobics when it hit Mother Earth and in a conclusion to that display I can proudly claim my rocket had successfully flown – an amazing five yards. I blinked several times and sniffed in acrid-smelling smoke. My disappointment was compounded when the other two rockets fared no better. They created a greater hazard to the flight engineer on the roof than any dream of their potential performance could emulate.

The experiment turned into such a bitter disillusion, it changed my mood from confident expectation to downright aggression. This was directed at my lack of ability. I couldn't work out what went wrong, although it certainly had something to do with my design. While lying on the roof contemplating the disastrous results, my thoughts were disturbed by a familiar voice calling out.

"Hey you! What are you doin' up there?"

I rolled onto my back and looked down onto a nosy neighbour's face. He was the last person I wanted talk to. Being on the roof was nothing to do with him, so why should he expect an answer. Besides I didn't like him.

"I said, what do you think you're doin' up there?" He repeated the question quite a lot louder and it included a more demanding tone in his voice. The man must have been attracted by the noise of the rockets as they fizzed, popped and went their individual way through the sky before thumping the ground.

Having just suffered a disastrous failure, I was in no mood to be polite, particularly to someone who intended interrupting a world-shattering experiment. "Minding my own business," I retorted while sitting up to give him my best sneer. Adults don't like being put down by kids, it gets right up their noses. Past experiences confirmed a suspicion that simply encouraged me.

"You come down from there you cheeky little bugger," the man shouted. He was obviously becoming very angry and frustrated at my nonchalant attitude toward his question, which was displayed by his red face and a waving fist.

"No!" I shouted before lying back to light a cigarette while feeling safe in the knowledge there was no way he could reach me.

The nosy neighbour must have come close to having an apoplexy. It showed as his frustration mounted. The red face became puce and both arms were rotating like broken windmills. "You damn well come down this minute or I'll tell your mother."

I remained on my back staring at the clear sky, exhaling smoke and wondering why the man had such a bad impression of me. He suspected I was responsible for everything going wrong in the world and for pulling up all his cabbages one night. A smile crossed my lips at that thought. We had enough cabbage to last a month. Uncle made a dozen big jars of what he termed as delicious and succulent Polish Sauerkraut. Fortunately for mother and me, he ate most of it himself. On the other hand, mother had great joy of having more cabbage than ever to destroy in the pot. It was good enough to eat, providing one had a spoon. That reflection prompted my return to the present and without looking down called out for him to go ahead. At that point I started banging on a fragile asbestos roof with the flat of my hand.

Moments later, mother came out squinting at sunlight with knitting still in her hand. The beginning of another recycled multicoloured jumper flapped a welcome to all and sundry. None of the colours suited me. The certainty of mother holding it up to measure the fit entered my thoughts and made me cringe. The only consolation would be wearing it to school because none of the colours matched the school uniform. My reputation of being a rebellious child would be further enhanced by mother's goodwill and prudence.

"Your son's on the roof and he's being very bloody cheeky," the nosy neighbour retorted. His pointing finger was like a schoolboy snitch dobbing in a mate.

"Please Miss, your son's on the roof Miss," I responded angrily before mother had time to say anything.

"Come down before you fall," her concerned voice called out.

"All right mum," I shouted and without hesitation stood up and tiptoed to the other side. Then, with a scream that would have shook a banshee out of its skin, I jumped seven feet to the ground. Both adults ran round to see if my scream had been for real but they never saw the broken body they expected. The only thing visible was my face leering at them from the bedroom window. Experiments that day ended and deep thoughts on the reasons for such unpredictable failures took over.

That evening, as promised, Uncle switched our television on. Meantime, the word got round that we had one of those magic boxes with moving pictures. Naturally I invited every member of my gang round to watch. However, there was insufficient room for everyone inside our front room. In any event, most of the gang, their family, friends and relatives congregated in the garden to watch through a window. Dave Clark and his mother from next door, Vlad, his brother and mother, Lofty and his enormous family and friends and anyone else who heard about the one and only television on the estate. The back garden filled to capacity as was our front room.

Everyone waited in excited anticipation while Uncle twiddled with knobs until a faint, out of focus, black and white fuzzy picture appeared. A mighty cheer rose from the assembled audience before it quickly settled to listen. Uncle turned the volume up and voices were clear enough to hear. The big problem was the picture clarity. It was so bad no one knew who was saying what to whom. That mystery continued for the duration of the program. No amount of fiddling by Uncle made the picture any clearer. Whilst the family can claim to have received the first television broadcast on Rudloe Estate, nobody has ever been able to figure what the program was about.

From my point of view, there were better things to do and set about applying myself into some serious thinking. There were no doubts the winged rocket theory would work, except an element in the design was missing. I firmly resolved to undertake some research. Next morning, I was in the library pouring over World War Two books but especially those pages referring to rocket-propelled planes, jets, V1 and V2 rockets. Most of my researched material referred to British Jets and German inventions with everything designed for warfare.

With paper and pencil in hand I wrote down any useful information while copying wing shapes. As soon as the pages were opened and studied, my original design fault became obvious. What I needed were smaller delta-shaped wings, tailplanes were also needed, with directional stability becoming the byword. I nodded in agreement with each passing sentence. Gradually, it all made perfect sense. My in-depth study became so engrossed I failed to notice my English teacher walking into the reading room.

Mike Macy made his way across the library until he stood close by. It was an unusual event for anyone to see me in serious study.

Nights in the Forest

He must have been watching for at least a minute before asking, "What are you doing?"

I immediately tensed up. During my engrossed research, he'd been able to catch me by surprise but that sort of question coming from a teacher seemed pretty stupid. My initial reaction was to say, milking a cow. However, a natural inclination to cause concern provided a more provocative reply, "Oh, hello Sir. I'm just studying the bomb-carrying capacity of rockets so that I can ..." At which point the book slammed shut with a resounding thump, my notebook was rolled up and I beat a hasty retreat. That left Mike with a look of consternation on his face while I retained a wicked gleam in my eye.

Enough study had been completed for the day anyway. Solutions to the problems I encountered were folded up in my pocket. Anticipation and excitement provided my legs with enough energy to run down the three miles of the Bradford road and back home. In my bedroom, several sheets of paper were laid out with only one question on my mind. How to determine any measure of success? The objective was to achieve rocket-propelled flight on a trajectory that would land the projectile on an egg packing station. That building stood some two hundred yards away on the other side of a playing field. If that could be achieved, I would consider it a success. From that moment all mental, physical and monetary resources were directed to that end.

The rocket would have to carry a bomb load, otherwise known as a warhead, of one or preferably two penny bangers, which meant a multiple warhead. A penny banger was the biggest one could buy over the counter unless one managed to acquire a Thunderflash. These were really difficult to obtain but they made a really big bang. Timing would be critical, particularly when lighting the blue touchpaper, since any bombs must not explode before the rocket departed its launch pad. The ultimate and almost impossible scenario was to have every warhead explode on impact.

With delta wing designs on hand, the remaining afternoon was consumed in cutting wing shapes from fine board then gluing them onto rockets. I made a point of allowing the glue to set overnight in spite of the urge to try the rockets straight away.

Morning saw me on the roof with three new rockets ready with recently researched, redesigned wings. Confidence in successfully achieving the objective of sustained flight returned with a vengeance. There would be no bombs carried during the second test sequence because aerial stability had to be established first.

The first new breed of rocket ready for testing was in its launching bottle with the blue touchpaper lit. I rolled clear to obtain a good view. A hollow whoosh echoed inside the milk bottle as a redesigned prototype took off. My ambition came to fruition. The joy of success can best be expressed in a number of words but a loud "Yahoo!" seemed to sum it up. What a glorious sight. The missile went straight and true for at least one hundred yards on a steady forty-five degree angle before a gust of wind turned it off course. I watched with a hand shielding eyes from early morning sunlight. The power died out, a descent started but there was no sudden dive, just a slow steady decline that carried the object out of sight. By my reckoning, had there been a bombload mounted, that descent would have been much steeper and bang on target. The following two rockets never matched the first one for distance or grace, nonetheless I was satisfied. A pattern for success had been established. It would be easy to model the remaining wings into a shape close to those of the first flight.

School next day was easy. Nothing could dampen my spirits or enthusiasm because planning the next stage had already begun. It consisted of mounting bombloads onto the remaining rockets. That's when the real fun would begin.

A week before Guy Fawkes Night I assembled an assortment of rockets with penny bangers mounted on them ready for firing. They made an impressive sight on my bed. Having used every available rocket and loaded each with bombs, a considerable number of bangers were left over. I had something special in mind for them. The idea of having one extra large explosion entered my subconscious.

John turned up to find out what had been occupying my time and offered to help in whatever project I had in hand, providing there was no danger in it. As usual, when any hard work had been completed, my friend would appear like magic and offer his services. That was annoying although there was nothing anyone could do to change him. His conditioning was established at birth. He had been late for that and would almost certainly be late for his funeral.

My plan for the biggest bang ever was to have a foot-long piece of one inch steel pipe filled with gunpowder and blocked off at both ends with screw-on caps. A fuse would be set in at one end. When lit, the steel tube would be dropped down the mine shaft at Top Wood. Simple! But then there's John and his questions.

"Why drop it down the shaft?" John asked.

"It'll make the bang sound much bigger."

"What mine shaft?" His persistence in questioning was irritating.

"The one at Top Wood."

"Is it going to be dangerous?"

"Not if it's dropped down the mine shaft."

"Are you sure there's no danger?"

"Well of course I'm sure."

"It sounds illegal."

"Of course it's not. Now, come on let's do some trials on these fuses." As a matter of fact, it would be very dangerous and absolutely illegal except there was no way I would tell John that and spoil all the fun.

The one inch steel pipe not only looked impressive it was also very heavy and strong. I considered painting it black to give it more appeal but dismissed the idea. No one but John and I would see it and its colour would have no effect on the performance. The first thing that needed doing was to separate every fuse from the opened bangers, which had their powder removed and poured into the steel tube.

"How are we going to test the fuses?" John asked.

"Not too difficult, although it could be highly dangerous," I replied turning around to hide my smiling face.

"Dangerous!" he exclaimed. A long silence followed before he added, "I don't think I want anything to do with that."

"Well, you don't have to if you're scared mate. I'll do it on my own," I responded still not turning round and biting my hand to control an urge to burst out laughing. On realizing the fun couldn't continue, I confided in John by telling him it was a dead simple trial and explained it. "Each separated fuse will be lit. A countdown will be made to determine how long each one will fizz. We don't even have to hold them. But the counting must start on the fizz not when the blue touchpaper's lit."

John's crossed eyes stared at a tiny bundle of banger fuse being held under his nose. His eyes flicked up into mine. He didn't say anything but nodded his understanding.

A row of fuses were placed on the ground. One by one their blue touchpaper was lit. I waited until the fuse started to fizz before counting, "One and two and three and four and ..." The count was carried out several times as each fuse burned out. "It's between five and six," I said slowly.

"What if it's a short fuse?" John asked with a concerned look on his face.

My friend always played on the safer side of safety because he had been brought up to never take unnecessary risks. I called him a pessimist and wanted to know where his sense of adventure was.

"Yeah, but what if that thing goes off before you let it go?"

"It won't," I replied sternly. Despite a confident front, it wasn't quite as strong as my words. With everything considered and taken into account, John could be right. For the first time that evening, a doubt entered my thoughts.

"But what if it does?" he persisted.

I thought about it while studying a fuse in my hand. Then picked up the heavy steel tube and flipped it over. "Ah well, in that case we'll probably be blown to bits. There's enough gun powder in here to blow up the Houses of Parliament," I responded while grinning at my friend's freckled face with wide eyes staring at the steel pipe under his nose. A concerned face grimaced back.

Nights in the Forest

Dusk developed by the time two intrepid heroes headed for Top Wood's testing ground. On our arrival, the darkness of night and trees surrounded us like a dark blue velvet blanket. We were standing close to the mine's ventilation shaft that plunged seventy feet straight down into the bowels of Mother Earth. John and I stood side by side looking into an obvious death trap. No one bothered to fill in the shaft or close the abandoned mine and from where we stood, it was a long way down to solid stone.

"Do you want to hold it?" I asked holding out the steel tube resembling a large galvanized stick of dynamite.

"No way!" he exclaimed stepping back. His eyes became round with horror with both hands held up in a gesture of surrender.

"Well, will you light it for me then?"

"Yeah, well, all right then. But you, gotta get rid of it, quick," he stuttered nervously.

"Great, you light the fuse and I'll count to six then let it drop down the shaft."

"Six!" he exclaimed in a squeak.

"Yeah, and why not?" I asked nonchalantly. We were standing very close to each other in almost pitch darkness. Our noses were touching. John looked directly into my eyes and in the dim light, I'm sure he detected a glint of madness in them.

"The fuses only last till five," he whispered.

"Okay, five it is."

"Maybe less."

I couldn't argue with that. He did have a valid point. Being on the safer side of safe meant letting go on the count of four, after all, my original idea was to try for a midair explosion. "You worry too much," I said softly while handing over the matches.

We stood face to face and very close to that deep hole in almost total darkness. The matches rattled in their box as John fumbled to pull one out. Two fell onto the ground. Seconds later, there was a scratching noise and a flare of sulphur lit our faces. We looked into each other's eyes over a quivering yellow flame. John's were as big as dinner plates. He was holding his breath. Both of us showed our teeth in a grin. I hesitated for a second before dipping blue touchpaper into the trembling flame. It immediately began to glow.

"Throw it," John hissed and gasped out the breath his lungs had been holding. He stepped back and almost fell.

I moved closer to the edge of oblivion. My plimsoll pressed on the crumbling edges of the hole. Several small pieces of stone tumbled over the edge and rattled down the shaft. I held my breath while holding that steel tube over it. The heart inside my chest made concerted efforts to beat its way out.

"Throw the damn thing," John muttered through clenched teeth. He began withdrawing into darkness.

I resisted throwing the damn thing and continued holding it at arm's length over the opening resembling a huge hungry mouth waiting to be fed. The fuse came to life. Its sudden fizz made both of us jump. I must have levitated about a foot above ground level when John shouted, "Throw it!" His eyes were wide and staring at the fuse as it hissed. His hands clamped over his ears as he stumbled backwards into the darkness toward what he assumed as being a safe distance. How safe he would have been from an exploding steel tube would be difficult to say.

While watching John reversing to safety I started counting in a loud voice. "One and two."

John's eyes slammed shut. He crouched into a lower position while yelling, "Throw it, you blinking idiot. Throw it."

"Three and four," I continued. Nerves were jangling along my arm and shaking the fingers. My heart pounded faster. I held my breath. "Five ..." the fizzing steel tube was released, "... and six."

The sound of that explosion was something that will be preserved in a special place where favourite memories of one's finest achievements are stored. Those echoing reverberations of sound rattling around the main chambers of the mines below our feet made the earth tremble. Exploding light erupting from the open mouth lit up Top Wood and almost blinded me. My ears twanged with noises and popping sounds while coloured lights with stars sparkled before my eyes. I had witnessed a truly magnificent spectacle. I could have been deafened and blinded for the rest of my life but those results proved to have been worth the risk.

John looked up in stunned surprise. His mouth remained wide open but he hadn't been privileged to the full visual and earth-shattering sound effects. A long silence followed while we absorbed the atmosphere.

I recovered from shock and came to my senses. Such a big bang was bound to attract attention. "Come on, let's get the hell out of here," I shouted in a voice sounding distant through noises going on in my head. John and I made our way through the trees as quickly as possible and once in open ground, we ran as fast as our legs could carry us for several minutes before we slowed down.

John was bursting to ask another one of those infuriating questions. "What was it like?"

His words were barely audible through a ringing in my ears and I pondered the question for a moment before replying. "It was fantastic mate, you should have seen it."

"I heard it," John said excitedly. Although how much noise he managed to hear through hands clamped over ears, was impossible to say.

"Yeah, but you should have seen it as well."

"Tell me, tell me what it was like?"

I stopped to give my friend a one-word answer. I placed a hand on his shoulder, gasped in a deep breath and shouted, "Indescribable!" before turning and breaking into another run.

Anthony Corbyn

Chapter Eight

Homemade Fireworks for Guy Fawkes Night

November the fifth was just around the corner with a grand finale that was mine for sure. I had worked hard and spent all my meagre pocket money on preparing for the event. Waiting was difficult and very frustrating because time moved slowly in those last days. The preparation work had been done too soon. No further trials were carried out and a final decision still had to be made. Should the rockets be fired during the day when they could be viewed and judged on their performance? Or, would it be better to set them off at night? Another question requiring an answer was whether to fire them one at a time making clinical assessments while analyzing individual performances. On the other hand, go the whole hog and fire the lot at once. I decided to postpone that decision until launch day. I felt sure, whichever one was made, would be right.

On November the fourth, John called to find out how my preparations were going and what time the grand finale would be. I remained undecided but felt a night-time event would be more spectacular. "It'll be some time before supper because we're having a bonfire in the back garden with some kids and neighbours. There'll be sparklers with Roman candles, that sort of stuff."

John nodded his understanding and agreed to return before supper. During our conversation his attention became attracted to the Thunderflash I rolled between my fingers. A naturally developed sense of concern wrinkled his forehead when he asked, "What you got there?"

"Thunderflash. There's just this one. I'm wondering what to do with it," I replied with a smile.

He stepped closer and looked into my eyes. "Oh, oh."

"What?" I asked.

"You've got that funny look in your eye."

"What funny look?" I responded with mock indignation.

John stepped back and delved both hands deep into his trouser pockets. "You always look like that whenever you're thinking about doing something you shouldn't."

The Thunderflash was placed very carefully into my shirt pocket as I walked out of adult earshot with a nod indicating John to follow.

"What you up to?" John asked and looked nervously over his shoulder before adding, "Whatever it is, no good will come of it, I can tell, I can tell."

I leaned against a wall looking left and right to make sure no one else could hear what I said. "You know that Scots family who live on the corner?" I motioned my head toward the house in question.

John followed my look. "Yeah," he replied slowly.

"The big mouth sod who thinks he knows it all?"

"Yeah."

I watched my friend's eyes close in anticipation of what he must have known would come next. I had his undivided attention so continued. "Always got the music up full volume and chased me once for bashing up his kid."

"Yeah," he whispered nervously.

A pounding in my chest permeated through me as warmth flooded in at the idea I intended carrying out with the Thunderflash. "I'm going to get my revenge on the old git," I hissed through clenched teeth.

"Oh no," John finally muttered.

"Do you want to come with me?" I asked while looking into a pair of eyes that suddenly flicked open.

"What are you going to do?" His apprehensive question required an answer before deciding whether to commit himself to an unknown adventure. In the first place, his mother would be upset if she knew he was with me, in the second place, it would be dangerous, in the third place, it was undoubtedly illegal. In fact, John wasn't supposed to get involved in anything to do with me. In this case, it was all wrapped up in a neat little package. It would require some very serious consideration before he made a decision.

"I reckon a banger on his window should do the trick." The Thunderflash, reappearing to emphasize my point, is no ordinary banger. I held it up and smiled.

John started shaking his head while shuffling nervously. From his point of view, my proposition exceeded every boundary imposed on him. We were about to become involved in some really serious stuff. If his mother ever found out, she'd kill him. He was thinking about it, had not said no, nor was he walking away. It looked as though John was having a hard time deciding.

I pressed home my advantage by adding some peer pressure. "Course if you're afraid, it's okay," I said and shrugged while turning away.

John took the bait. "What time?"

The emotion of relief swept through me because I did not want to perform that particular expedition on my own. "After supper, it'll be a bit late but safer when we do it." I stepped closer until we were once again nose to nose, eyeball to eyeball. "Are you in?"

John's nod touched my forehead. We went inside to discuss the plan in the privacy of my bedroom.

During a typical pitch-dark November night we crouched behind the garden hedge of my enemy's house about twenty yards away. The very cold evening had clear skies without a moon. It provided perfect conditions for such a clandestine operation. Curtains at the windows were drawn but a small chink of light showed through giving a clear indication of our target. Inside the house, loud music blasted out over raised voices. Everything those people from Scotland did, disturbed the peace.

"Good, they're having a row, it'll help cover our sortie," I said and glanced at John's face. It had taken on the scared, determined look of a soldier readying himself for battle. "I wish this was that steel bomb we exploded last week," I added rolling the Thunderflash under his nose.

"What do you want to do, blow up his house?" John asked in an exasperated whisper.

"Yes, that's a good idea for later. Tonight let's just blow out one of his windows," I answered as the garden gate was pushed open.

John tagged along close behind as we tiptoed up the garden path toward a window. My friend favoured the bedroom because no one would be there, apart from which it made an easier target with much less of a chance of getting caught. I listened to his suggestion, called him a lily-livered chicken and explained my purpose was to cause the maximum disturbance. After all, it was a revenge attack on someone who chased me with the intention of doing some harm and who deserved it. Tonight was payback time. Blowing out a window seemed bad enough. However, the front room where the music blared while everybody enjoyed a noisy argument seemed a good place to start.

We followed the plan discussed earlier. Neither spoke as I held the Thunderflash against a window pane. John pulled a length of masking tape off and pressed it over the explosive device to secure it against the glass. Our eyes met. John looked as shit-scared as I felt. Despite it, a bright light of excitement shone in his eyes. His hands were shaking as he tore off another strip of masking tape. I took the roll to free John's hands and watched him place that second strip of tape firmly over the Thunderflash before nodding my satisfaction of the device being secure. I struck a match. Without hesitating I lit the seven-second duration fuse. It gave us just enough time to scuttle down the path and hide behind a hedge to watch the results. Our excited gasping produced clouds of vapour while we peered over our victim's hedgerow but didn't have long to wait.

When the explosion happened, the accompanying sound of shattering glass added to my sense of satisfaction. A long moment of silence followed as though the world had been stilled by our dastardly deed. That brief moment in deciding what to do next was interrupted by a deep voice booming out, "I suppose you thought that was bloody funny."

That mysterious voice thundered out the darkness from nowhere. Its interruption to solid silence negated any decision on what to do. Never in my short life had such a sound provoked a

Nights in the Forest

more earnest desire to make a run for it. My reflexes were much sharper than John's. I got away first while my friend was left gathering up his shattered nerves to leap after me.

We charged through Bottom Wood in almost total darkness, we scrambled over thick tangles of undergrowth that tore at our clothing and skin. We smashed our way through anything we were unable to leap over as if our lives depended on it. For all I knew, it did. Terror stricken, nothing that got in my way could stop me putting the greatest possible distance between myself and that voice. My legs were moving like over-revving pistons and none too soon the trees were cleared with an open field appearing before me. Although open ground would expose me, it gave an opportunity to open up full bore. I gave it everything I had left.

The sound of heavy breathing, other than my own, was getting closer and became a nightmare everyone shares. Run, run as fast as you can but it makes no difference how hard one tries, the actions are always in slow motion. The knees turn to jelly, the heart leaps into one's throat, and visions of an avenging beast breathing fire get closer and closer. The image becomes exaggerated with wings and razor-sharp talons. It's impossible to escape. In a dream, one might wake in a sweat. On that particular night though, the horror dream had transformed itself into reality.

Notwithstanding my active imagination, that heavy breathing was on my shoulder, those footsteps came closer and were pounding the ground faster than my own. What chance did I have against a full-grown athlete with the legs of a gazelle? I glanced over my shoulder to face my avenger.

John was passing by without seeing me. His nose pointed skyward and from an open mouth heaving gasps produced clouds of vapour that billowed like fire from a dragon. I couldn't understand the force giving his legs that much power. He was bigger and heavier than me so it made no sense. Perhaps his fear of getting caught was greater than mine, or put simply, he could run faster.

Moments later we crashed headfirst into a hedgerow too dense to break through. We had no alternative but to follow it until we reached a gate and leaped over. The pair of us continued running along a road for several minutes before collapsing into a ditch. I fought desperately to bring my breathing under control because any gasping sound and vapour might give me away. Several minutes passed. Deep breaths were taken. A pounding heart was contained within my chest.

As usual, John broke the silence with, "Who the hell was that?"

"How should I know," I replied.

"Do you think he could see us?"

John's question convinced me his fear must have been one of recognition and I answered to reassure him by softly saying, "Not a chance mate, it's much too dark."

"He must have been watching," John responded with a worried tone.

"God knows, I didn't want to stop and find out, did you?"

"No flamin' fear. From the sound of his voice, he must have been ten feet tall."

John was still gasping for air and his description of the man who intruded on our clandestine mission was certainly a fitting one. I smiled at the idea and said he must have been at least that big before adding, it sounded as though he was four feet wide with a hairy back. My comment caused both of us to start giggling.

"What are we going to do now?" John asked in a voice that turned from humour to one brimming with concern.

"Wait here for a few minutes to make sure he never followed, and then go home," I stated in as articulate a voice as could be made under the circumstances. We continued lying in the ditch under the hedgerow in silence. It was dark and cold yet appeared safe. No one could spot us provided we remained quiet and still. After we heard nothing for a while, neither footsteps nor a challenging voice, we ventured out very cautiously. We followed the hedgerow and used it as cover, just in case. When it eventually came to an end, a high stone wall confronted us.

"What is it?" John asked while touching the hard surface.

"A wall," I declared with obvious irritation at such a stupid question.

Nights in the Forest

"What do think it's for?"

I assumed it had been built to keep people out and told my friend what I thought its purpose was for. We stood side by side looking at the formidable red brick obstacle towering over us. In my opinion, it simply represented another challenge as I gazed at the top of the wall. "Come on let's get over it."

"What for?" was John's incredulous response.

I asked if he was curious to find out what was on the other side but my friend didn't really want to know and asked why I hadn't had enough excitement for one night. Personally, I thought one exciting element of our night's adventure was over and a new one presented itself. John's question was considered futile because I had already embarked on a way to scale the obstacle and called on him to give me a hand. A tree had been cut down close by, which provided a branch long enough to overcome the wall. John and I managed to drag the broken limb to the wall and climbed up. A few minutes later we were sitting high up looking into a large walled garden. In the distance at the far end stood a large multi-story house with lights on and I pointed while whispering, "That must be the manor house."

Those big old houses were owned by the gentry of their day and they always had large walled gardens. The rich wanted to retain a wealthy independence by ensuring any fresh fruit and vegetables remained in their own gardens, which would be available to them alone. They needed to protect their lot from hungry peasants like me whose mother had no chance of being able to afford such luxuries as plums, asparagus, cucumbers and other such exotic fruits and vegetables. All the gardens I ever nicked stuff from grew things like cabbages, Brussels sprouts, turnips, carrots and potatoes. Such fare suitable for lower class common folk never needed protection. The walled garden John and I looked on had all that and so much more.

We climbed into the forbidden zone using a fruit tree growing against the wall. As John and I began looking around, a dog barked in the distance and car headlights swept the darkness. We both dived for cover. Moving light caused shadowy trees to dance with each other. Someone must have been leaving or arriving.

Anthony Corbyn

My friend and I crouched close to the ground. I pointed out an extensive greenhouse built against a wall and gestured we make for it. The unlocked glass-panelled door opened slowly before I eased through the gap. Once inside we quickly became aware of a difference in temperature inside that big heated greenhouse. The type of greenhouse we entered was quite unusual but provided a nice warm place to explore.

The pair of us stood still until our eyes adjusted to dim light. Despite being inside a greenhouse, it became appreciably darker because there was only little starlight filtering through. A canopy of dense leaves was within reach and I touched them but couldn't figure out what they were. I lit a match to satisfy my curiosity to reveal something I had never seen before – grapes! There were huge bunches hanging like green chandeliers above our heads. John's eyes were bugging out like organ stops as he reached up and plucked one free and gleefully stuffed it into his mouth to chew the round green morsel. A second later a swift spit confirmed they were not ready to eat.

"They're not ripe then?" I asked.

"Sour as shit," John replied. He spat again as we wandered through that greenhouse savouring the warmth and security it offered. "We could pick some and take them home," John whispered. It seemed his initial fear of extending our adventurous evening evaporated when the prospect of collecting some rich person's food for free became available. The fact it was inedible bore little significance to acquiring it, particularly when it was free. From what I knew, it seemed appropriate to remind my friend, they were almost certainly Christmas grapes. I went on to add that as such, they would not be ready to eat before then. Having delivered the full extent of my knowledge regarding grapes, I reached up to touch the nearest bunch.

"We could hang them up and wait for them to ripen," John said quickly. He seemed determined to have something from the night's escapade other than the memory of being scared half to death. He wanted something to show for the night's effort and it sounded like a good idea.

Nights in the Forest

I never thought grapes would ripen once they were picked. Nevertheless, we began gathering the harvest. Grapes for Christmas, I heard people talk of it but till then had never seen it, although on that night I discovered how it was done. On Christmas Day my family would share in a bounty the Squire was good enough to provide. It turned into a busy night and from my point of view, I had already earned whatever could be carried. With as many bunches as our jumpers could hold, John and I made our way over the wall and headed for home until we came to our parting of the way.

"We had a good night, eh John."

"I don't want too many of them. I'll be old before my time," he replied.

"Ha!" I exclaimed, "How often can you go home on a cold winter's night with a jumper full of grapes?" and then began laughing with relief for the first time that night.

"It may be alright for you," my anxious friend said as he looked up and down the dark road, "But I have to think of what to tell me mum when she asks where these grapes came from."

"That's easy. Tell her I gave them to you," I suggested while adjusting the overflowing pile of grapes in my overstretched jumper. "If she wants to know where I got them from, say Uncle Willy gave them to me. That should do it."

"I'll see you next time I can escape," John said and giggled as he turned for home.

By the time I arrived, mother had gone to bed and Uncle was in the kitchen having a drink and a cigarette. The black and white television's maiden voyage lasted all of two nights before a frustrated mother came close to throwing it out the window. Having a television was great, being able to see some pictures, whatever colour, would have been better. The "box" held pride of place in a corner of the room as a flowerpot stand. While carefully moving toward my bedroom, Uncle turned to me saying, "Hello boy, you vant a drink?"

"Er, yes please Uncle. Hey, look what I've found," I said before unloading a jumper full of grapes onto the table.

Uncle looked dumbfounded. Then congratulated me as being the only person he knew who could find grapes in the middle of winter. He rubbed his hands in a gesture of delight before plucking a grape and popping it into his mouth. Uncle was worse than John when it came to being impulsive and I never had time to stop him. It took less than a second for the grin on his face to disappear. Uncle's puckered-up mouth looked as though he just sucked on a green lemon and muttered, "These things, zey are not ready to eat."

"No of course not, they're Christmas grapes, they'll be ready then," I smiled into his puckered face with watering eyes and began rolling a cigarette.

"Maybe, maybe," Uncle muttered and smiled as he poured a drink for both of us. "To take the taste away eh, salute," he added and raised his glass high. The glasses barely touched our lips when there was a firm thump on our kitchen door. In a single swift move Uncle scooped up the grapes, placed them in the pantry, shut the door with his foot and sat back on the chair before calling, "Come in."

The kitchen door opened just wide enough to allow a policeman to peer in. "Good evening Sir. Sorry to disturb you but I saw your light on and knew someone must be awake."

"Come in, come in," Uncle shouted and waved at the officer standing in our doorway, "you are letting in the cold." Uncle must have noted my obvious discomfort at the intrusion of a man in blue. I wondered how the hell they were able to find out so quickly. The policeman came in and stood behind me. Uncle quickly offered our late night caller a drink. I lit a cigarette.

"No thank you Sir, I'm on duty," our uninvited visitor replied.

"What brings you out in the cold at this time of night officer?" Uncle asked.

I took a deep drag while an internal struggle to compose myself went on. At least the policeman was behind me. Nicotine-impregnated smoke was released from my lungs in a slow steady stream. My heart slowed. A shaking hand steadied to remove the cigarette from pouted lips.

Nights in the Forest

"Did you hear any bangs tonight, Sir?" the policeman asked in a very polite friendly tone.

Uncle took a sip of drink, which gave him time to think. "Ah yes, many bangs eh," he started waving his arms about in wild disorientated gestures. "Bang, bang, many bangs, zey should vait until tomorrow, tak?" he shouted and immediately started leaning heavily on his Polish accent.

"Well, yes Sir," the man in blue confirmed and took a pace back, "but this was a big bang about an hour ago." Our friendly policeman raised his voice as people are apt to do whenever confronted with a foreigner whose English was a little suspect.

Uncle had nothing wrong with his hearing and could speak the language very well. Nevertheless, the cunning old devil always relied on his accent to give a false impression, particularly when cornered. He pointed at me, "Boy und me ve talk, drink smoke, talk some more. I not listen for bang."

"Has the young man been with you all evening, Sir?"

That question made my heart leap. The cigarette was replaced between my lips and another long drag taken. I shot a quick glance at Uncle who was in his element and enjoying every second of the situation. There's a word that comes to mind for that kind of person but I refuse to say it.

"Tak, tak, ve sitting talk and drinking and shmoke," he answered, lifted the bottle and asked "You shure?"

"Thank you, no."

"Zo vyfore you cum eh?" Uncle asked.

It sounded as though Uncle had developed a deeper Polish accent. Some words were sticking together with a slur, which became prominent and definitely wasn't there when I came home a short while before.

"Someone put a firework on your neighbour's window and blew it in."

The best shocked expression I'd ever seen appeared on Uncle's face. He stood up quickly and slammed his glass on the table in a prelude for the verbal assault which followed. "Thish ish an terrible tink for doing. You musta catch dis peoples und punch 'im." A fist pounded our flimsy kitchen table, illicit booze spilled over Uncle's glass. At that stage of the interrogation Uncle staggered a little before sitting back down with a heavy thump. His closing argument included a finger pointing at our visitor and telling him to catch the filthy swine.

"We intend to," the man in blue said while rapidly retreating toward the door. If our visiting policeman had a nervous disposition, he was showing it very clearly in his eyes.

Uncle gulped down his drink, then immediately poured another. I reached for the bottle to top up my glass and became aware of my drinking companion avoiding any eye contact.

"It was not only criminal but extremely dangerous," the policeman said firmly while continuing to reverse with increasing speed. He already had one hand reaching for the handle.

"Tak, tak," Uncle bellowed in a voice that shook my glass and rattled the bottle on the table before offering his services. "If der is anyvon ve canst doing, you mush letting me knowing eh. I kill zis bastard. Na zdrowie!!" That said, Uncle emptied the contents of yet another glass down his throat. He gulped, belched and with bulging cross eyes stared over crooked glasses at the policeman.

That action seemed a cue for our visitor to leave. He thanked us and made his way out. Less than a second passed after the door clicked shut. Uncle and I scuttled to the window and watched the blue uniform walking quickly toward his pushbike before Uncle turned to me. "He gone, now you are telling me vat you bin up to zis time, eh, eh?" He started chuckling and sat down to pour another drink.

I was already feeling the effect of his potent brew and sucked on my cigarette with a feeling of relief while reaching for the recharged glass. "Uncle, you're never going to believe this," I began with a smile lighting up my face. However, it was nowhere near as big as Uncle's.

On November the fifth a momentous decision was needed with careful calculations and considerations to be taken into account. It's a well-known fact that historical events will always be adjusted to suit the needs and wants of society at the time. Everything depends on whether heroes or terrorists were required, which depended on what point of view was taken, or whose side one was on. I found it particularly curious, why the whole country should be celebrating an individual who tried to blow up the Houses of Parliament and subsequently executed him for failing. The authorities called it treason but there were many odd things about adults I found confusing.

Outlaws become heroes, there's nothing new in that. For example there was William Bonney, otherwise known as Billy the Kid. He was an American killer and a psychopath. However, that never stopped writers glorifying him in comics and films as a hero of the American Wild West. Billy was interpreted as a cowboy, although in reality, was a total nut case. England had Sir Robin of Loxley otherwise known as Robin Hood who was a historical English bandit who robbed the rich to give to the poor. Since all his gang of merry men were poor, it became easy to distribute any ill-gotten spoils. Then there was a character called Ned Kelly, an Australian bush ranger who became a folk hero and made a name for himself by shooting policemen while wearing a bucket over his head. I could go on and mention numerous other murderers and thugs who were knighted for unglamorous deeds. Whatever they did made no difference to me anyway.

After careful consideration I came to a decision. The words of a prophet or someone close to him once said, "Rather a lion for a day than a mouse for life." That thought was sufficient to clear my mind. The display would be a mass firing. Every rocket would be lit at once whatever the consequences, come what may. The launch site would be our front garden although it should have been the roof. However, logistical problems associated with having a multiple launch site from such a precariously delicate platform proved insurmountable. Uncle point-blank disallowed it.

A long line of milk bottles were planted along the flower bed where the ground remained soft enough to bury them with their necks protruded at forty-five degrees. Each bottle was loaded with a rocket late at night just before launch time. Some carried a single banger "bombload" while larger rockets carried a double load.

The bangers were taped on in such a way that rocket propulsion would ignite their fuses after takeoff. By my paper and pencil calculations each one should explode during or shortly after their flight path ended. My calculations seemed like sound reasoning and I was confident in that belief. My only prayer was that none of the bangers would go off before the rocket carried it a safe distance.

John came to watch and assist in the launch. His presence required a short discussion on how we should go about it before I handed my friend a lighted cigarette to use for touching off those fuses.

Mother and Uncle stood well back. Most of the invited assembly including Dave Clark and his family didn't turn up. Only Lofty and his parents were there, as was Vlad and his brother Victor. Everyone who turned up was unsure what might happen once the display began. A certain amount of anticipated disaster added tension as John and I began from the middle of the line. We worked our way outward as quickly as possible. As the last rockets in the line were being lit, the first ones began to whoosh into the night sky.

At that precise moment, God only knows why, the wind velocity suddenly increased beyond expectations or the weather forecaster's predictions. On the other hand, it might have been due to a slight miscalculation on my part. On reflection and to be perfectly honest, wind speed and direction were left out of my calculations. Nonetheless, I remain convinced the change in wind speed and direction was responsible for the following events.

Some of the bombs may have been a little too heavy for the rockets' capabilities to deliver their payload beyond the danger zone. There may have been some fault in their propulsion units as well. I did try explaining to mother after she calmed down sufficiently to regain some control of her shattered composure. I have it on good authority, there are some three hundred and sixty degrees in a circle. On that particular night, those rockets were determined to explore the potential of each one.

One unit shot up almost vertical, a practice well outside its geometric design and expectations. It became unstable and returned to home base. That one really upset mother and came close to singeing what was left of Uncle's hair. He managed to

Nights in the Forest

avoid becoming decapitated by throwing himself prostrate onto the ground when the sound of shattering glass drew everyone's attention. The still very much alive rocket now proceeded to set fire to my bed.

That had never been in the plan; it simply wasn't supposed to happen. Uncle scrambled to his feet and rushed into the house while I shouted, "Look out for the bombs." As providence would have it, he was either out of earshot, too brave, stone deaf or dead drunk. From the way he was staggering, I would say the latter. On the other hand, he may have been in too much of a hurry to receive the warning. The audience outside heard a loud bang followed by some very angry Polish curses. A second bang was accompanied by a yelp with a further series of Polish curses that sounded like, "Yer yunray pyer yurney" or words to that effect. The bedroom window flew open. The spent rocket with broken wings and a smouldering blanket fell into the garden.

Nevertheless, despite the occasional inadvertent mishap, most of the display performed reasonably well and according to my scientifically prepared plan. When the rocket's propulsion died, fuses on the bangers were already ignited. That small additional thrust gave the missile greater distance before exploding in midair. The sight and sounds provided a magical show for everyone. The cacophony of events were too numerous to note them all at once with each rocket travelling its own course. Their trajectory was dictated by wind and other unnatural causes well beyond anyone's control. I wanted to give mother and Uncle that vital piece of information except, as I said earlier, who listens to a juvenile delinquent?

One exceptionally big and very expensive rocket flew an extremely low trajectory weighted down by an extra large Blockbuster penny banger. Perhaps its lack of ability was affected by an unexpected downdraught; maybe those short delta wings had insufficient lift to gain height and attributed to its long low level flight path. Whatever the problems that projectile encountered, it made a perfect three-point landing, if that's possible for a rocket. It skidded along the road and stopped about two inches short of an old man taking his dog for a walk. The man appeared fascinated by a violently fizzing object at his feet while his dog, well past its sell by date, had its head cocked to one side. It appeared curious as to where the thing came from and what it was. That dog leaned forward to have a sniff. The problem with dogs is they do not understand things that fizz. His master, on the other hand, became aware it might represent a danger to both of them. The old man's timing could not have been better. He kicked at that fizzing object exactly the same time it exploded. The decrepit animal howled, turned tail and ran while towing its owner along at a pace he could not possibly achieve on his own.

I did nothing but stare at such a comical sight that was certainly worth remembering. There were many lessons learned that night, with at least two never to be forgotten. In the first place, never take a dog for a walk on November the fifth and secondly, don't kick anything fizzing at your feet.

Everyone watched the last rocket loaded with a single banger dive in true kamikaze style to the ground and explode on impact. "That's just the way all of them should have performed," I said to John as a sense of satisfaction finally swept over me.

Later that night, Uncle, John and I stood outside gazing at the stars and absorbing the profound silence around us. Uncle proceeded to roll himself a cigarette and smiled while watching me make one for myself and place it into my mouth. I turned to face the man already holding out his lighter. "What do you think?" I asked as my roll dipped into the flame.

"Not bad," Uncle replied. "Not bad. But you should hear vat I am doing ven I your age."

"Yeah," I said exhaling a cloud of smoke, "are you going to tell us about it?"

"You never believe, come I tell you anyvay. Ve have a drink now yes, and I tell you a story from Poland."

John and I followed Uncle with a fresh level of excitement surrounding us at the prospect of another story by the man from Poland. My ginger-headed friend ambled in a little confused and disorientated. John knew if his mother ever found out he had been party to the night's events, he would be in deeper than deep shit. Still, as he informed me later, he had a wonderful time and it was well outside normal events.

"John, sit down and have a drink. We did a real good job tonight and you deserve one," I said while pouring the drinks.

John sat down, took the glass offered and had a sip. His eyes opened wide and his mouth fell open in shock as Uncle's homemade alcohol burned. He was still gasping for breath as our night-time story began.

"Now zen boys. You must svearing never repeating vat you hearing tonight because I am know ze police in Poland still look for me." His bulging eyes traversed from me to John in turn as we held up our right hand and swore an oath not to tell. Uncle nodded his satisfaction before commencing. "Well, in zis case, I am telling you." Our storyteller took a long deep drag on his cigarette and leaned forward. "It vas a long time ago in my home town in Silesia. Mój Boże it is like yesterday. Zis farmer he is having a dog. O Jezu, but zis dog he is big like zis ..."

Anthony Corbyn

Chapter Nine

The Canoe

There were and still are many ways in measuring success. For me, however, it always meant taking into consideration two aspects of measurement. Did one acquire more of an accomplishment in achieving many goals in life compared to the person who managed a big one?

My search for adventure and the meaning of life in general got me into many scrapes. However, much of what conspired developed from curiosity and a need to fulfil an ambition some adults never understood. Many projects were short-lived or petered out on completion; this was also misunderstood and caused by numerous sets of unfortunate circumstances. It was a fact, once my curiosity became satisfied the urge to continue pursuing the finite ends of a project fell flat. Therein, I think, must lie the difference between reaching a goal and being driven by obsession where, having achieved an ambition, one must continue beyond it. That kind of attitude has never been part of my makeup.

Reading about days when men used spears or bows and arrows to hunt inspired me to build a canoe. It stood to reason that since a river flowed through my hunting area, making a canoe was a good idea because it extended my hunting range. Game would be unaware of a hunter approaching them in a boat hidden by riverbanks until it was too late. From a hunter's point of view, it was something worth trying. With the seed of an idea planted, germination didn't take long to become well advanced. I puzzled for days on what alternative materials to use besides those immediately available. It became a case of doing the best one could with whatever was on hand. My philosophy has always been, if what one wanted was not on hand, find it. After all, that's what grown-ups were saying all the time, in their unchallenged opinion – "The end justifies the means."

Anthony Corbyn

After careful consideration, I decided on a specific course of action. The frame would be made from willow branches, since they were strong, flexible and readily available. The covering proved a difficult problem. Eskimos used sealskins originally but that material was unavailable. However, the decision to make a canoe had been made, so alternative material was needed.

My search led me past a house on the outskirts of town near the village of Neston. Recollections of past days came flooding back when John and I stole greengages from the owner's garden. They were absolutely delicious but gave both of us stomach ache and the runs from eating too many. The next house beside the post office was a rich person's house. That much was obvious because not only did it have a garage, there was a car in it, too. Only people who were well off could afford such luxuries. They also owned a television and a real aerial, not one made of wire coat hangers. It had been professionally attached to the chimney stack, so they must have been rich. I bet John that their television screen would be bigger than the one we had at my house.

In the front garden was a large canvas tarpaulin covering a winter stockpile of logs, which was far too big for its function. My calculations enabled me to work out that a piece big enough to make a small canoe would not be missed. A cunning plan formed on how to relieve those rich people from a small piece. I knew John never had the gumption to entertain the thought of helping me borrow something. He always retained a reluctance to help with any ideas along those lines, so I called on Lofty instead. His responsibility was simple. He would act as lookout. On reflection, I should have known better. Although a good mate, when it came to Lofty being sharp, that was another story.

We were close to the house when my instructions were given on the tactic he should employ. "Lofty, you stay here mate. Watch the road while I go and get that piece of canvas I need. Okay?"

Lofty nodded, and thereby gave the impression he understood and would comply with those directives. Later, I blamed myself, since my instructions were quite obviously not clear enough. He followed them literally and watched the road, most of the time his eyes remained on a square of bitumen near his feet.

Nights in the Forest

During the daring act of obtaining an essential part for the construction of my latest project by cutting away some superfluous canvas required, a car pulled into the yard. There was no warning whistle, no shout of a car coming, nothing! Naturally, there was little option but to take off like a rabbit bolting from its hole with a ferret close behind. I passed Lofty still standing where he'd been directed to keep lookout. He continued watching the road at his feet and was unable to understand my remark about his level of intelligence, nor the need to run for it.

The sound of a car rapidly reversing spurred Lofty into action. Seconds later he ran beside me panting and asking what was happening. I looked over my shoulder to see the car making rapid progress toward us and yelled, "Go left Lofty, go left across country, see you later."

People under stress are apt to hesitate and lose their ability to think in a calm rational manner. Lofty was no exception. In his case he zigzagged several times in a confused state before the functioning part of his brain finally worked out which was left. He immediately turned right. In doing so, he barged into me and I almost lost my footing. Without time to argue or correct his inadvertent mistake, I turned left into someone's pebble driveway. Loud crunching noises hailed each footstep as I shot past the front garden. The only entry to the back yard was down a narrow alleyway. Those crunching sounds turned to hollow echoing and heavy breathing on entry into the yard. At one stage I passed a woman hanging out some washing. A surprised look covered her face and without time to explain my predicament, I leaped over a fence. I took advantage of open country to make good speed with no idea if the occupant of the car actually followed Lofty or me. I continued running until reaching the safety of Top Wood. After sitting in the undergrowth for half an hour waiting for my mate, he inevitably let me down by not turning up. In fact, he never came to my house for two days. It was no more that could be expected from someone who had a hard time working out his left from right. On the other hand, when he eventually showed his face, my canoe was almost finished.

Undaunted by the unfortunate loss of essential materials I decided on going ahead with the project. I went to the river in Wyvern Valley and collected sufficient willow branches to make the frame. Meantime my mind continued pondering on what to use as a covering and where to acquire it. Most of the first day was spent looking for the right trees to cut the right number and size of branches for the keel, ribs and toe rail. Once they were cut, I carried them home. As usual, mother's curiosity needed satisfying when she wanted to know where I'd been all day.

"Can't you see mum, I've been collecting wood to make a canoe," I said reassuringly while pointing at the pile of willow branches.

Mother looked at the branches lying on the lawn and seemed satisfied with my answer because her muttered reply of "That's good son," was as much to herself as to me.

After assessing several alternative options on how to construct a frame that gave the right shape, the solution was quite simple. The keel was planted into the ground at both ends to make a bow shape. The ribs were then bent over the keel with their ends pushed into the ground to secure them in the correct position. The toe rail was pinned to the ground alongside the ribs. Having accomplished the right shape, everything was tied together with some strong twine found in Uncle's shed. I felt sure he would not mind if he ever found out.

One major problem remained. What to use to cover the frame? I sat on the ground smoking while looking at the perfect skeletal frame of a canoe. My brain continued working overtime. I feel absolutely certain it was a renegade brain cell that reminded me of a nearby egg packing station having a truck depot. Trucks, as everyone knows, carry huge rolls of tarpaulins to cover their loads. My mind ticked over at a steady rate, estimating and reassessing the size of material needed.

Late that night, dressed in my darkest clothing, I blackened my face with some of Uncle's boot polish the way commandos do before going into action. I felt certain Uncle would not mind about the polish either, if he ever found out. When totally prepared, I set off to lighten a load on someone's truck. "Not by

Nights in the Forest

much, not by much, not even enough to be missed," were the words used to console my conscience. Despite being convinced it would be okay, doubts remained in my mind, perhaps Father Sullivan would not approve of such actions during my next confession. With the certainty of a penance being increased to several Hail Mary's and the expression of "the end justifying the means", it helped modify any feelings of guilt.

I walked past the truck depot making sure no one was about while noting which vehicle carried the required material. A large trailer was parked in a convenient dark corner of the yard with a big roll of canvas securely tied on it. I jumped onto that trailer like a cat leaping onto its prey. That huge roll was much heavier than anticipated, except it never deterred me. With a lot of effort I set about unrolling it, cut a piece off, and then rolled the main lump back up. My boot-blackened face had a relieved smile; it must have been shining with sweat while my eyes gleamed in moonlight. With sufficient material to finish my project across both shoulders, I carried it home.

Early morning saw me stretching canvas over the frame, and with whatever remained of Uncle's twine I stitched it on with mother's big wool darning needle. During my euphoric state I decided to tell Uncle about the twine after explaining it had been taken for a good cause. He laughed at my confession and told me I was welcome to anything he had, then reminded me to ask next time. During the finishing stages Lofty and John made an appearance. Lofty actually turned up two days late, while John lived up to his reputation of arriving when there was nothing left to do. He also became very adept at avoiding work whenever he arrived early, which in John's case was – never!

The subject of the chase Lofty and I were involved in did not come up, so it was assumed Lofty made good his escape. My two friends stood beside each other gawking at my latest creation, which, even if I say so myself, looked absolutely fantastic.

John had never been shy about making critical remarks and as usual was the first to make a comment. "It's a funny shape."

"It's a revolutionary design," I muttered trying to avoid being irritated by John's ignorance of quality craftsmanship. The design had been forged by inspiration, hard work and individual effort. Apart from those indisputable facts, John had just dented my ego. The finished canoe happened to turn out the way it had because of the willows' resistance to bending into the direction they were required to.

"Will it go?" Lofty asked with a small measure of enthusiasm.

"Well if course it will," I replied indignantly.

"How?" John asked.

"With paddles of course. Derr, it's a canoe," I answered with hands on hips. There were serious doubts in my mind about John's level of intellect, despite giving the impression of being reasonably well educated. Although coming from a broken home, he was subjected to some pretty serious rules of engagement with whom he selected as friends. Perhaps those rules only applied to me. That did not surprise me and it may well have been the reason why any brain cells in his skull were constantly malfunctioning.

"It's a funny shape isn't it? Which end is the back?" John added. His knack of criticizing anything he couldn't understand surfaced by persistently asking irritating questions. However, one must give credit where credit is due. If there was something John was very good at, it was asking infuriating questions.

"The stern," I emphasized in an attempt to show John how ignorant he was of nautical terms, "is this end. That is the bow," I stated firmly while pointing at the other end. I knew that because lots of research had been done in the library. The pointed end is the bow and the stumpy flat bit at the back is called a stern.

"It looks back to front to me," John retorted softly. He was rubbing his chin and looking sideways. Shifty people, who don't know what they are talking about, do that sort of thing. He must have become aware I did not welcome his destructive critique. The fact his impression was correct had little if anything to do with it.

"Me too," Lofty supported but obviously had no idea why. That was hardly surprising when one considered recent events and making any comparisons between the two usually ended up by being equal.

"Just goes to show how much you two know about design," I said in defence of a classical education in design engineering. My researching through mountains of books, and then spending at least an hour in the local library taking notes and procuring designs, then making copies on tracing paper before redrafting an alternative shape and building it according to my latest ingenious design. Or perhaps, as it is more commonly known, I made a balls-up.

"Where are the paddles?" John asked.

"I haven't made them yet," I answered. In fact, with one thing and another they slipped my mind and a solution to that problem remained open to suggestion. Up till then inspiration remained stuck but I had no intention of revealing that inadvertent lapse of preparations to my companions. We geniuses are apt to keep secrets from idiots.

"When are you going to sail it?" John asked.

Sail. Now that had been something I considered. Putting a sail on my canoe may not have been difficult although it created additional problems I could well do without. A canoe is a canoe, not a sailing boat. "Tomorrow, if the weather holds," I answered confidently. John wanted to know if he could accompany me. Naturally he would be welcome. Other than having company on the trip to the river, I needed help in carrying the canoe. Lofty complained that he would not be able to come with us. His parents were having some visitors they wanted him to meet. He sounded like John making an excuse and it caused me to remember how my two friends were so alike in many aspects of their persona.

"Well, maybe next time then," I said and sat down.

He nodded, then smiled before sitting beside me. The three of us settled beside the finished canoe and talked about past adventures while sharing Uncle's tobacco. As Catholics, we compared the sins we committed and which ones we would be confessing to Father Sullivan at confessional that evening. My sins were quite big compared to John's fib to his mother about not seeing me. Lofty wanted to confess his improper thoughts about the girl next door. God already knew about my "borrowing" some much-needed material off the back of a truck. He must also be aware of my using Uncle's expensive very important twine and boot polish. Therefore, if he already knew my sins, there was little point in confessing them to Father Sullivan in that confessional box. I had no problems with that analysis. Any confessions to the boss upstairs would be made in the privacy of my bedroom before going to sleep. It seemed prudent to keep that sort of thing strictly between us.

On Sunday morning after church and before John arrived, the problem regarding two canoe paddles had been solved. The solution consisted of a long piece of wood with two paint tin lids nailed on the ends. The paint lids were found in Uncle's shed. Despite being lifted from tins of paint, I felt sure the paint inside would be perfectly okay, providing someone didn't kick them over. It was the best I could manage given the time and materials available. As long as it worked, what difference did it make what the paddles looked like? A Morris Oxford went just as well as a Rolls Royce but the Rolls was more aesthetic, that's all. My canoe never had a name but it was beautiful, and I had no doubts about it working.

Soon after his arrival, John took up the stern and with me on the bow, we set off on the long walk through Wyvern Valley down to the river.

Once in Wyvern Valley, we followed the well-trodden path leading to a lane that ran toward the river. On the way we stopped frequently for a chat and smoke breaks. I leaned against a tree and looked at John lying flat on his back in the sun. His freckled face was bright red and if he took a deeper breath there would have been an explosion. Body parts would be feeding the wildlife for weeks. I asked if he was tired.

"Nah, just enjoying the sun," he replied.

I lit a cigarette and looked among the branches where a squirrel suddenly appeared. We were fairly quiet during our journey and had not disturbed the wildlife, which gave me an opportunity to watch the tiny agile animal leap from branch to branch until it was out of sight. "Shame I didn't bring the air gun," I whispered softly.

Nights in the Forest

"You say somthin'?" John asked in a dreamy faraway voice. In less than another minute, my companion would have fallen into a deep sleep because any kind of exercise always made him feel tired.

A long silence followed while my senses went on the alert. A soft scent of fresh grass was drawn into my lungs. I caught the faint aroma of cow dung hanging in the air. Leaves above rustled and long stringy stands of weeds swayed. An unseen bird in the forest fluttered through some trees close by. I drew on my cigarette and watched exhaled pale blue smoke disappearing on the breeze before replying. "Yeah, looks like hunting would have been good today." My reply caused John to sit up. His curiosity was roused and he wanted to know what made me say that. I waved a hand in a wide sweep. "There's a lot of game about. Haven't you seen it?"

My friend's head swivelled from left to right. He saw nothing. He shrugged and finally commented nonchalantly, "Looks dead to me."

I closed my eyes in despair and found it hard to believe that anyone could sit amongst so much and still not see it. I took another long drag but said nothing. I dropped the butt before pressing it out with my foot while saying, "Come on lazy, let's get this ship launched," and lifted my end of the craft.

John, never one to be hurried, rose slower than growing grass and ambled to the other end. On lifting the stern, a nod confirmed he was ready before we moved off. To raise tired flagging spirits, I suggested we sing and, although John remained reluctant, when the third verse started, he joined in.

> Nick nack paddy whack
> Give a dog a bone
> This old man came rolling home
> This old man he played three
> He played nick nack on my knee
> With a nick nack paddy whack
> Give a dog a bone
> This old man came rolling home.

Chorus followed chorus until we carried the canoe to a wide slow-moving section of water before tentatively launching it. The materials were quite light, in fact, the canoe was light enough to carry on my own, and it floated very high.

A small square of wood was placed in the bottom before I gingerly climbed in. It wobbled, which meant clinging onto riverbank weeds for a moment while convincing myself it was just a question of balance. John stood watching apprehensively with one hand over his mouth and one on his head. It looked as though he was about to make a comment but decided against it, which was just as well because it was the one thing I didn't want right then. A few minutes later I was happily paddling up and down to the sound of John's incessant questions. Having established a level of stability, I began enjoying the fruits of my labour while putting up with a load of questions from my friend.

"What's it like?"

"Great," I replied.

"Does it leak?"

"Don't know."

"Can I have a go?"

"Yes."

"When?"

"Later."

"Come back. Where are you going?"

By the time he asked that question, I was paddling away faster, with John's last words ringing across the valley. What a wonderful little craft it turned out to be. The more I paddled the quieter my world became until several minutes of silence elapsed before looking back. I'd gone round several bends in that twisting river and arrived at a large almost still pond surrounded by overhanging trees. Sunlight filtered through branches onto crystal clear water around the isolated spot. Birds in those trees were hardly disturbed by my presence. My intrusion on their piece of paradise was looked on with curiosity. A plop close by indicated there were fish in the pond. I remained perfectly still while my little craft drifted toward a riverbank until it nestled against an old tree lying in the water.

Nights in the Forest

All my work and the hazards involved with accumulating building materials during the past two days were suddenly justified. My previous thoughts of the river holding no secrets were proved wrong. The spot I discovered could only be accessed by water. I leaned against that dead tree trunk to rest and watch the wildlife around me. Any daydreaming didn't last long because a distant voice intruded into pleasant thoughts. John must have been getting anxious about my disappearance. Nonetheless, reflections in that heavenly place continued for a few extra precious moments before pushing off to paddle downstream toward John's yelling.

On my arrival he began interrogating me before I climbed out to secure the canoe. I reached for my satchel lying where John discarded it as he came to the riverbank.

"Where'd you go?"

"Just round the corner," I replied while looking into the bag.

"Yeah, but you were gone a long time."

Time tends to meander slowly when you're waiting for someone. I knew it because of my friend's habit of taking his own time always kept others waiting. That failing would never be corrected. I looked up to answer, "No I wasn't."

"Can I 'ave a go now?" he asked enthusiastically, reaching for the line tied to a branch.

"Yes alright, but don't go past that tree," I said before sitting down to make a roll-up.

While preparing my cigarette, John clambered into the canoe and clung to the bank. He let go, the craft wobbled. He grabbed for the bank and shouted, "It's very unstable."

"Not when you get used to it." I called and half-expected John to roll the thing over and fall into the water. That made me wonder if the canoe would sink, if John could swim and if I would have to rescue him.

It took several attempts to balance himself before becoming confident enough to allow the craft to drift away from the riverbank. He dipped one tin lid into the water and the canoe wobbled. John remained still for a few moments before paddling gently. As my friend's confidence grew, his stroke rate became more vigorous until, with a whoop of joy he splashed through slow-flowing waters. John left no doubt he was enjoying his newfound freedom. I looked about. Any game that may have been around would certainly have taken cover from the noises my friend made. While he was having fun, the question of whether we should carry my canoe home or hide it among the bushes needed serious consideration. It would be easy, being small it could certainly be shoved under a nearby bush. I took a stroll and looked for a suitable hiding place. There were plenty of cowpats everywhere with an obvious trail running along the riverside. People came past the spot and I mused on the possibility of it being a farmer. If anyone found my canoe they would more than likely want to use it. Whoever they were would have a good time with it and not particularly concerned about sinking it. That idea was horrifying. Too much time and effort had been put into the project to have it obliterated or sunk by someone having fun. That left no alternative but for John and me to cart it all the way back home.

John continued paddling up and down for half an hour before his enthusiasm wore off. He finally came ashore to stand aside for a few moments, nodding with a smile of satisfaction on his red face. I watched the display of self-hero-worship with mild amusement before calling for him to come and sit down, offered Uncle's tobacco tin and watched the delight on his face at making his own cigarette.

"Well, what do you think of her?"

"It's damn good mate, we did it, didn't we," he answered before lighting the cigarette and taking a deep drag.

I was about to correct John on his formal proclamation of "we", but satisfied myself with agreeing. After all, his help would be needed to carry it back. And it was uphill most of the way. We continued smoking while deliberating who should take the lead on the return journey. I quickly came to the conclusion that John realized he was not obliged to help carry my canoe back. He made his point clear by insisting the choice of who went first was his.

We were strolling along with the canoe suspended between us talking about when we should do it again. However, with my primary ambition satisfied, I came close to concluding our discussion by either giving the canoe to John or leaving it under a bush by the river. On reflection, as things turned out, either alternative would have been best. However, on that day we continued slogging it out up through the valley and home.

As time went by, I found it impossible to raise sufficient enthusiasm or energy to carry that canoe back to Wyvern Valley on my own and John couldn't be persuaded to assist. It sat in the garden becoming overgrown with weeds as she waited to add a sequel to her maiden voyage. The sight of it eventually provoked mother into fits of annoyance at the "mess" until an ultimatum was eventually issued. "Get rid of that rubbish or I'll set fire to it," she shouted.

The canoe had already served its purpose, and I gave mother a box of matches and told her to go ahead, knowing my decision would upset John. The fire started very quickly, since the vessel's wooden frame and canvas covering had become drier than tinder. It only took about one minute before the flames engulfed its entire fragile structure. I watched swirling white smoke curling ever upwards. Without a breeze to disperse it, it climbed higher and higher. It looked like a fitting signal to the end of an era that included a maiden voyage. The flames roared for a few minutes, then died to leave a pile of grey ash amongst tangled blackened weeds, which left me with one thought. "Best way to go."

Anthony Corbyn

Chapter Ten

Starfield House

A little red Renault Dauphine drew up outside the house and from my bedroom window I watched an attractive woman climb out. Our long anticipated visitor had finally arrived. The first thing that impressed me was the length of her legs as she got out the car. It also prompted my heart to skip a beat when she straightened her skirt. She pushed on the wrinkles until her hands smoothed over the full length to her knees. Without any doubt, our visitor had exceptionally good looks and I wondered what she was doing here. It must have been the reason mother told me to stay in. Curiosity prevented me from going out, despite it being a perfect day for taking Lassie to the forest on a hunting trip. There were few things, if any, preventing me doing what I wanted. Although on that occasion an inquisitive mind chained me to the house with the idea that it might prove interesting. Mother greeted our visitor at the door while I listened from my bedroom to various comments and responses of a soft feminine voice.

Some time passed before mother called my name. By then my curiosity had developed into a devilish mood. Mother and our visitor had been talking about me like some kind of inanimate object without once considering why I continued doing things that annoyed everyone in authority. Their conversation reflected a typical approach to a juvenile problem by adults. Their defence to any questions was always "Do as you're told" without explaining why. I soon discovered their reasons for never giving an explanation. More often than not, an answer could not be justified or they never had one. In my opinion the classic case of many adult attitudes and answers consisted of a "Do as you're told, you're too young to understand" hypothesis.

Now that I found difficult to understand but an example of hypocrisy becomes clear when an adult tells a young person they're too young to smoke and in any case it's illegal. That particular critique was usually followed by the smoker blowing out a cloud of smoke whilst saying those immortal words, "It's not good for you." When I'm old enough it's permitted and therefore not a problem. That opinion struck me as very odd. If it's not allowed because it's not good for me before my birthday, how come it's okay after?

By the time I met our visitor, that person in authority waiting in our sitting room, my mood had become aggressive. I walked into our front room to confront the good-looking woman with an attitude of pure defiance. Her charming nature, posture and good looks simply added fuel to my burning desire to rebel.

"Hello, Paul, isn't it," the sweet voice said as she held out her hand.

I reached for it with the intention of squeezing hard to impress on the woman how strong, masculine and independent I was. Its cool gentle grip was soft, white, and very clean compared to mine. Her nails were manicured with a pale pink lacquer that enhanced her overall appeal, as did her perfume. I inhaled the fragrance, it smelled like spring morning with dew still on the ground, and tantalizingly exotic. Any masculine display or rebellious intentions simply evaporated and were replaced with my best smile and gentle squeeze. She looked deeply into my eyes, my heart sank. All resistance along with any thoughts of rebellion faltered. Feminine guile and beauty overcame all.

"My name is Miss Brown," she said before sitting down again.

I stood before her while she lectured on my bad habits of not going to school, annoying neighbours, a poor disposition and rebellious attitude toward authority, causing mayhem and inciting my friends to follow my bad example. After a few minutes of verbal administration in attempting to alter my ways, she ended the lecture by stating in all sincerity that I'd been, a very naughty boy.

That final statement ending her long dialogue did it for me. I stepped back to give my best couldn't give a damn, cocky, feet apart, hands on hips stance specifically designed to infuriate adults. My eyes were staring hard throughout the lecture, first at her breasts then the exposed knees. I knew it unsettled Miss Brown because she kept pulling at the hem. When my eyes shifted back to her breasts, she was unable to resist glancing at her blouse buttons to make sure they were still done up. My sharp eye latched onto a tiny piece of pink lace attached to her bra and remained fixed on it. The stare became blatantly bright with lust. It was impossible to hide, even if I wanted to.

"Did you hear what I said?" she asked quickly in an obvious attempt at recovering the initiative. "You have been a very naughty boy."

"Yes, but not half as naughty as I'd like to be with you," I responded and almost choked trying to hold down a fit of laughter. Although the statement was blurted out, I meant every word. Adults seem to forget, young adults and sprouting teenagers like me have a lot of unrestricted hormones leaping about inside growing bodies. Those male hormones have a detrimental effect on youngsters' thoughts and some physical reactions are nature's way of signalling we are ready to mate. Almost any female will do. Even males, if one were that way inclined.

Miss Brown blushed. She could not have been more than twenty-three and from what I discovered later, I was the first assignment in her career as a probation officer. That attractive officer was vulnerable to any kind of crude verbal assault by a young hooligan who took the initiative by destroying any sense of authority that existed. "How dare you!" she exclaimed in an attempt to hide her embarrassment by pulling rank, the hem of her skirt and closing a developing gap on her blouse, prompted by deep breathing – all at the same time. She also used whatever authority was left by standing up, to tower over me. Miss Brown must have been aware of my contemptuous view toward her authoritative position, even though I had obviously taken a liking to her.

"I dare," were my last words before laughing aloud. The entire scenario suddenly became very funny as I turned and staggered away almost doubled up in a laughing fit.

Mother remained stunned at my outburst with a hand over her mouth. She'd been privy to seeing that side of me before but never toward a visitor.

"Paul. You come back here this instant. I haven't finished with you yet. Come here!" my pretty young probation officer demanded firmly with a face flushed from the humiliation of my casual dismissal.

"But I've finished with you," I called back. The door slammed shut on my laughter, which continued all the way to my bedroom. That must have been a very unsettling experience for my probation officer and it may also have been a contributing factor in starting the wheels of authority turning against me. It became a futile attempt at grinding down a free spirit and putting it in its place, wherever that might have been. The wheels had already been turning for some time, yet I was still free!

Several people came to visit mother during the next couple of weeks and my disruptive presence was no longer required. Decisions were being made about my future without conferring or including me in their discussions. It represented a typical attitude of many adults in authority and the primary reason why there's always going to be conflict between me and them. Not long after, the same Renault Dauphin pulled up outside the house. Mother began fussing about, crying, making excuses on my behalf and saying it had all been a mistake before asking Miss Brown if she really was going to take me away.

"Don't worry mum, just think of it as me going on holiday. I'll be able to visit you," I assured mother before turning to my probation officer for confirmation.

"Well yes. Yes of course he will," Miss Brown replied. Her response was directed to mother with a reassuring hand on her shoulder. However comforting the words may have been intended, I detected a note of doubt in her voice. That angel of authority had been given the task of taking me away. From the tone in her voice, she had no idea what would happen after that. Nevertheless, those assurances were enough to calm mother down and put on a brave face while waving me goodbye.

Meantime, Uncle kept a low profile during the entire proceedings. The authorities have strange attitudes and are apt to come down hard on lodgers. They were very suspicious of "uncles" and visiting real relatives who stayed too long in one place, especially if they contributed to housekeeping expenses. In our case, the tax payer carried the burden of supplying money to our kitty, and any illegal increment came from Uncle.

My probation officer and I were on the road when Uncle rode up on his big Norton Dominator as the Renault stopped at a junction. He looked down at me, blipped the throttle, gave me a wink, then raced away. His signal was there for anyone who understood it. From that moment, my secret supporter would always be there should he be needed. The thought made me feel good and something worth remembering.

Before setting off, mother instructed me to put on some nice clothes to give a good impression on whoever was at the other end of my journey. The clothing was easy to select. I picked my favourite black jumper with a wide diagonal red stripe across the front and pulled it on. It was my rebel flag that contrasted vividly with Corsham Secondary Modern School's uniform and got right up every teacher's nose. I'd been told on numerous occasions not to wear it by the headmaster, except his objections simply encouraged me to disobey. Long curly hair slicked down with Echo margarine substituting hair cream came straight out of mother's larder. My number one, best tight-fitting, latest fashion drain pipe blue jeans hugged every contour of my lower body. From every juvenile's point of view they looked cool. When they were brand new, their stiffness made me walk like a duck with my legs apart, although once they'd been washed, I could swagger in them. Any youth who walked that way would receive derogatory remarks from adults. That didn't matter because young girls were impressed and looked at you the way you wanted. It was easy to make them blush by putting one's hands into pockets and thrusting your hips forward.

Miss Brown changed gears, looked left and right and avoided my stare covering every move she made. Judging from her agitated movements, it must have had an effect on her. "I want you to behave yourself while you are at the House," she said softly. Her eyes remained fixed on the road. It was the first time the word "House" had been mentioned. It seemed as though a deep secret had finally been let out of the bag and the subject could suddenly be talked about, but only in whispers.

I asked what it was like for no better reason than having a genuine interest on my part. During the next ten minutes Miss Brown gave a glowing report on the House and how it functioned along informal lines. The building was a little way out of the village with lots of room to play outside. There were no bars on the windows, which made it a nice big house where boys and girls lived happily together in a family environment. She explained how everyone shared in the maintenance, digging in gardens to grow food, collecting vegetables and fruit, even eggs from a big chicken hut. Miss Brown went on to assure me that she felt confident I would settle in very quickly.

I took a spontaneous liking for Miss Brown even though she was far too old for me. Nevertheless, my question came out anyway. "Will you come and visit me?"

We had stopped at a road junction. She looked across with soft brown eyes that melted my heart and said, "Well of course I will, as long as you behave yourself."

Those additional words stabbed into my being and made me wish she never said them. They were tantamount to moral blackmail. However, it didn't stop the ardent desire to kiss her full on the lips. The yearning went well beyond friendship. Those juvenile urges and imaginations became so intense that my body started reacting accordingly. A growing bulge became painfully suppressed by tight-fitting denim material. Fortunately, by the time we reached our destination, its physical display had subsided sufficiently so as not to be embarrassing. Besides, my rebel jumper was long enough to cover everything below the waist. We came to a stop on the wide gravel driveway of Starfield House, not far from Trowbridge, the county town of Wiltshire.

Miss Brown leaned across to unlock the door, her face came close to mine. I instinctively leaned forward with every intention of stealing a kiss, but she pulled back and hissed, "Behave yourself." Her eyes flicked across mine with a stern look. Nonetheless, I felt certain there was a very feminine look of curiosity hidden below their severe surface. Perhaps she was tempted to find out what it would be like.

I swaggered across the driveway toward a large stone building looking up at windows. They were full of young faces peering down on our approach. I followed Miss Brown up several steps to the front door. Those stairs provided a perfect opportunity for a close-up look of her buttocks and they were well worth studying. The view certainly influenced my thoughts toward the female anatomy from that day. From my brief visual encounter, an inbuilt disinterested attitude towards female rear ends altered to devoted admiration.

We were side by side heading down a long corridor toward a door marked "Office". Our brief walk toward it gave me an uncomfortable familiar sensation, which was exactly the same as that experienced when a notice marked on the door read "Headmaster".

Miss Brown knocked and opened it to the words "come in" being issued from the other side. We were ushered into an office where my escort was directed to sit. The same directive was not given to me. My thoughts recalled past experiences that followed the same instructions, so it became easy to close my mind against those current circumstances. The man sitting before me looked as much like my old headmaster as anyone could. The situation called for reverting to what I always did under those same circumstances. I stood at ease, put on a dead straight ahead stare and shut down my listening devices, took a deep breath and slowed my heartbeat. That physical and mental posture always did the trick for me.

The impression I arrived at during the interview confirmed Miss Brown had just made her first delivery of a prisoner. From my immature point of view, she had a lot to learn about the person running Starfield House for juvenile delinquents. The man sitting before us never even liked children. A paper-thin sneer splitting his lips was a dead giveaway. Cold pale blue eyes never looked straight at whoever he talked to. From where I stood, the man had no compassion, humour or understanding. We were in his domain, therefore beware anyone coming into it who had a mind of their own. Confrontation between us was on the agenda. However, my confidence in an ability to handle him grew stronger with each passing moment.

My pretty probation officer's lovely eyes betrayed her true emotions. A hint of sorrow, a puzzled look of disbelief, the realization she had unwittingly led her charge, her defenceless little lamb, into a den run by a wolf. I wanted to reassure her that as the best survivor and hunter there was on planet earth, a den of lions would have been a more appropriate challenge to her charge's abilities. I never took long making an assessment of my position within a group. All situations were never as bad as first impressions. I quickly realized Starfield House had numerous possibilities. It also provided a place where I was able to confirm once and for all, adults were naive, even stupid, if they believed controlling a free mind can be sustained by simply issuing a threat. That type of crude logic always failed to impress me. After all, wasn't that the reason I was there?

Starfield was sited just outside a small country village near Trowbridge. It is a place where the road goes straight through. A small convenience store served as a post office that nestled in the centre of a row of cottages. The village was surrounded by numerous farms with undulating green pastures and acres of greenhouses. It had a train line running past, although I never saw a train stop. To be perfectly honest, the steady chuff chuffer chuff of steam engines appeared to increase their speed. The engine driver must have been keen to get past as fast as possible, apart from which there was no station to stop at anyway. The greatest benefit to the residents was the road out with only two choices, left or right.

Starfield had been established to place young teenage boys who were rebellious and parents had lost control of them, separated or died. Some had gone to hospital with nervous breakdowns, which were almost certainly caused by their beloved sons. Then there were young girls who were of similar age. They were at Starfield House because of promiscuous behaviour and according to rumour, some had even become pregnant. So, we dregs of society were thrown into the cooking pot like so many vegetables. From what I recall, it represented the recipe for a stew that was bound to boil over. I considered myself privileged to share the company of thieves, vagabonds and general good for nothings, all with equally free spirits. By the end of my first day it began feeling like a home from home.

The authorities, who included the odd adult intellectual, in their absolute wisdom put young hot-blooded, rampant, uncontrollable males together with equally young or older hot-blooded promiscuous females. Both genders were equal in their determination to have anything they wanted. Every teenager confined within its walls had more rampaging hormones than the pot called Starfield could safely restrain. From a teenager's point of view, things were perfect. I was in a pressure cooker and the gas was turned full on.

On my first morning, in a dormitory of six male delinquents, I sat on my warm bed smiling. There were terrible thoughts of disruption going on in my mind already. Later the same morning one of the Aunties showed me round the place. It seemed only natural to ask why we had to call them by that name.

"What else would you call us?" came the expected adult reply.

Auntie took me round the building to the dining area where I had breakfast earlier, then pointed out some extensive gardens. She showed me the playroom, which contained a strange phenomenon that really baffled me. It contained a large pile of mattresses in one corner for "the children" to play on. I could understand it if we occupants had been five years old, but thirteen to sixteen year old delinquents of mixed gender have a much clearer idea and imagination of what could be done on mattresses. This was particularly true when one of our company of delinquents remained at the door as lookout.

The same room contained a table tennis table and Auntie offered to teach me how to play it one day. She led me into a walled garden and introduced me to the gardener. He represented the typical stereotype gardener of the era. He wasn't tall, had a swarthy complexion, spoke with a broad West Country accent and wore a cloth cap pulled down to cover his eyes. He was bow-legged and probably had rickets or some such disease that bow-legged gardeners get. He wore an oversized, well-worn Harris Tweed jacket that hung over slopping shoulders, with leather elbow pads that were coming free of their stitching. His trousers must have belonged to a clown and he had a pair of boots that must have come from an army disposal depot. His wrinkled face grinned and he shook my hand before sticking an equally old briar pipe back in his mouth and moving off. Uncle always taught me that appearances were deceiving. He was right.

In that high-walled inner sanctum there were apple, plum and pear trees growing. In between those trees were neat rows of raspberry canes, strawberry beds and black currant bushes including a full range of extra special vegetables. The only thing I couldn't see was a heated greenhouse with grapevines growing inside. Still, my active mind continued making notes where everything grew for those nights when I climbed over the wall to sample some "borrowed" goods. A particular objective that came to mind was those overloaded bushes of ripe black currants. It's not as if it was something I hadn't done before.

We paid a visit to a large playing field with swings and goal posts planted at each end. Auntie told me the warden, Mister Bowshot, encouraged any kind of sporting activity. The next area was a large open garden where potatoes, cabbages, carrots and sprouts were grown next to a fenced in area where dozens of chickens were kept. "In here we have plenty of chickens so there are always lots of eggs," Auntie informed me. I experienced an urge to suppress the image that came to mind of happy not so far off days when stealing eggs had been a source of nourishment. Sucking out the raw contents had always been a pleasure not available at home. The milkman wouldn't be delivering any eggs with milk at the Starfield House doorstep. But that didn't stop me wondering how many freshly laid eggs would be available during a night's foraging.

Two donkeys were kept for anyone willing and able to ride them, since according to Auntie they were a bit frisky at times. The last spot we paid a visit to was where several doves were kept. They were very pretty white things with big fantails. However, my mind not only rested on how good they looked but what they might taste like. Previous hunger prints unforgettable images in the mind that remain constant reminders for one's imagination to work on.

During the next couple of weeks in that heaven-sent place, the innocent grew up and virgins became non-virgins. Life at Starfield proceeded at a steady pace. Up till then, it had not experienced any unprecedented event in its history. I could see the peace of that place coming adrift sooner or later and under my influence, it would be the former.

Over a month later I sat on the swings singing to myself and contemplating the situation while trying to work out a plan to create some disturbance worthy of my talents. When one has a reputation, one is duty-bound to live up to it by subjecting the local community to a level of alarm and despondency.

The place functioned like a large family with a big vegetable garden, a hen house, two donkeys, push bikes to ride, swings to play on, and much more. All the boys slept in one dormitory opposite the girl's dorm and we all called the women who looked after us "Auntie". For the life of me no one could tell me why they didn't have real names. Only the warden Mister Bowshot had one, no one else. With a name like that I would have been instructing all my charges to call me Uncle.

Starfield House quickly lost its appeal as a stable environment and became my prison. Old Pigface, as the head custodian was also known by inmates, would learn that despite his power, at least one inmate wasn't impressed. Things were underfoot that would tip the balance and create some mayhem. To any spectator the place looked well planned and orderly, despite what was going on unseen at night.

Nelson Haden Boys Secondary Modern School in Trowbridge was a good bus ride away. Whilst I verbally objected to going, it became impossible to have any days and nights in the forest to hunt without being detected. It also turned into one of the toughest schools I ever attended. Any kids from Starfield had to put up with being pushed around, bullied and hounded by other students who targeted us for scorn and ridicule.

Anthony Corbyn

My problem was an infallible belief that I was as good if not better than anyone who came up against me. That belief resulted in the age and size of adversaries growing each day and my reputation for being a fighter grew with it. It wasn't difficult to achieve because by comparison to most opponents, my stature was indeed quite small. However, retained within this wiry body was a powerful desire to win no matter what the odds. An enviable but unwarranted reputation soon built up and as explained to the headmaster on more than one occasion, "The fight wasn't started by me Sir, honest."

Actually I was scared to fight because one day I knew the odds would inevitably be stacked against my ability to win. The result would be receiving a damn good thrashing. It reached the stage where my adversaries were almost always bigger than me. A typical example of the current situation occurred while queuing up for a bus after another day in boring classes.

Someone shuffled up behind and pushed me forward. Like most people I don't like being pushed but it's the sort of thing that makes anyone really angry. The shove was ignored and I continuing talking to my friend. Another push in the back made me spin round to confront whoever did the pushing. A youth about a foot taller grinned down on me although his face was not familiar. I attempted to ignore him and moved away. However, my friend knew what was happening. He became increasingly nervous and it showed in his posture, wide eyes and agitated reactions.

A much harder thrust followed and it couldn't have been anything less than deliberate provocation. My heart suddenly picked up speed and began pounding against rapidly expanding and deflating ribs. My mouth dried, my stomach churned and my legs began to weaken. They were symptoms not conducive to a pleasant ending of the day because I knew what other emotions were about to follow. They were a prelude to an inevitable event.

"Come on, let's get outa here," my friend whispered nervously. He clasped hold of an arm and we immediately began moving from the queue with me allowing him to lead the way.

Nights in the Forest

The tall youth wasn't in the mood to be denied, he followed. The pushing altered to open vocal taunts and number one school bully made a move and there would be no help from dozens of onlookers. As far as they were concerned, it had nothing to do with them, besides there hadn't been a good fight in the schoolyard for ages. School fights were part and parcel of entertainment and helped break up the monotony of learning.

The gangly youth sneered and closed in before spouting what could only be described as a challenge. "Wasa matter then squirt, scared or sumfink is yur."

My companion clearly had no intentions of becoming involved. He started walking away while attempting to pull me along with him. That would not have done any good because number one school bully had selected his target. Moving away only provided him with an incentive to pursue his potential victim who was fearful of him. Most teachers knew the problem existed but they were vague in their solutions to solving the problem. Walk away, report it, talk your way out, join a group and stay with them for safety were a few of the suggestions. In case they were unaware of it, I could have told them there's only one way to stop a bully. Beat seven bells out of him every time he indulges in such a hostile activity. Primitive methods are normally the only course of action against primeval beings. Banning them from school simply puts them in another area to carry out what they are good at.

Any recollections of what happened next are a little vague but fear isn't that far removed from anger. When the final shove came, it landed as a punch between my shoulder blades and was accompanied by a voice in an echo chamber. "You ain't nothin' but a yeller bellied motherless little bastud who cums from a broken 'ome."

I clearly remember turning with a clenched fist and seeing a surprised look on my provocateur's face. Uncle's words were ringing through my mind. "If you have to fight be sure your punches are the best you have and above all, make yours the first." As my first punch landed, a red mist closed my mind. Hate, vengeance and blind rage swept away any vestige of sanity or fear.

From that moment I have no recollections of the event. It was my nervous friend who recounted what happened. "Your scream turned the heads of everyone in the queue. We all watched in amazement as your body went into a frenzy of kicks, punches and bites. When that bully fell, you were all over him like the pox, smashing your fist into the kid's face so many times it was impossible to count. Your left hand closed around the poor sod's neck while you were sitting on his chest." He took a deep breath before concluding with, "Mary mother of God, just watching scared the living shit out of me." So ended my friend's description of what happened.

The fight didn't last long. It took two teachers to drag my screaming, kicking, arm-swinging, wriggling body off the victim. That action by the teachers resulted in them sustaining injuries to their own faces, groins and shins. Their attempts at calming me took much longer than the actual fight. No sympathy was extended to the pupil who was much bigger than me. Both teachers demanded we shake hands and forget whatever or whoever started the fight. I adamantly refused and angrily demanded a rematch so I could finish the job properly without interference. Had I been given the opportunity, there was every intension of killing my opponent.

They carted the tall youth off to hospital to have stitches in a bite wound on his face, a broken nose repaired and two loose teeth removed. It appears that other facial bruising and bump on the back of his head, caused by its perpetual bouncing against the schoolyard concrete, would heal over time. That unfortunate incident helped confirm my unjustified reputation and for some time pupils left me alone. One of the teachers, however, decided that such aggression should not be wasted on simple academic studies. An invitation from our physical training instructor to join the boxing team was presented to me. "I saw you fighting son. You would make a good boxer, plenty of spirit with no fear and a good strong punch." That's what he said.

Ha! That's how much he knew. I thought it was a load of crap. My inclination at that stage was to say no but after some persuasion decided to give it a try. I no sooner agreed to his training program than my coach put me in the ring for a few lessons. There were rules, more rules than one could poke a stick at. I was constantly being told that I could do one thing but not do this or that. There were more rules about what one could not do in the ring than what you could. It made very little sense. My fighting had always been carried out with one objective – win no matter what. From that day, my fighting abilities were under control and I had to abide by a set of rules drawn up by some Marquess who came from Queensberry and died about a million years ago. Training consisted of punching a punch bag, ducking and weaving, jabbing out the left, counter punching with the right. My training took place each day at lunchtime for a half hour.

The first boxing match happened a week later. A lot of screaming kids packed themselves into the sports hall. Everyone was baying for blood, anybody's blood. None of them cared one way or the other whose blood it was as long as it wasn't theirs. According to my coach, one week's training had honed my fighting prowess down to the razor-sharp edge of a champion killer. "This fight's a good opportunity to prove just how good you are when the odds are even." At least that's what the trainer shouted as he led me toward the ring past screaming crowds. In the other corner another similar-sized youth stood waiting to prove who the better boxer was. It took about a split second to recognize Nelson Haden Boys School's champion.

A horrible feeling of being manipulated by teachers surged inside to make me feel sick with anger. I was unable to understand the point of trusting people who were responsible for controlling situations when they did that sort of thing.

My opponent and I were brought to the centre of the ring where the referee gave us instructions about fighting fair. We were to break when he told us and go to a neutral corner if either one were knocked down. Although he said quite a lot, most was inaudible during the screaming going on around me. Nonetheless, I distinctly remember his last words of encouragement before returning to my corner. The referee's specific instructions were, "When the bell goes, come out fighting." Those words fixed inside my head like shit to a blanket.

Anthony Corbyn

My trainer, coach and confidant attempted giving me some last words of advice on defensive moves. His words were also barely audible over the screams coming from the spectators. It made no difference anyway. I was focusing on my intentions, concentrating all evil thoughts on that school champion and distinctly recall looking at my opponent's back in the opposite corner. When the bell sounded, "Come out fighting" were the only words reverberating through my brain. I shot toward my opponent like a rabbit chased by a ferret. The first punch, in true Uncle instructive technique, landed just as our school champion turned. Perhaps he never heard the bell, maybe he thought, like everyone before I would be waiting for him in the centre of the ring. However, an evil temper flared at the comment about even odds. It was my first boxing match, and against the school champion!

My gloved fist pounded onto the champion's nose. The initial force bounced his head back against corner ropes. His head came forward from the rebound to meet my head coming in on the attack. The collision of my forehead against his nose could not have been avoided even if I wanted to. I attempted getting out the way as our school champion, now totally stunned by such a ferocious premeditated attack, staggered sideways. He stumbled along the ropes with blood pouring from his nose and a cut above it. Seeing an adversary in deep trouble, as a fighter I felt duty-bound to go after him full bore. My mind was no longer in the ring but back in a schoolyard. Rules in the boxing game were for others, not for me. I closed in very fast and delivered a volley of punches designed to break concrete blocks. While the left glove came up in a series of short sharp uppercuts to my adversary's face, the right chopped down like a hammer on the champion's neck. By all the rules of physics, he should have gone down from the number of blows belting into him. However, with an arm firmly clamped over the middle rope, he simply couldn't fall, which was tough titty on him.

Maintaining that bludgeoning assault to his head with both fists on a defenceless champion continued. I was breathing hard and seriously considering kicking him between the legs. They were wide open and inviting. It would put an end to his misery and any potential children he might want, but what the hell. I closed in, hammered another rabbit punch to the back of his neck, and took a deep breath to steady myself for a well-delivered kick. Suddenly, I became airborne; the ref lifted me off my feet and carried me away. I was able to remember, according to the rules your opponent remains a legitimate target until he falls to the canvas.

I'll never be certain why the champ won that fight, after all, he never even threw a punch. Our school champ didn't so much win the fight but had his hand lifted due to my disqualification. I tried explaining away the accidental headbutt, and as for my knee to the groin, it had nothing to do with me, he fell on it. Yes, it's true, there had been a series of rabbit punches delivered at a frantic rate, which had been done in ignorance of so many confusing rules. No one told me it was against the rules to deliver punches to the neck while one's opponent had trapped himself on the ropes. In fact, I clearly recall being told to stay away from them.

The disappointment of my disqualification stunned me to such an extent I insisted on retiring. My trainer said it would be a shame because he had faith in such fighting qualities and it would be such a waste of enormous potential. However hard he tried to persuade me otherwise, I didn't want to fight. Another tournament was arranged a short time later and my refusal to take part became subjected to a string of derogatory remarks. The comments were particularly bad from those who wanted me to fight, the teachers and coaches. They were saying, "I thought you were a brave boy" or "You don't want your friends to think you're afraid, do you?" or "Only cowards back away from a fight." That last callous remark came from the coach himself. There were many other comments dropped into conversations during times of persuasion, despite my just wanting them to leave me alone. The boxing team trainers were determined not to be cheated out of their desire to obtain some spectacular entertainment. The team coach must have become desperate because he enlisted the help of another student who befriended me.

Mike invited me to his home in Trowbridge to meet his parents and have a meal. We had dinner and talked about everything in general although before long the subject of boxing came up and the question why I didn't want to box. It was not a subject I wanted to talk about although my newfound friend persisted.

The following day during a lunch break, Mike had another go at persuading me. I eventually agreed by saying, "Okay. I'll do it, but you have to be my sparring partner."

Apparently, Mike was not keen on having his face bashed in just for the fun of it. The thought of being my sparring partner had no appeal to him at all. The alternative of seeing me battered, bruised and spread out like strawberry jam on canvas seemed to make him deliriously happy. Somewhere down the line we struck a deal with Mike eventually agreeing to spar with me. It would be a light-hearted affair with no malice or anger involved. "No aggression must be displayed in the ring against a sparring partner," he kept reminding me as we bobbed up and down before any punches were thrown. I had no idea those instructions were for Mike's benefit so duly conformed to his misinformation of a misinterpreted rule. Before long the training period was over and another boxing tournament began.

I sat watching my opponent climb into the ring. His appearance staggered me. He was much taller and obviously far heavier than me. "Is this the supposed fair fight where contestants about the same height and weight pit their boxing skills against each other?" I took a deep breath and looked my trainer in the eye. "How can anyone call this a fair fight?"

A smirk developed across his lips when he saw the look on my face and muttered back, "Well now lad, let's see how well you do when the boot's on the other foot."

A tortured mind started racing and wondering if they thought I was an idiot, or if they were relying on me being too naive to understand what they were up to. The whole scenario was an obvious ploy to teach one unruly pupil a lesson. Although teachers aren't allowed to satisfy their primeval instinct in giving an obnoxious student a good beating, they had the facilities to get someone else to do it for them. The guise of a supervised sporting activity called a boxing tournament held a perfect venue. An angry frustration inside me had never been suppressed for so long

Nights in the Forest

without a necessary blow-out or a calming influence those days and nights in the forest provided. After being cajoled into fighting, tricked and kept in place against my will, something had to give. Above all else, I had been denied a hunting trip for weeks. The entire system began piling up far more feelings than anything ever experienced before. Something needed doing about it and the fight fiasco became the last straw.

When the bell sounded for boxing to begin, the tremor shaking my body didn't represent fear or apprehension. A sneering smile on my trainer's face turned that feeling into rage. In the opposite corner, my opponent stood up and began advancing with his gloves held high. Although he may not have been aware of it, he was about to become the recipient of unbelievable anger. A pang of sympathy surfaced because he may have stood a chance had he been more than, just twice my size.

I remained stationary, hands by my side, with my body coiled like a compressed spring waiting for someone to press the release button.

The lanky, ginger-headed youth with gloves held high bounced up and down in front. I never moved but watched him bobbing and throw a half-hearted left. He weaved for a few seconds, threw a couple more left jabs, then put on a wonderful display of shadow boxing. Left and rights came within inches of my face in rapid staccato. The crowd, including my trainer, my opponent's trainer, the referee and corner men were screaming for blood. Hit him, kill him, smash the little prick, were some bits of advice being handed out by everyone inside or outside the ring. The referee finally stepped between us and encouraged me to defend myself. My boxing stance with raised gloves and slightly bent legs for balance was taken up, except I remained rooted to the spot.

My opponent's first jab fell short, so did the second. That kind of provocation wasn't enough to stimulate the start button inside a fermenting volcano. A puzzled look covered his face while he continued playing by that unwritten rule of not hitting someone smaller than himself or a defenceless person. I remained stationary with my gloves raised when another jab touched me on the shoulder, a sort of, come on let's start fighting, punch.

Anthony Corbyn

That turned into the last thing needed for my starter button to be pressed and whatever restrained my coiled spring suddenly let go. I leaped at the unfortunate youth. I began kicking, headbutting, punching and biting – all at once. The young man was naturally taken completely by surprise, since that's not the sort of thing that happened in a boxing ring. His defence system came apart under my onslaught. He fell backwards onto the canvas with me adhered to him. One glove was firmly behind his head. The second pounded his belly. A knee came up between his legs and remained locked into that position while my teeth fastened themselves securely into his face. A lot of screaming erupted with some of it coming from me. Most of it from the person I became strongly attached to.

The referee rushed across to pull me off along with two trainers leaping in to assist. By the time they managed to separate us, I had inflicted a considerable amount of damage to all parties concerned. My adversary had a tear in his face that would require stitches. A lot of blood had been spilled, some of it mine. The headbutt delivered to an unfortunate foe split open his mouth but the teeth cut my forehead. Two deep indentations in the shape of teeth were where all my blood came from.

During their valiant attempts to separate us, our referee received an elbow in his eye and my trainer got a well-deserved kick in the groin. I went completely berserk, which made it difficult for anyone to restrain and calm me down. Needless to say, the crowd went absolutely wild. They got what they wanted with more than enough entertainment and blood to satisfy everyone till the next contest. My fight was the shortest but almost certainly the tournament's most talked about. The boxing promoters had their spectacular piece of entertainment, then banned me from the boxing ring as being totally unpredictable and dangerous.

I couldn't understand why they placed me in that category. Surely those two aspects of a boxer were his greatest assets. The situation suited me, for a while. A long time after the tournament no one was game to try me out in the schoolyard. Despite not being provoked into fights, I had a heavy heart. There were no adults who could be trusted, in the first place I never wanted to

Nights in the Forest

fight and later discovered that Mike had been used to persuade me back into the ring. That was hard for me to bear. A friend in the making used an embryo of our friendship to trick me into that boxing ring again.

During those long evenings at Starfield House things began settling into a sort of mundane home style living. One aspect of life included a weekly program we were permitted to watch on a black and white television, it was called "Quatermass and the Pit". The story line included finding a spaceship buried deep underground. Naturally, only the elder inmates of the establishment were permitted to watch some crude unfolding drama, which I never found particularly horrifying. The beings enclosed within that buried spacecraft looked like giant grasshoppers. They were able to influence human behaviour, especially their walking, which turned into a sort of lolloping gait. While earthlings loped about, all manner of household articles flew in different directions. I found Quatermass and the Pit highly entertaining in a comical sort of way and thought, "The Poltergeists" would have been a better title to those periodical mischievous acts performed in the story. When not watching television, playing games in the playroom or riding donkeys, we ate regular meals. These included meat and two vegetables for dinner.

Meat was an item on the menu at home that only appeared after one of my successful hunting trips, unless mother managed to scrounge a tin of imported ex-army bully beef from a neighbour. On one occasion Uncle shot a sufficient number of blackbirds with my Airsporter to provide at least four birds each. Blackbirds are quite small when you pluck all their feathers off. We used to sing a song at school about a king having twenty-four of the little beggars baked in a pie. There were special occasions during Christmas, Easter, or other important religious festivals on the Catholic calendar. On such auspicious days a frozen chicken would be roasted with the carcass boiled for soup the next day. In the roasting pan would be a selection of potatoes and carrots from the garden. Our bread would be smothered, very thinly, in Anchor butter all the way from New Zealand. Plum jam from the Co-op topped off the festive fare. On other special occasions such as birthdays when my hunting was poor, Uncle purchased a tin of Argentinean corned beef. We may have been poor, but from the variety of food appearing on our table, it seemed as though the whole world had a hand in putting it into our mouths.

Chapter Eleven

Back to the Forest

Attending Nelson Haden Boys School became a tiresome bore supplemented with innumerable problems involving pupils and teachers harassing me. On the other hand, Starfield had lots of activities to keep my mind occupied. These activities included secret meetings in the playroom on that pile of mattresses where innocence was lost to the experienced. My attraction to Beverly came about simply because she had red hair. I named her Ginger in memory of a previous encounter with a similar looking red-headed girl. Beverly was sixteen. She'd been sent to Starfield House as an uncontrollable promiscuous teenager. We soon developed a bond of friendship and some boys were convinced she already had at least one baby. Beverly cannot be described as pretty as the ginger-headed beauty who captured my heart on that hot summer's day at Penny Pool. However, Beverly had plenty going for her and was not afraid to show it. She also had the attribute of being sixteen, which meant she could buy cigarettes. That alone encouraged me to cultivate our friendship. It seemed wrong at the time but when one's a smoker, certain hypocrisies are permitted.

We met in the walled garden one afternoon by chance after I had been practicing with a homemade dart and hoped to use it as a hunting weapon. Beverly wandered in to look at the abundant fruit bushes. Her sudden appearance compelled me to duck out of sight. After watching for a few minutes, I moved out of cover into a position that would enable her to see me sitting on a low stone wall surrounding the compost heap.

"Hello, what are you doing here?" she asked during her approach.

"Oh nothing much, just sitting in a quiet spot thinking."

She sat beside me with the warmth of her body pressed firmly against mine. Beverly had on previous occasions made evocative comments, which suggested she fancied me. It was intriguing but okay because I felt the same way about her. On that particular day, she sat beside me in the walled garden while our so-called Aunties were preparing tea. It also meant most of the other kids would be gathering at the table waiting to be fed. At least we wouldn't be disturbed for a short period of time. It seems Beverly was out to corrupt me one way or the other. Our meeting in the garden became an inadvertent golden opportunity for her to make a move. She looked into my eyes and asked if I wanted a fag.

"Yeah, that'll be good," I replied.

The ginger-headed girl held out the droopy Woodbine like a piece of bait. I was obliged to reach across to take it. "What do I get for it?" she asked, pulling it away from my grasping fingers.

"What do you want?" I responded. Then quickly became acutely aware of the situation developing into unfamiliar grounds.

She leaned forward, pressing even closer. Her face and lips were almost touching mine when she whispered, "If I give you this fag, will you give me what I want?"

"Yeah okay," I replied as nonchalantly as a dried-up mouth would let me. Visions of a red triangle sprang to mind. We'd frolicked about on that pile of mattresses in the playroom a few times. I was convinced those seemingly unintentional glimpses between her legs were deliberately allowed. "What do you want?"

We ducked behind that compost wall to sit on clean ground while Beverly lit a cigarette. Our eyes remained looking into each other's while sharing the illegal tobacco by passing the stub between us. Beverly leaned forward and looked deeply into my eyes as her fingers closed around the remains of our cigarette in my mouth and pulled it free. "I want you to come to my bed tonight," she whispered.

That answer prompted a sudden release of smoke in a sharp puff as my poor little heart went into double time. The butt was quickly retrieved and another long drag taken before blowing smoke into the air, but much slower.

Beverly smiled while waiting for an answer. My nod prompted both of us to start giggling and make sexy provocative remarks to each other. I had funny feelings running up and down my body while a growing urge prompted my legs to cross. Both hands ended up jammed between them.

Later that night while lying in bed waiting for the big house and its inmates to fall asleep, imaginary visions of that red-headed girl across the corridor became increasingly erotic. I also realized, what we were about to do was a massive breach of behaviour. It was another item on my list of misdemeanours to be performed that added to the thrill.

I slipped out of bed and nipped across a corridor toward the girls' dormitory. One small light cast my shadow along silent corridors. Beverly had informed me that her bed was the first on the right through the door. I eased it open and peered into the dimly lit room. She looked sound asleep. That did nothing for my machismo. It indicated the girl of my dreams had grown tired of waiting and dropped off. I moved toward the bedside and touched her shoulder. Beverly's eyes popped open. A smile spread broad lips across her face. She put a finger to her lips as bedclothes were pulled back in a clear open invitation.

Her naked, covered in freckles body made my heart leap. My mouth suddenly dried up. The stiff member between my legs became even more erect inside blue striped, brushed cotton pyjamas. I slid in beside her and felt heat radiating from her body and whispered, "Gosh, you're hot, aren't you."

"Burning with desire," she hissed while drawing my head closer for a kiss.

When our lips met, my thoughts became very erratic. Nevertheless, I clearly remember of wanting to thank Miss Brown, the authorities and everyone responsible for sending me to heaven. I groped for a breast. Her body stiffened as I started twiddling a nipple. My own body shuddered as her hand fumbled its way through the opening of my pyjama trousers in its search for my erection. When our kiss broke, we were panting for air. I gulped as she grasped my penis and whispered, "Do it to me."

It didn't take long for Beverly to have her way with me, except my pleasure was very short-lived. A sweeping sensation of satisfying warmth pulled me into the depths of relaxation, deeper than I ever thought possible. Even in such a euphoric state my instincts were warning of possible dangers. A feeling that nothing good would come from such sweet satisfaction only served to keep those warning chimes tinkling in the distance. They were the same warning bells I swore never to ignore. My position was not one I should get caught in. But any senses controlling self-preservation had been dulled by a need to prolong the existing pleasure for every possible second. Nevertheless, it proved impossible to prevent sleep engulfing me. That avenue of sweet darkness drew me into oblivion. In what seemed like a split second, the lights came on, Auntie came in and heaven was instantly exchanged for eternal hell and damnation.

Morning saw me standing in front of my mentor who could not look me in the eye. That was normal and nothing to do with me and what I had done, Mister "Bow shot the lot" never looked anyone in the eye. A protracted silence evolved until he fired his first question. "What the hell do you think you were doing?"

"Sir?" I asked, unable to understand the question because anyone with a modicum of intelligence would have known what I was doing. I did!

"You blithering little tyke! Why can't you just behave yourself and stay out of trouble." Mister Bowshot – I preferred his nickname Pigface or that one just mentioned – continued staring at a pile of papers on his desk. He retained the reputation of never looking anyone in the eye no matter what he might be talking about.

"It wasn't my fault, Sir," I responded firmly. Christ only knows how many times I said that without changing anyone's opinion. Any of my denials never altered the course of events bestowed on everyone concerned, particularly me.

"Oh I agree. Nobody with your level of intellect can possibly be responsible for anything they do. That's why you're here." Pigface took a deep breath before concluding that part of his totally uninteresting dialogue by spluttering out a derogatory remark, calculated to put me firmly in my place. "You are nothing but a bloody irresponsible, trouble making, little bloody idiot. You're a dirty little sod, aren't you?"

Nights in the Forest

Although one was tempted to obtain a great deal of pleasure by conforming to his description, I was hardly in a position to deny what he claimed. I stood firmly to attention to deliver my reply. Raised my chin, gave my best couldn't give a damn expression and said, "Yes Sir." His tirade continued in a softer if somewhat reduced tone, although any vehemence beneath the surface remained firmly in place. Naturally, it was my fault with little point in making any kind of defence. Who would believe me? Despite the derogatory expressions and verbal contempt being thrown at me, deep down I felt a victory had been achieved.

After returning from school, I discovered Beverly had been removed to a safer place. I wondered for whose safety that statement applied to. However, she did leave a legacy behind. Included in my memory of our very brief exciting encounter, which remains logged forever, she left a note and half a packet of Woodbine cigarettes under my pillow. I made my way to the toilet to read Beverly's farewell that informed me, how nice "it" had been and hoped I enjoyed the fags.

Things got really tough after that episode. Whilst most inmates considered me really cool for actually having slept with Beverly, the Aunties including Old Pigface maintained an especially careful watch on me. There were nights when I became aware of one Auntie standing guard outside the dormitory, waiting to catch me at it again. There was no chance of that. I had no desires for any other girls in the dormitory and they didn't fancy me either. In the meantime, our warden sought me out for every problem that arose.

Miss Brown came to see me shortly after. She was not the least bit surprised at my predicament but sympathized and understood that juvenile rampaging hormones were at fault, not me. Miss Brown now appeared in a new light. I became besotted by her more than ever since one brief intimate lesson in life gave me an insight into how good things could be.

My pretty probation officer took the culpability for my actions. That attitude of hers went beyond my comprehension. She sat demurely beside our joint accuser while I stood there with a blank stare ignoring every word shouted at me. When Old Pigface finished his berating, he dismissed me with a wave of the hand and a muttered, "Get out."

Miss Brown's eyes were full of a new understanding. She finally appreciated my earlier comments about the man who ran the institution, not liking children. On leaving the room our eyes met. Old Pigface was on the other side of his office door. I poked my tongue out, held a thumb on my nose and wiggled my fingers, then gave him a universal two-fingered salute, which, for those who do not know it, happens to be a Cub Scouts' salute the wrong way round. Miss Brown covered her smile with a hand but both eyes were overflowing with humour. I blew her a kiss, and she winked back. Ecstasy was mine. I left the building and ran across the playing field shouting with joy. Every trial and tribulation over the last couple of days had been worth it, just for that wink. Unfortunately, those few moments in Bowshot's office was the last time we ever met.

Nights were colder as winter closed in and we inmates were given a small allowance of pocket money to spend on whatever we wanted. In my case, every penny went on bangers. They were hoarded in a safe place until there was a large bundle. Meantime, I set about building a bomb casing by inflating a small balloon, covering it with a strong mixture of sand and cement, then waiting for the concrete to set before withdrawing the balloon. I then poured the accumulated gunpowder into that hollow concrete ball. It resembled a bomb seen in cartoons, especially when the small hole at the top had a fuse inserted. The steel tube made for Top Wood's mine shaft had been replaced by a concrete ball. After a few days, the bomb was complete and looked very satisfactory. Nevertheless, my secret late night visits to Starfield's garden shed had not gone unnoticed with my security breached by another inmate. In this rebel's book, what he did represented treachery of the highest order. My betrayer became as low as any human could get. Snitching on a fellow prisoner to gain favour with Pigface deserved nothing less than a damn good lesson.

I stood before the camp commandant. The bomb sitting on his desk looked positively magnificent. While standing to attention, a voice echoed through a vacant recess in my mind. That voice remained convinced of how much better the bomb would look if it had been painted black. Numerous cartoon characters were depicted in comics carrying the same kind of round black ball with a fuse fizzing at the top.

Before long, intensive investigations revealed who had been treacherous to my cause. Preparation for some kind of retribution of the lowlife that ignored the principles of life was under way. My idea was simple and could in no way be attributed to anything other than an accident. While we were climbing the stairway of a double-decker bus one morning, it was more by design than a quirk of fate I managed to get in front of my intended victim.

Later that afternoon, on my return from school, I stood in the office being told to explain the circumstances regarding how I slipped and fell against the person behind me. That person unfortunately went head over heels, also known as arse over tit, down the stairs sustaining severe bruising and a mild concussion by the time his insignificant pile of twitching skin and bone landed on the road.

"It wasn't my fault," I stated firmly at the end of my explanation.

Old Pigface never believed a word, although it was impossible to prove otherwise. The traitor was removed a few days later to prevent any further accidents and never seen again. It occurred to me that everyone in that place was being removed for one reason or another.

Starfield House developed its own institution by forming an independent structure isolated from outside influences. Starfield made it possible to produce fare from its own vegetable garden, fruit trees and large hen house for eggs. Any country person will tell you, hen houses, no matter what size, attract rats.

It didn't take long for the inevitable to happen. One afternoon while collecting eggs, an Auntie saw the one thing she never wanted to see. Her scream sent every chicken and girl collecting eggs scattering in a variety of directions. Precious eggs were dropped in a flurry of panic as girls ran toward the house. Once inside the building, all doors were locked before everyone converged at the kitchen window overlooking the infamous chicken run. According to every female in the building, our chicken area had become infested with rats, plural not singular.

That night one girl swore an oath that she'd never eat another egg. Our topic of conversation at supper eventually concentrated on horror stories about rats and bubonic plague. Those at the table also revealed how rats were the kind of animal who always went for the throat whenever cornered. I must have been the only one who knew the truth but had no intentions of telling anyone. Like most wild animals, they will almost always run away from humans. On the other hand, since horror stories were the order of that evening's storytelling, I felt obliged to submit one of my own to the assembly.

"Did you know," I began softly to draw their attention and avoid attracting one of our Aunties bustling about, "Rats will gnaw at the soles of your feet while you're asleep. It's a fact. Honest to God. Not only that, but it's very hard trying to get to sleep while rats at the bottom of your bed sink their teeth into your bleeding feet."

Some subdued nervous laughter covered a sense of fear, which I encouraged with another one of my stories involving a family of rats. My descriptive comments had one girl's eyes bugging out her head.

Next morning, a call went out for volunteers to go on a rat hunt. It turned into a male only expedition. Girls aren't into doing that sort of thing. After school, five brave heroes gathered to carry out their noble, deadly dangerous, heroic deed. The rat hunting team surrounded the chicken hut. Our manliness was boosted and supported by girls and Aunties cheering us on from the safety of the kitchen window. Not only that, we provided each other with constant peer pressure by yelling, "Kill the rats, kill the rats," as our war cry while advancing toward the chicken hut. We closed in. We were armed with a variety of weapons including clubs and sticks. My primary weapon was a pitchfork. On reaching the wooden structure, our vengeful cries were silenced. The bold approach proceeded at a much slower, cautious stride. Inside the hut we carefully moved chickens aside and looked under bales or into nooks and crannies. A tense silence developed with one or two rat hunters careful not to expose their necks. Jumpers were pulled up to the chin. Suddenly! There was a high-pitched scream. A girl at the kitchen window was pointing. "There it is, there it is," the hysterical girl yelled from a very safe position.

At that point, mayhem and chaos took over. Chickens flew in all directions, three of the brave warrior rat hunting party decided that valour could best be served on another day as they scattered in headlong retreat. From the way they were running, one would have thought the dangerous animal had been lying in wait to leap onto them and infect them with bubonic plague.

The rat scampered along the same trail as one unfortunate youth whose screams were drowned by shouts from girls providing a multitude of confusing instructions. These included, "Run for your life. Run faster it's catching up. Go the other way. No not that way. Don't stop, run, run."

The old rat, which would have had a hard time chasing a chicken egg, continued scurrying along as best it could. That poor animal was more scared than the boy in front who, at that stage, reverted to blind panic. He hammered on the kitchen door demanding someone let him in.

That rat ran directly across my path just a few yards away. Holding some sort of a spear in my hands brought visions of those days hunting on Buffalo Field in Wyvern Valley. My arm went back and in a smooth motion, the pitchfork was launched. There was nothing wrong in my timing. A twin-pronged spear glided through cold October air and a moment later Mister Rat was pinned to the ground.

Its sudden screech silenced screaming girls as they watched in fascinated horror at the animal's twisting and biting. The tenacity it displayed proved rats have a powerful will to stay alive. The pitchfork handle quivered and the urge to finish the job was accomplished with a club from another hunter to put an end to its struggle for life. I felt like a conquering hero with the trophy held up on my spear for all to see. We remaining heroic hunters marched in triumph toward the window full of girls' faces. Their screams echoed through the house, especially when I rattled the corpse against a window pane. Some time later, when the excitement died down and the rat was buried, an Auntie congratulated me for killing it. But she remonstrated with me for staining the window with blood. Cleaning that window was a small price this hero happily paid for claiming the esteemed position of rat killer. My episode of heroic worship didn't last as long as I would have liked. Things quickly settled into what the girls called normal events like playing with dolls, skipping and hopscotch – girly things.

To add a little colour to our surroundings, Starfield had a number of what were called white peace doves. They were known to me as pigeons whatever their colour. They fluttered about for no particular reason other than to look good and receive admiring looks or comments from girls. We weren't allowed to eat them, despite my insistence they made very good eating, especially the young ones before they started flying. That suggestion brought about a good deal of hostility from every female and earned me the alternative nick name of Baby Dove Eater. The name enhanced an already embellished status among the boys and older girls. There was something ego-boosting about being looked on as a rat hunting baby dove eater. Although, being centre stage, whatever the circumstances, felt good.

One day, however, a fine-feathered, much-loved member of our community must have picked up some poison bait. The dove flapped about in convulsing agony. Nobody knew what to do about it, except me. I insisted we kill it and put it out of its misery. It was a beautiful bird, a white dove, a symbol of peace, Ban the Bomb activists used it as a symbol. How anyone could kill it, was just one of the comments made in response to such a proposal. One girl wanted to make it better by giving it a drink of water while another came up with the suggestion of keeping it warm and calling a vet. Nobody could bear the thought of putting it out of its misery, except one of the Aunties. She eventually drew me to one side, handed the bird to me and whispered, "You look after it but don't let anyone see."

Nights in the Forest

I turned and walked away with the dove held firmly under my jumper. Once out of sight, its neck was twisted and I muttered a prayer for the creature as it was buried in the garden.

"The time has come to leave." That thought had been festering inside me for ages and by the weekend my mind was made up. I would escape and get as far away from Starfield House as possible.

Old Pigface himself put the idea into my head by suggesting I join the Royal Navy. I clearly recall filling in an application form that absolved my mother from any responsibility. Mister Bowshot was nominated my legal guardian before I gave him a sample of my urine. The bottle had a small opening and to my embarrassment some piss landed on his office floor. It really wasn't my fault. My misfortune, however, seemed to amuse the warden who said, "Hey, have you just missed the boat?" Then chuckled to himself. It must have been the first time I heard him laugh. Laughing at someone else's misfortune provided an intimate detail on that man's sense of humour. If one could call it that.

I hadn't missed any boat but there had been more than enough discipline at Starfield to last a lifetime. The idea of joining a navy, any navy, was a good one. My ambition centred on joining the Merchant Navy with the intention of leaving England. Uncle once told me that when one had an ambition one should always keep one's aspirations high. My plan would cause more consternation than anything I could think of because it would prove very difficult to find me. It would also be lots of fun getting Old Pigface into trouble. The first stage of my master plan was to take a bike ride and visit mother. The visit went well but mother wasn't told my clandestine visits were not permitted. "I'm not going back tonight mum," I told her soon after my arrival.

"If you don't go back tonight, will you stay here?"

"Well, I'm not sure yet, maybe the forest eh. What do you think?" I smiled to reassure her.

Despite those reassurances, mother began having doubts. "How long will you stay down there?" Her question preceded a preamble of offerings including the availability of a room, warm clothing, food, even access to Uncle's hidden supply of drink. I knew where he hid it anyway but the offer was appreciated.

"Oh mum," I said while slowly putting an arm over her shoulder, "You don't have to worry about me. It's not like I've never done it before." My comforting comments made mother relax and her concerns for my safety evaporated. "Mind you, I could do with a nice cup of tea." That request cheered her up. Providing mother was doing something for the wayward son she loved, it made her happy.

The same afternoon I was loaded down with gear setting off toward my favourite place in the forest. I felt confident that when the authorities came to our house, mother would tell them where to look. It didn't take long to arrive amongst welcoming trees deep in the valley. Late afternoon air was crisp and sharp and it meant finding a warm secure place for the night. A small barn with a winter stock of baled hay provided an excellent warm shelter but also a perfect hiding place. By removing several bales close to the roof, a recess was made. The entrance to the cavity became filled by pushing a bale into it like a cork in a bottle. No one would be able to detect my position. There were numerous nail holes in the barn's corrugated iron walls, which made it easy to look out on the world outside.

Shortly before dark and after preparing my bed for the night, I sat near a rabbit warren, waiting for a meal to appear but before long, my bum become numb from sitting on frozen ground. The wait severely tested my patience yet served to remind me of Uncle's advice when he said, "A successful hunter is a patient one." Daylight faded quickly with shortening shadows as the dimming light of night surrounded undulating countryside and darkness closed in. Before long, it was too dark to see anything more than fifty yards away. However, a small movement attracted my peripheral vision. Two small points close to the ground were twitching. An animal's hunger and its need for a feed prompted it out to sniff the atmosphere. I levelled the gun barrel at the movement and held my breath in anticipation of something about to happen. Suddenly, a rabbit popped out. With both eyes open, I squeezed the trigger. My small bore shotgun shattered the silence.

Nights in the Forest

It prompted me into a scrambling run to pick up my dinner without stopping as I passed. A gamekeeper patrolled the forest and a noisy gun going off at any time of day would attract his attention. We came close to meeting on more than one occasion. Fortunately, each time, I was dressed for the hunt in green camouflaged jacket and hat. My positions were always sufficiently well hidden to watch his ghostly figure move silently past. He never saw who fired that last shot, although from that day on, I became careful not to hang about after firing my gun.

Back near my hideout, I set about preparing an evening meal. If the gamekeeper did come out, I never spotted him, but then he wouldn't be a good gamekeeper if he was seen first during the hours of darkness. While the rabbit cooked over a small fire inside a deep hole to hide the flames, the scent of roasting meat drifting on crisply clear night air to wet an already fierce appetite. The rabbit, which had been cooked over an open fire, was eaten slowly with every tender morsel savoured. Slithers of meat had a smoky flavour with a touch of burned crispiness on the extremities. At the end of a satisfying meal, I sat back to enjoy a cup of tea and a cigarette.

I huddled over the fire with a blanket draped over my shoulders, endeavouring to capture some heat rising from smouldering embers. My thoughts centred on the luck in finding my small bore shotgun which Uncle reclaimed from the police. A gun, a box of shells, a blanket, cigarettes, spare food and drink, a belt with my own hunting knives and hatchet strapped around my waist, and a freshly cooked rabbit for dinner. All that and the freedom to roam the one place I could not be happier in. It was hard to believe such good fortune.

Some time went by as the bones were chewed or sucked on while a peace and contentment encompassed everything that had been missing for months. When the last bone was sucked dry and thrown onto the ashes, I lit another cigarette before standing up. I filled the fire hole in and then placed a large flat stone over the spot before heading back to my hideout. By the time my tired cold body pulled a bale into the entrance, it was ready for sleep.

Warm bales soothed my body as it curled into a ball. Within minutes, the land of dreams welcomed me.

Another auspicious day began with an early morning sun sending long slivers of golden sunlight through nail holes. It highlighted a cloud of dust erupting by my movement to take a look around. My challenge to the authorities had been made and it simply remained a question of waiting for them. I even told mother where I would be so they knew where to look.

With blanket rolled up, pack secured and gun in hand, I set off on an expedition to explore unknown territory in the valley. My meandering took me past the old haunted house, which didn't look anywhere near as intimidating during daylight. Once across the river in Wyvern Valley, the wooded area ahead was almost unknown. I took some time exploring the woodland known as Deer Forest. During my adventures just one ambition remained, to hunt down one of those elusive fallow deer. I never even saw one. That had a lot to do with never going far enough into the new area before. My wanderings brought me to a wide clearing with a large oak tree growing in the centre.

I stood still to absorb a feeling one can only describe as magical with a mysterious sense of secrecy so strong, it filled the air about me. Only keen hunters and people close to nature know what that feeling's like. I felt it before, although on this particular occasion it became very intense.

While moving like a ghost through the early morning sunbeams and shadows, I recalled Uncle telling me, "When the feeling comes you will know it, do not waste a moment and spoil it." I slowed and almost stopped when the cry of a pheasant on silent crisp air prompted me to lower myself onto the ground. The pack on my back was removed. My weapon checked to ensure it was loaded. The safety catch was released. The hammer cocked and my head turned aside to listen. It became important to pinpoint that pheasant's position and blend into my surroundings as any good hunter should.

In the distance another pheasant answered as I crawled to the edge of a clearing to lie on the ground under a bush. Although the undergrowth limited total visibility, my eye detected a slight movement between long blades of grass. The silent disruption encouraged me to inch forward. Senses became intensely alert as the shotgun fitted into my hands as it always did on such occasions. The gun barrel was eased through branches and I waited.

Minutes later the biggest cock pheasant I ever saw appeared on the other side of that clearing. It was huge and strutting his stuff while calling out. When those sounds he made echoed across the valley, it made my heart leap. The bird looked fantastic with magnificent colours in stark contrast to the undergrowth.

From its direction, the pheasant would come past my position and be well within range. I watched that strutting walk over my gun barrel, which traversed in line with its moving target. The pheasant occasionally stopped and stretched to its full height. His head swivelled slowly in a display from the master of the forest that he remained on constant alert for danger. When satisfied everything was safe, he moved a little further. A beam of sunlight filtered through a gap in the branches and sparkled on plumage around his neck.

I felt like an intruder in his domain but continued watching in fascination. Any kind of disturbance in the bushes made the pheasant stiffen in readiness to take cover. When another bird fluttered above, its beating wings sent him ducking under overhanging ground cover. For a few moments he remained out of sight. However, I knew that his automatic reaction to noise meant waiting for a short while before he reappeared.

The barrel continued following the cock pheasant until it came within range. I felt certain of a good clean kill. Suddenly, the bird sensed danger. It stretched to its full height and remained stationary while looking directly at me. In that moment our eyes met, my heart skipped a beat, the big bird hesitated and I squeezed the trigger.

Before the echo fell silent, I jumped to my feet and raced to pick up the kill. Knowing the area was close to the gamekeeper's cottage, I felt a desperate need to move on. A steady dogtrot for ten minutes saw me well clear and close to the river where a secluded spot was found to sit and view my work. It wasn't the first pheasant I killed, except it was certainly the biggest and best looking.

A perfect long tail feather was extracted and placed in my cap where it served as a reminder of my successful hunt. For the first time, a feeling of guilt pervaded my mind. Killing such a beautiful creature never gave a sense of satisfaction, although that night over a small fire, I enjoyed the fruits of my hunt.

Earlier in the afternoon, I spotted some people moving about near the river but stayed well clear. It had been a rewarding interesting day and there were no intentions of spoiling it by talking to others. A culmination of the day included finding some fallow deer tracks, exploring a new area, enjoying a successful hunt followed by an enjoyable meal. There was even half a pheasant left over. The end of a perfect day meant bedtime and a warm comfortable barn waited for my return.

The track into and out of the valley had been little used, which allowed treetops to grow over it. Despite having a low overhang, the track was easy enough to walk along even at night, especially on such a clear starlit one. I moved silently but my contentment hadn't dulled those ever alert instincts. The smell of Virginia tobacco smoke gave an early warning signal. Anyone smoking on such a clear still night provided me with an alien scent to the environment clearer than honeysuckle on a summer's night.

I stepped off the track, waited, and listened while considering who it might be. Initial thoughts focused on the gamekeeper. He knew that sooner or later whoever had been poaching on his patch would have to take the narrow track leading out the valley. That thought was dismissed as very unlikely. If the gamekeeper was on the lookout, he wouldn't be smoking however much he wanted to. Therefore those people in hiding had to be townies. Except, who were they and what were they doing? I wondered if a couple was seeking some privacy where they could carry out their forbidden activities. From any point of view there were far better places for them than a forest trail on a cold night. Numerous alternative ideas on who they might be were considered while sitting on the track. Several minutes passed as a need to satisfy my curiosity grew. The time came to strip down in preparation for flight. My gun, belt with knives and hatchet attached along with the pack were hidden under a bush. Instinct kept telling me to back away and return to the certain safety of a night in the forest. Curiosity had the better of me and that part of my mind demanded satisfaction. That curiosity continued growing until it took over common sense. With that dilemma in mind, I became convinced, by being careful the ambushers lying in wait would not be any the wiser of my visit. Their trap had been set on a bend behind a clump of hazelnut bushes. If my sense of smell had not detected cigarette smoke, their ambush might have succeeded. An active imagination came to the conclusion that those people lying in wait must be after me. It was the only answer available after eliminating any other alternative on why they were there.

A sense of adventure thundered through my body without any way of telling if it was fear or excitement. Whatever those feeling might have been, it felt good. It was easy to double back and get behind the bend before closing into listening range. As luck would have it, a large drystone wall had been built along the bend, which afforded me sufficient cover to get close. By carefully inching toward the wall, I came close enough to overhear a whispered conversation. Despite being relatively near, it remained difficult to make out the words. On hands and knees I crept along my side of the wall before easing onto the ground and concentrated on slowing my breathing and heartbeat.

The first words that were clearly audible were, "How much longer are we going to wait here Sir?" The familiar voice of a big Welsh sergeant was almost a comfort to hear, even though it belonged to someone considered as my enemy.

"Until it's time to go," was the uncompromising answer.

"We won't catch the lad Sir, not at this time of night. He'll be settled down somewhere nice and snug by now, so 'e will."

A long pause in their conversation followed. My breathing and heart rate came down. However, the ground was hard and ice-cold. Someone on the other side of the wall lit another cigarette. I thought the sergeant should have known better.

The other voice spoke after blowing out a lungful of smoke in a steady long hiss that sounded like a whistle. "What do you suggest we do, Sergeant?"

From the tone of his voice, he was obviously a townie who had become more than a little grumpy on a winter's night getting colder by the minute. Anyone with common sense would be sitting on a comfortable sofa, in front of a warming fire, listening to the radio, drinking hot chocolate on a night like this.

"We should go 'ome Sir. The lad will come to 'is senses and return when 'e's ready," the sergeant said. That familiar Welsh accent promoting common sense made me smile.

Another long silence followed with more cigarette smoke drifting on the air with a smell so good it stirred me into drawing in slow deep breaths. At that moment I would have killed for a cigarette. Those men were only a few feet away. By raising myself onto both elbows, I could see the top of a trilby hat and police helmet within touching distance. The dark blue shape was topped with a silvery point. The devil inside nudged my bad side. It told me to spring up and scream. That would scare the living daylights out of them. Despite an overwhelming temptation, I decided to stay put, restrain myself and listen to what they had to say.

"He's a ward of the court, Sergeant. Must I remind you, our duty is to catch him and return him where he belongs? After all, he is only a boy." No one could argue with that kind of adult logic. The sergeant did not comment, although my thoughts were the same as his. "Don't you agree?" the uncompromising stranger asked in a final question that demanded an answer.

My favourite police sergeant paused long enough to consider the best way to answer it. He took a deep breath before saying, "Oh yes Sir, if you have an army to spare."

"What do you mean by that?"

"I know the lad. This is 'is hidin' place you see, an' he knows it better than anyone. It'll take an army to flush 'im out. Even then you can't be sure." The big Welshman drew another deep breath before continuing. "Experience tells me to leave 'im alone, he can look after 'imself, be back 'ome in 'is own time. So he will."

Nights in the Forest

I was nodding in agreement with his thinking and wondered why all grown-ups were not like that big Welshman. Although I considered him the enemy, I was silently praising him from behind a crumbling wall in the dark with a lump of it digging into my ribs. It was getting damned uncomfortable and my fingers were already stiff from cold at that point. Nevertheless, I agreed with the sergeant's comment of just leaving me alone. However, that kind of statement did not go down well with the other person.

"That's a fine attitude toward an escaped ward of the court. Would you happen to have the same attitude if he was an escaped criminal?" The question reverberated on cold air in a hoarse accusing whisper.

"Maybe not Sir, maybe not."

One had to agree with that stranger's words but it sounded as though the policeman had doubts. Several minutes of silence elapsed. My entire body became stiff from cold percolating up from the ground and through my clothing. I ground my teeth together to stop them chattering before the stranger muttered, "I've had enough of this, let's get out of here."

They moved off and stumbled their way up the track to leave one stiff body to prize itself off frozen ground and sit on the wall. I rubbed my hands together in a vigorous action to warm them while listening to voices fading away in the darkness.

After sitting on the wall for a minute, their voices had faded into infinity and the forest returned to absolute silence. My hands were warmed up when I jumped down to collect several cigarette butts off the ground. They were Player's not Woodbine and some were big enough to smoke without removing the tobacco to roll in cigarette paper. There were quite a number, which told me both men must have been there for some time. Or one was a chain smoker. One of the stubs was smoked before I collected my gear and made for the barn to spend what remained of the night in warm comfort. Sleep, however, did not come easy. The big sergeant's last words, "Maybe not Sir, maybe not," kept echoing through my mind. They logged themselves deep into the subconscious and persisted in disturbing me. Perhaps it was the disappointed tone in his voice and the reluctance on my part to admit there might be some truth in what the other man said. Whatever it was, those penetrating words remained embedded into the corners of my mind and festered doubts about what I planned next.

Four days later I stood before the camp commandant. Both hands were locked behind my back with the best couldn't give a damn look while Old Pigface ranted and raved. "Do you have any idea of the amount of trouble you caused everyone," he shouted with a face turning purple. He appeared to be approaching an apoplexy during his angry outburst. "You're a bloody fool. What the hell do you think you have achieved?"

Whilst not being absolutely certain, my escapade must have cost him as many sleepless nights as I was away enjoying myself. I had heard everything he said before and all the shouting never impressed me one little bit. The pasty excuse for a human being was always complaining about the problems I caused, which was primarily due to my adventurous nature. It made my heart sing to think it put him to so much trouble. What just happened was an appetizer, a taste of an achievement yet to be accomplished. My ultimate plan had already been prepared. If he thought he was having problems with me before, there were bigger ones coming. I mused the plan over in my mind and was more than happy to receive an abrupt dismissal from my mentor.

Chapter Twelve

Training to become a Seaman

Nothing had ever been as daring as my next plan and well beyond anything attempted before. It required a tremendous amount of planning because it was nothing like just getting up and leaving. Taking a few days off and going hunting in the forest may have been one thing. On the other hand, my ultimate plan of disruption was something totally different.

I needed to know exactly what was needed and where to go before pursuing my eventual goal. That prompted me to make frequent visits to the school library to acquire the necessary information. Everything was there. By the middle of the week, a small bag was packed with some spare clothes hidden outside under some bushes by the road. It would be easy to register into my first class then skip school. The next stage was to return and collect my bag of clothes from where it had been hidden. With that accomplished there was nothing stopping me from heading to the big bad city of London more than a hundred miles away.

Leaving school after registering meant nobody would be aware of my disappearance until later in the day. That would happen when I never turned up at Starfield House. Mister Bowshot would report me missing to the authorities who naturally assumed I did the usual thing and headed for the forest. As usual, a search party would be dispatched to carry out their duty, have their usual quick look before giving up to wait. By the time anyone realized I hadn't returned after a week, the level of searching would be stepped up a gear. By then, this reprobate will have disappeared into another world. By mid-morning, the first stage of my plan had gone without a hitch.

I made it to the A4 London road to stand with my thumb up. It didn't take long before a noisy old Bedford truck ground to a halt and I climbed aboard. My gratitude for the warmth of a noise-filled cab was given to the driver as he shifted into gear to move off. A battered, worn-out cloth cap sat lopsided on his head. His dark features were covered with a weekend's growth of beard, which gave him the appearance of a ruthless gangster. A cigarette stub smouldered away at the corner of his lips and the grin revealed nicotine-stained teeth as he muttered, "Where you goin' kid?"

I took an instant liking to the image of a hit man. My answer was delivered with as much self-assurance that could be mustered. "London," I declared confidently.

"Ah right you are then. Which part?"

"A place called Gravesend. Do you know where it is?" I asked cautiously.

"Really!" the personification of a gangster at the wheel exclaimed. The engine roared as if in support to his exclamation. A huge hairy hand shifted the vibrating gearstick into a lower gear to take a steep incline. "What you goin' to that poxy place for?" The cab shuddered before a long steady whine filled the cavity from the engine beside me as it struggled to haul the load uphill.

The question seemed genuine and I saw no reason for not telling him some form of the truth, although a little embellishment might be called for. "Going to join the Merchant Navy," I said with my confidence remaining high. A smile lit up my face, my arms were crossed and I looked directly into his eyes.

His eyebrows shot up. "Hey! I was in the Merch," the driver responded with a faraway look in his eyes before paying attention to the road. "That's where the training depot is, ain't it?" The truck reached the crest and picked up speed. That long vibrating gear leaver was gripped by his massive hairy hand and I noted a wedding ring. The clutch pedal surrendered to a thrusting boot. He grunted as the gear lever was pushed forward and the engine note settled to a steady rumble.

"Yes, that's right," I shouted. After answering his question, it seemed like a good time to add a little embellishment. By the time my story ended, that worldly wise driver thought a young man going off into the world to help his poor old mum with some money to pay the bills was very commendable. He considered my idea as a very Christian thing to be doing. After talking for a while, I wanted to know how long it would take before we arrived at Gravesend.

The question made his laugh sound like a bad cough. He wound the cab window down and flicked his cigarette butt out. A cooling gush of fresh air replaced all the warmth before he closed the window and answered with, "Well, if I drop you at the truck depot it'll take you all bloody day. Hell, but you're a good kid so I'll drop you outside the gates of the training school. How does that sound?"

I looked at the tough looking gangster of the highways and couldn't hold back a smile. "Are you sure that'll be alright?"

"Auright!" the driver exclaimed, "Well of course it'll be auright."

Some way down the road we stopped at a roadside café where the driver bought me a meal and a mug of tea. The tea looked and tasted much the same as Uncle made, very sweet, dark brown and strong enough for the spoon to stand upright in. The meal consisted of a typical truck driver's snack. Two extra large sausages, two eggs, two tomatoes and two slices of toast smothered in some kind of fruit jam. Later still, on the outskirts of London, the driver made a detour and parked in a lay-by for half an hour to share a flask of coffee. We chatted and smoked in the silence of the engine being switched off.

Mid-afternoon saw us outside the gates of the Merchant Navy training depot and I climbed down from the cab after thanking my newfound hoodlum for the lift. The truck engine roared in response. With a nonchalant wave of his hand and a thumbs up signal the driver and his truck moved off in a cloud of dust and plumes of blue diesel smoke.

My attention was diverted and I turned to see a guard standing behind closed iron barred gates. The first thought that crossed my mind was "prison". Nonetheless, once my identity papers were shown, the gate opened. Someone steered me to a place called a bunk where I unpacked my possessions onto it. Nautical terms were soon rolling off my tongue in no time at all. A "bunk" is the navy term for bed but the word is also known as a load of rubbish to "landlubbers". That word is a derogatory expression used by seamen for unfortunate people who live on land. A "bunk up" can be interpreted in two ways. The first is to help someone onto a higher level, while the second refers to having quick sex. My learning curve on nautical terms was skyrocketing and I had only been at the training depot a few hours. On the first day, teatime was not for another hour, which left me plenty of time to have a look around. I also reflected on how my plan had been successful and what could be done to ensure it continued being that way. My thoughts returned to the start of such a complicated plan.

To perform any clandestine visits home, I asked Old Pigface if it would be alright to borrow one of the pushbikes to go for a ride. Those requests were never refused, since it meant being out of everyone's hair using up surplus energy. He never once asked where I was going or where I had been, so much for care and attention and being a ward of the court.

Mother always welcomed me like a long-lost son, despite it having only been a few weeks. During those surreptitious visits the purpose was to meet up with a regular lodger at mother's house called Billy Sproul. He was an Irishman with as easy-going an attitude as any sailor should have and we got on very well. Bill was in the Merchant Navy and he became a key player in my plan by unknowingly providing information I needed to acquire a new way of life.

Once the papers arrived, getting mother to sign them was relatively easy. After all, she could not read but was more than happy sign her name to almost anything, just to prove she could do it. I tricked her into signing a document informing the authorities I was in effect two years older. It was a major step in the plan that needed carrying out before going any further. Two weeks later the acceptance papers came through with instructions to be at Gravesend on a given date. Up to that point, it had been quite easy to achieve my deception.

Having lived by the motto, "he, who travels light, travels faster" I could have left the same day but bit the bullet and waited. Two weeks later saw me hitching a lift to London with no intentions of ever returning. A whole new world waited for me and I planned to grab it and hold on with both hands, no matter how many problems it caused others.

I arrived at a place where boys were turned into men, and they trained to serve on ships that travelled all over the world. From any person's point of view, the Merchant Navy training depot was where the world began, where the ends of the world could be reached and where it was all within my grasp.

My reminiscing thoughts were disturbed by a bell sounding like a siren going off. It made me jump, shattered my daydream and shredded every nerve. I scrambled to join the general rush for food being served in the dining hall. It was early evening and I knew another alarm would be sounding at Starfield House when the wayward ward of the court had not returned from school. Search parties would be sent out in the morning but it would take more than a single search or an extended wait for my return. Mother would worry for a while, but secretly, she would be glad her son escaped and be proud of my escalating endeavours. By the end of the week, Uncle would be reassuring her about my being competent enough to take care of myself. The fact none of the authorities had found me simply meant, I found a better hiding place. Uncle would simply inform mother, her son would return in his own good time. Mother would agree, relax and wait in Uncle's reassuring certainty.

The first task our trainers put on their new batch of recruits was marching in step. That was the first thing that made no sense to most of the junior seamen. Why did a career in the Merchant Navy require everyone to keep in step? Secondly and more to the point, why did thirty young men have to keep in step wearing Wellington boots? I wanted to be a steward and wearing Wellington boots in the dining room did not seem right. Nothing in the adult world made any sense in the past and it was safe to assume the Merchant Navy would be the same, if not worse.

It did not take long to discover, the training school was chock-a-block full of society's misfits, upstarts, morons, young hooligans, dropouts and teddy boys. They were all there to prove their manhood and the main reason I liked the place and fitted in. The majority held the undisputed, unchallenged opinion that any authority needed to be tested, questioned or generally ignored most of the time.

Our marching instructor was a weasel-faced man who may have been small of stature but had a very wiry physique. That man became very prone to screaming, mostly on the parade ground, especially when "his troops" turned the wrong way. His reactions were easy for those under his command to provoke. Simple and apparent misunderstandings on our part sent our instructor into wild gesticulations accompanied by vivid descriptions. "Left, you ignorant bloody imbeciles, left, left," he would scream while performing versatile gymnastics. Our instructor would then bring us to a halt and openly declare we were all a load of snotty-nosed little prats. He would take a deep breath and call us stupid, tight-arsed, little pricks. At which point he would gasp in another lungful of air before inferring there wasn't enough brains between the lot of us to fill the skull of an ant. Our gallant leader of men ordered everyone to raise their left foot to demonstrate which side of our anatomy was on the left. Naturally, some of us, including myself, deliberately lifted our right foot which prompted a new interest in the term associated with our birth rite. Our instructor came close to having an apoplexy on many occasions, despite being a resilient little guy with a heart of stone.

There were many things to learn at the training depot. Apart from everything else, lots of friends and enemies needed to be made and we only had six weeks in which to accomplish it. I personally thought that six weeks left barely enough time to achieve everything.

One sporting event included entertaining the crowd by having a boat race. It was another thing I found difficult to understand. Why put half a dozen young men, the majority of which were skinny little runts, into a lifeboat designed to hold seventy people? Those six unfortunate brave souls were pitted to race against each other up and down the River Thames. Lifeboats are not built for speed. I assumed it had something to do with teamwork, following orders, competition, discipline, that sort of thing. Apparently, that brainchild had been developed to show everyone, by working as a team, we would all be successful.

Nights in the Forest

That may have been true. However, the first boat across the finish line was the yellow team. Everyone witnessed the entire event. We all heard the coxswain screaming "in out, in out, in out" at the top of his lungs. There was little if any rhythm happening at all by those being shouted at. No teamwork, no coordinated effort, no listening to orders, absolutely no discipline whatsoever. Those of us ashore were witnesses to six young men rowing as fast as they could in their own time. From my vantage point on the river bank I never saw two oars dip into the water at the same time. Chaos reigned supreme in their isolated little world. The only person keeping time was the coxswain screaming his instructions like a clock. The tick tock being "in out, in out", yet they won anyway. Now, there must be a lesson in that result somewhere.

The boat race represented part of a festival that happened every year and the women's associations gathered support from the community to make it a success. Our physical training instructor decided to put on a boxing tournament with the boxing team representing a highlight of the entertainment. Like most young men who fancied themselves as fighters, I put my hand up when volunteers were called for. Until that day I never heard the expression, "never volunteer" and up till then I never knew why. After all, volunteering seemed reasonable because if memory served me correctly, I was undefeated in the ring and the primary reason why my hand shot into the air. It was an ideal opportunity of proving that fighting by the rules could be the successful, rewarding experience a coach emphasized some time ago.

A festive mood infiltrated the area with lots of people from Gravesend there to enjoy the day's events, including the blood sport of boxing. I watched two of the bouts before entering the ring and knew when it came to boxing there were far too many rules. A total week of training and preparation for the event was about to prove how well founded my effort had been. Among the cheering crowds were women with their children who were enjoying themselves. The weather remained sunny and warm, thus ensuring a good crowd to have fun at the amusement arcades.

I stood in my corner clutching the top rope and became aware of that familiar sound of a crowd baying for more blood than any solitary human body could possibly contain. I sat on the stool while two corner men made sure my boot and glove laces were secure while another pair screamed conflicting advice into both ears.

"All you have to do in this fight is box. Keep the left hand working, jab, jab, jab. Remember to duck, don't forget to weave, bob up and down, no rabbit punches, don't hit below the belt." That advice came into my left ear.

In my right ear came some alternative advice. "Don't listen to 'im, that bastard don't know nufink. Swing them right 'anded 'aymakers into his pox-ridden face. Bust sum oh they spots. The little shit's blind in 'is left eye, 'e'll never see 'em comin'."

I listened intently but quickly became confused with that additional advice.

Before standing and moving to the centre of the ring, yet more advice was meted out. This included: no kicking, no biting, no elbows, no knee to the groin, no headbutting, don't do this, don't do that, go to a neutral corner if my opponent goes down. That final instruction made me wonder if it was because my adversary had fallen over, because according to the information relayed, I hadn't hit him yet. Everything required to win in a real fight was forbidden. I blinked, looked my trainer in the eye and asked if it would be illegal to punch my opponent. There was no way of knowing if he heard anything I said above the screaming crowd.

A mouth yelled in my ear, "Left jab, keep jabbing out the left. Don't let him come near you. He's got a vicious right, box him but whatever else you do, don't ..." Those last words of advice were lost as a roar erupting from the crowd coincided with an electric bell. The crowd was expected to go totally berserk – they did. My coach lifted me off my feet and pushed me firmly toward the centre of the ring. I staggered and nearly fell. Even the ear-splitting mayhem surrounding me could not mask the final contradicting instruction by coach number two when he yelled, "Swing that furkin' right."

Nights in the Forest

The referee hardly said a word before the fight was on. I took a deep breath as a wild haymaker whistled past my face. It missed but that punch was what I was supposed to be doing to my opponent. I became determined to follow the rules and make a proper fight of it by stepping back to regain my balance, and then follow one of my trainer's instructions. My left fist constantly shot out so often it resembled a piston pumping at full throttle. I bobbed and weaved, clung onto my opponent when he came in close. While in the clinches, some solid counter punches were delivered to his midriff with my right. I deflected some heavy punches with my arms and several on the shoulder but managed to avoid getting any deliveries to the head. It was tempting to bite his ear and lift my knee into the groin. Spitting in the eyes and headbutting was also a severe temptation but neither was carried out.

The fight was near the end of the second round. I began thinking it was relatively easy and confidence began rising like a shining star. Suddenly, a right-handed roundhouse, also known as a haymaker, came through the air. The speed of which could not be measured with the naked eye but the impact caused by its collision with my nose was devastating. I became one soundly thrashed individual who suffered huge losses of blood, a swollen nose, battered pride and deflated confidence. Perhaps the crowds were correct after all. That boxing match was a hard lesson learned and would never be forgotten. I decided that when it came to fighting, the only thing the rule books were good for was for throwing into your victim's face to distract him while you kicked him where it really hurts.

The fight may have been lost but I still received a prize. The reward for all the blood loss, effort and damage it created, was a cigarette case. My thoughts dwelt on the prize as the shiny metal object was turned over in my hand. If anyone wanted a contradiction that pointed out the height of hypocrisy, it was being held in the hand of a defeated boxer. The masters persuaded everyone in the boxing team to give up smoking. They informed us how the disgusting habit filled one's lungs with tar, made one cough, short winded and gave one cancer. So what did they do? They handed

Anthony Corbyn

the loosing boxer a prize in the shape of a cigarette case. Final proof, as if any were needed, that the adult world is rampantly stupid.

Meal times were always disorderly. One needed to make a concerted effort into getting to the front of any queue waiting to be served. An excessive amount of bias happened as to who got the best of whatever was being dished up. It has never really been any different and an accepted part of life in any animal kingdom. Whenever your mate was dishing out sausages, the natural course of events was for him to give you the biggest. One could also expect to get the unbroken egg or the piece of toast that survived a sacrificial burning, but one was also expected to do the same when the roles were reversed.

On a particular occasion, the new intakes were given a large bowl of fresh cherries for pudding. The problem confronting those serving behind the counter was how to distribute those luscious fresh cherries fairly. Some were bigger and juicier than others. Some had a darker red colouring while others were black. It's a well-known fact that black cherries taste best. Everybody knows that.

Nobody will ever be sure who started the fight. Obviously one of the servers favoured a friend and selected a handful of coloured cherries, which his friend preferred. I distinctly recall a voice calling out, "Hey, that's not fair," which was evidently true, while a hand reached into the bowl. "Give those back," the server shouted and attempted to retrieve some special cherries committed to a friend. Bedlam broke out in the time it takes to bat an eyelid.

That enormous bowl of cherries became the centre of the known universe with the entire assembly wanting their fair share. Not to be outdone, I dived in and closed a hand on the biggest, softest, sweetest, blackest cherries in the bowl. To ensure their successful journey they were stuffed into my mouth while grabbing another handful with my free hand. When it came to survival of the quickest, those boys around, under and on top of me had a few tricks to learn. Within seconds, cherries were clattering across the floor like hundreds of marbles. The not so ripe ones were tested and those not meeting the taster's standard became missiles hurtling across the mess hall and splattered against the walls.

Before long, such a noisy mêlée attracted an officer who commenced abusing everyone after being called to attention. The assembled reprobates stood among the squashed fruit with hands full of evidence. In some cases, including my own, our mouths were also crammed to bursting. I made valiant attempts to chew and swallow. But it proved very difficult separating the stones from the flesh when one's mouth was chock-a-block full. Some were destined to disappear down the gullet whole. My friend stood rigidly at ease with his hands behind his back and started unloading cherries one at a time. In the silence that followed the officer's tirade, everyone heard the plop, plop, plop of solitary cherries landing on the wooden floor. Nobody knew what the noise was, except those standing behind the offending noise maker and they were fit to bursting into hysterical laughter.

Our catering officer gulped in a huge lungful of air. His face turned bright red. Veins in his neck stood out as bulging eyes traversed our faces. His attention was drawn to the overturned tables and chairs and one big empty cherry bowl amid the scattering of squashed fruit on the floor. Traces of cherry juice trickled down the walls. His final comment of, "You lot are nothing but a bunch of bloody animals," was roared across the room.

His accurate description brought an immediate response from my friend. With cheeks bulging from being overfilled, he was unable to contain himself. His mouth burst open like an exploding grenade. Shrapnel in the shape of green, red and black cherries erupted out his mouth as he screamed with laughter. That evoked a domino effect for the rest of us who started rolling about laughing our heads off. The catering officer lost any resemblance of authority and left the room when he decided to go for help.

I did my best to eat as much of the fruit in my mouth with a determination that emphasized how such a special treat should not be wasted. As with all things in life, the good times are paid for with something. That afternoon, everyone in the camp was paraded for a severe dressing down with all social activities for the week suspended. On reflection, I thought the cherries were well worth it.

In the fourth week, small groups formed to visit local pubs. And whilst it may have been illegal, if I sat in a dimly lit pub with a cigarette in one hand and a pint of Watneys Red Barrel in the other, a blind landlord might pass me for eighteen. As new intakes, we were enjoying ourselves, although as in any town or community, we were the outsiders in uniform with money to spend.

Gravesend had its own local gang led by a character called Number Seven. That's the number he had imprinted on his T-shirt. This gang was always on the lookout for small groups or single youths in a Merchant Navy uniform they could pick on. The advice given by our instructors from day one was, never go out of camp alone and never venture far from the depot.

One particular evening, my friend Felix and I were returning to the depot. We turned toward the gates to see our way blocked by about a dozen locals. They were obviously waiting for stragglers going home to roost. At the head of the group, a youth strutted about with hands on hips, an inflated chest and a number seven printed on his T-shirt. The pack spread themselves across the road with no intention of letting anyone in uniform pass. Felix and I slowed to weigh up the odds and discuss our chances of breaking through. The distance between us and the safety of the gates was less than twenty yards but it might as well have been twenty miles. There really were no options to consider. With somewhat sharper survival instincts, I left Felix standing there saying something about shit before he turned on his heel to follow.

A roar from the pack of hounds echoed up the street as their tails went up. The chase was on. Felix and I headed for the myriad of dark narrow streets and alleyways providing the backbone of Gravesend. Having made it round the corner, we were out of sight of our pursuers for a few vital seconds, when my friend decided on his own course of action. He hung a sharp starboard (right) turn into a pub. The last thing I saw of him that night was his backside as it disappeared under a table before the door slammed shut.

I ducked into a narrow alley and became plunged into a darkness that could best be described as almost pitch black. Naturally, it forced me to slow down. At least my dark blue uniform blended in. My heavy breathing came under control, which was more than could be said for my heart while I desperately searched for an escape route. Although my mind reverted from its state of turmoil, there was no panic but it developed a desperate need to think fast. I wanted something to give myself some extra protection, some kind of a weapon.

In the darkness I discovered a recess in a wall, made by a supporting column, which provided some extra cover. It also gave me a little time. That element represented small comfort in the knowledge of the pack finding me soon. I struggled to regain some self-control and composure by concentrating on self-preservation. A memory flash prompted the removal of a sock. It would make an effective cosh if filled with sand. I kneeled to scrape some grit, dirt and small stones off the driveway to pour into it.

Rapid footsteps echoing through the darkness were poignant reminders of the hounds closing on this fox. My heart rate picked up, I began taking deep breaths through gritted teeth while my body shook as fear turned to rage. I pressed into the darkened recess to wait as a pair of vengeful hounds came round the corner. They faltered under a pale forty watt street light looking up and down the junction. There were four ways to go and only two of them. I was weighing up the odds when one of the youths hissed, "You go down there, I'll go down here, we'll flush the little shits out."

My body pressed harder against the wall and deeper into the darkness as I prepared to defend myself but the weighted sock did not feel heavy enough. Still, it had a good length. At least it gave a small advantage with only one of them left to deal with. On reflection, it would have been better to stand still in the darkness and allow my pursuer to continue creeping past. After all, he was moving from light into darkness. His eyes would take time to adjust as he began moving past. I should have remained perfectly still but the anger inside was not content to remain motionless and allow a perfect opportunity of vengeance to slip by. I took two long strides toward my victim. The weighted sock swept through the air in an arc. Its descent was as close to supersonic as I could make it and aimed at the youth's head. I was not exactly sure where it landed but the impact made a loud whack. My victim fell screaming in pained surprise at such an unexpected attack out the darkness. That shout must have alerted his companion and once again the vengeful demon in me should have been ignored and I should have made a run for it. However, the anger inside refused to subside. I swung the sock again and aimed at the figure's head as he was lying face down. The second blow splattered onto the young man's face as he turned to see who was attacking him. Luckily for him my sock had not been made with top quality material because it burst on impact with his nose taking the full brunt of a smelly sock full of gravel. Some went into his wide eyes, which must have created temporary blindness. At that stage everything turned to my advantage with common sense shouting, "Now! Make a run for it."

However, the resentment within had not been satisfied. It screamed defiance and insisted I deliver a boot into the hound's stomach with every ounce my small body could summon up. The unfortunate victim had all the wind knocked out of him. He was left gasping for air with blood pouring from his nose and at the same time blinded with gravel. In that moment of silence, the sound of running feet could be heard echoing down dark alleyways. With my anger finally satisfied, I bolted while stuffing what remained of an empty sock into a pocket.

Moments later I emerged into the light and directly in front of the camp gates. By good fortune rather than design my sense of direction had taken me full circle, unfortunately for me, so had the hounds. It made perfect sense because that's what I would have done in their shoes. After all, sooner or later it's where I would end up. Things became really sticky at that moment because I was in the open with nowhere to run. At my back, down that dark alley, at least two very angry youths would kill me if given half the chance. Facing me was a fate worse than death that began advancing with smiles on their faces.

An eternity seemed to pass, when suddenly, the main gates flew open. A well-formed group in columns of three, dressed in dark blue uniforms, emerged at the double in perfect step. They were led by a beady-eyed, weasel-faced marching instructor. His ratty little face was alive with expectation but more than that, it was looking for a fight. He held a pickaxe handle at the ready and was shouting, "Hup, hup, hup," in double time and to my utter relief, the pack disappeared like chaff before the wind.

For the remaining term at Gravesend Merchant Navy training depot, my marching improved in leaps and bounds along with a newfound respect for a little guy who had a big mouth.

Another interesting aspect in the training program was the ever-present lessons about sex. It was one area where no punches were pulled. The Merchant Navy seaman has a reputation of having a higher than average sex drive. Hence, whenever travelling overseas, he must have a woman in every port. At least, that particular woman belonged to him while in port.

Sexually transmitted diseases among sailors have always been a problem, despite the efforts of trainers advising to their trainees not to do "it". As for the amount of bragging that went on, everyone had more than their fair share of regular sex from prostitutes, girlfriends, their wives or other men's wives. They had abundant opportunities, they were young men loaded with testosterone and money in their pockets. Apart from which they had a reputation to perpetuate. And who was going to stop them?

Another heavy emphasis directed toward potential seamen during their training was not to have tattoos. From what I saw, there were few trainees or sailors who didn't have at least one tattoo.

During the course of our social activities arranged by the officers, we congregated in the gym to watch whatever movies were hired. Most of them were old war movies about this or that sea battle, "Sink the Bismarck!", "The Cockleshell Heroes", convoys, where the Merchant Navy supply ships were constantly being sunk by German submarines known as U-boats. It was all great fun but we yearned for something different such as a western or a movie about an invasion with tanks and infantry, anything to do with the army. That never happened but one memorable seagoing adventure film was the latest Warner Brothers film "Moby Dick". The film star Gregory Peck was the actor seeking revenge on the white whale known as Moby Dick. It was great fun to watch and some spirited support was given to those whalers during the storms they encountered at sea. Naturally, it's the end that everyone remembered. There's a terrific part that leads to the final confrontation between the whale and the hunters. The hero, Captain Ahab (Gregory Peck), launches an attack. Harpoons fly and the whale is riddled with harpoons and lines. Ahab ends up taking on the monster single-handed until he becomes entangled in the lines and drowns. From memory, the ending showed a solitary coffin floating on the ocean and it left the impression of signifying something. But I've never been able to figure out what it was.

Sundays never seem to change wherever one was. It's a day for visits, for a family get together, meals, a fight, a walk in the park, rest and an opportunity to reflect on the past week while generally winding down, thus making the first working day an inevitable uphill climb. On one particular Sunday, I sat in the park close to the training depot watching ships on the River Thames setting out to sea. My mind filled with dreams that I hoped would be realized in the near future. There were new frontiers to cross, new horizons, a new world to be explored. On the other hand, I also wondered what was happening back home. My reminiscing meandered along overhanging forest tracks where profuse numbers of game waited. The swimming hole near the old haunted house could be clearly seen in my imagination. It was an inviting scenario that tempted me to change my mind, except resistance to it remained firm. With only one week's training left, excitement began to show among the intake. Departure from the depot would be our first step in a new life and we would all have ships to sail on. A new life waited to embrace me. The pictures were clear in my mind's eye. A sundrenched beach had palm trees casting shadows over smooth silver sand. Bright blue skies reflected on shimmering turquoise waters. A fishing line was bated and waiting to catch another fish while an ice-cold cola kept me cool and quenched my thirst. The only thing to be heard while I swung gently in my hammock was a soft lapping of rippling seawater along the shoreline.

"Hello." The sound of a voice broke through my daydream.

I blinked and looked round to face a girl sitting beside me. Her beauty stunned me. Perhaps it was the sun glinting through her hair, maybe my eyes were still adjusting to the light. I had no idea what it might have been but that vision of beauty with bright green eyes took my breath away. My only reaction was to stare at her and hope my mouth hadn't fallen open.

"What's your name?" she asked softly.

Suddenly, love struck me to the core. It pierced my very being. I became tongue-tied and muttered something that couldn't be understood apart from my name.

Her eyes lit up. "I hope you don't mind but you looked miles away and I just wanted to ask you something."

"Ask what?" My brain used the few seconds available to recover and re-engage a mouth into acting in a way it could be understood. However, despite a rapid recovery, my natural reaction to any question had always been to assume the defence.

"Well," she said slowly and leaned forward, "I want to know what you were thinking about, that's all."

Those lovely bright green eyes looked directly into mine. They were the highlight of a wide beautiful face. The allure she presented took away any resistance. My mind, body and soul were hers the instant our eyes met. I looked away feeling sure my face flushed bright red while staring at her. I concentrated on a small ship manoeuvring down the river. "I was just wondering where that ship's going." That was the best reply I could come up with while pointing at the small vessel steaming down the river.

She moved closer. I could smell her. It wasn't scent, that girl just exuded the pleasant aroma of clean fresh spring air. With a heart racing and a mouth completely dry, it made me wonder why that always happened whenever a good-looking girl came close to me. "You must be one of the boys from the training school."

I nodded and felt sure if I tried to say anything it would come out all wrong. We sat in silence for a few moments, watching the small ship as it made its way down the river until it disappeared round the bend.

"Do you think it's going far?" she asked in a whisper.

"Who knows," I replied feeling a little easier, "it's a small ship so it won't be going too far."

"Shall we go for a walk," she said and stood up.

I found myself standing without making a conscious effort. We walked for a while and she began telling me about herself and the large family she came from. During the short time we were together, we ate ice cream and talked until the sun dipped behind the treetops. For no apparent reason, we were holding hands in the certain knowledge that eternity was ours. The constant walking on air, then stopping to look into each other's eyes, should have lasted forever but the world doesn't stop turning for anyone. In fact, I barely had time to ask when we could meet again. My heart pounded in anticipation that her reply would be "soon".

"Next Sunday, same time same place," she answered and squeezed my hand. Elongated shadows drawn across the park almost touched the water's edge. A tear was developing in her eyes when she added in a whisper, "I have to go."

We shared a long moment of silence. I felt helpless in doing anything that might extend our being together for one more minute. With a mind of its own, my hand went behind her head and drew it toward me. Our eyes closed as our lips met. For a few trembling seconds, heaven belonged to me. When we parted she turned quickly and with a final wave of her hand, hurried away.

The final week turned into a blur of slow motion studies. There were long boring interviews accompanied by assessment programs but the only thing on my mind was a green-eyed girl named Ann. It dawned on me that Sunday would be the last chance to see her before returning home. A week of seven days can really drag until Sunday eventually came back. Soon after breakfast, with a kitbag packed, I sat on the park bench waiting for her. In my pocket were a bus ticket home and a boarding pass for a cruise liner waiting to depart on her maiden voyage. I would be a steward aboard and it would be a new start for both of us. I also had a pen and some paper to make a note of Ann's name and address with about a million other things I wanted to ask. When we had been together, time seemed to travel so slowly. While waiting to see her again, it flew by. Ann was late, which meant that each delayed moment was lost forever.

My bus was due. She still hadn't turned up. A deep sense of disappointment flooded through me. I gazed at the seat while walking to the bus stop. It looked empty and forlorn. The sound of a bus engine rattled down the street. My eyes remained fixed on the bench while praying she would at least show up. I slowly began making my way toward the bus stop until I threw the kit-bag over my shoulder and made a run for it.

I climbed aboard, still looking behind with a slither of hope in my heart. The bus pulled away and like that small ship we watched, I kept that seat in view until it finally disappeared behind the treeline.

Anthony Corbyn

Chapter Thirteen

In the Merchant Navy

Uncle and I settled into some serious drinking, smoking and talking. As usual, he never questioned my reasons for doing anything, yet was always there to help and offer advice, although any final decisions were left to me.

It was well past my bedtime when Uncle laid me down in a state of semi-consciousness. The final train of thought running through my head as I slipped into a deep sleep was to get up on time. However, the amount of alcohol I consumed dulled my excellent internal clock. When my eyes eventually opened to the sound of a dawn chorus, there were no doubts in my mind – I was late!

After leaping up I ran into the double bedroom to shake Uncle and mother awake. We staggered about rushing to get ready. My bags had already been packed and mother made frantic efforts at preparing some breakfast, which at that stage I became too excited to eat. Uncle had a hard time focusing because he still remained under the influence from the last nightcap that must have been a really big one.

I stood beside the Norton Dominator motorbike urging Uncle to hurry. In the confusion, mother's questions regarding what was happening and what time would I be back, were among the multitudes left unanswered. "Uncle will explain when he returns," were my last words shouted as Uncle opened the throttle. We sped away leaving a confused looking mum waving goodbye. The Norton Dominator's six hundred cc engine gave a deep throaty roar from a plentiful supply of power. Within minutes we were cruising along the open road at a steady speed with the wind in our faces and a kitbag strapped to my back. Being on a motorbike is the best form of transport.

I leaned forward and tapped Uncle on the shoulder then indicated he should go faster by opening an imaginary throttle. He nodded and eased the throttle open just a touch and the engine between our legs responded with a deeper growl. We hadn't been going long before Uncle pointed in the mirror and drew my attention to the unmistakable blue flashing light cresting the horizon behind. Uncle did not have a licence, he had never passed his test, he was definitely speeding and if caught would undoubtedly be in big trouble. The driving offences counted for nothing compared to aiding and abetting a runaway ward of the court.

Without needing any instructions on what to do, a blip on the throttle was the signal for both of us to lean forward. I gritted my teeth, shut my eyes and hung on tight. The mighty engine roared, and suddenly we were accelerating at a frightening rate. A change into top gear resulted in the engine settling to a steady growl. We were going flat out along a straight road. Suddenly, a shutdown, a blip on the throttle, a change down in gear as we approached a bend, then acceleration round the bend while leaning hard over. With eyes shut tight and both arms wrapped unyieldingly around Uncle's waist, I began praying. The bike came upright, its throttle was opened all the way, vibrations filled my body, shutdown, change into top, throttle wide open again.

I saw power poles flashing by with a constant whoosh, whoosh, whoosh. My heart pounded with every change down and consequential lean over on the bends. After a frightening five minutes, the bike suddenly slowed down as we pulled into a bikers' café. Uncle parked the Norton among a row of bikes and we dismounted quickly to enter the premises. Uncle ordered two coffees before the door slammed shut. Seconds later, we were sitting at a table among a group of bikers with very hostile stares. Outside, a police car raced past with lights flashing and siren blaring. Everyone in the café watched in silence.

Someone about the size of a house in worn leathers strode across the room and stood over Uncle looking down on his pudding basin-shaped helmet. Uncle's overall attire, apart from the out of date helmet, included a brown corduroy jacket, a white silk scarf, fawn horse riding breeches and jet-black calf-length boots. If anyone looked out of place in that café, it could not have been anybody else but Uncle.

Nights in the Forest

Another police car flashed past before slowing to a stop. The police inside the vehicle with blue flashing lights looked at the café, which drew the attention of several bikers who stood up. A deep voice growled, "The pigs are after someone."

I was unable to help myself and said, "They're after us." Uncle kicked me under the table anyway.

The bikers looked at the two most conspicuous people in the room. The big one standing behind Uncle had tattoos up his massive arms and looked like an ideal bad man and the epitome of defiance. He was huge, wore a leather jacket, a full beard and had long black greasy hair down to his shoulders. Above all, the giant was really very ugly. He looked extremely impressive, especially when he roared, "You?" The big man directed his single-worded question at Uncle who maintained his cool and shrugged. "Why dya stop 'ere?" came the aggressively added question, spat out with clenched fists resting on hips.

Uncle took a deep breath and sipped his coffee. It provided him with a momentary delay while his mind worked out the best answer. "If you want to hide a tree, first find a forest," he said pointing to the row of bikes outside.

"Did you guys 'ear that?" the big man bellowed. Then burst out laughing as the mood amongst the bikers turned in our favour. We were joined at the table by several men offering cigarettes and asking why we were wanted by the police.

"We go a little too quickly," Uncle replied.

"We were doing over a hundred miles an hour," I blurted out in an attempt to impress those oversized rebels of the road surrounding us. The confession of going over the magical ton brought a cheer from every biker in the café. They began waving to the occupants in the police car until it moved off.

"They won't be back, you'll be safe now," the big bearded one said.

"Yeah, but ve must going soon. Boy here he must catch his ship. He is in Navy," Uncle said.

Although easy to say, we were unable to leave until each member of the biker gang sat astride Uncle's bike. A lot of comments went back and forth as first a Triumph Bonneville, a big BSA

Gold Flash, two older but immaculately maintained Matchless bikes and two Velocette MACs with their fishtail exhausts were admired. All the bikes had been modified to some extent with ape hanger handlebars or drops. Forks were elevated, ribbons festooned the handle and crash bars. More bikes stood in line waiting to be examined but I reminded Uncle of the time by saying, "We must leave now." My persistent reminders finally received a positive response with a nod.

The bikers escorted us to the turnoff for Southampton making such an enormous impression on me, I vowed that one day I'd become a biker. Their bike horns blew and engines revved in a farewell and good luck salute. Suddenly we were on our own again heading down the road to Southampton without speeding.

On our arrival at the docks Uncle dropped me off at the gates. I stood facing him for several moments until he held out his hand and said, "Good luck boy."

"Thanks for the lift Uncle."

He turned away and without looking back sped up the road until, a few seconds later Uncle disappeared out of sight into the traffic.

A security officer directed me to the signing on shed where ships were allocated to crewmen. The entire dockside complex was a hive of activity because, with a national seamen's strike on, nobody was going anywhere. No one stopped me making it to the window where I pushed my papers through. It took about one moment for a voice to say, "You're late, the Oriana has a full crew, wait over there, I'll see what other ships might be available." His statement stunned me. There had to be some kind of mistake. They must have known I was on my way. The SS Oriana was allocated to me, but my rebuttal received nothing more than a shrug of the shoulders. The harsher realities of life weren't something new. Previous experiences taught me that being late or at the back of a queue meant you missed out.

A lot of men were coming and going through a pair of battered old double doors. The bustling room's atmosphere was suffocating with dense tobacco smoke, noisy cursing seamen creating tension and dispensing strange smells. Above the chaos going on, a familiar voice filtered through the haze. I stood up to weave my way into another room. With some difficulty I suppressed the joy of seeing Billy Sproul but managed to remain cool. "Hello Billy," I called in a voice loud enough to be heard over the cacophony of noises.

Bill looked up. A broad grin spread across his delighted face. "Well I'll be buggered, young un. What in blazes are you doin' here?"

"Joined the Merch," I answered firmly and inflated my chest with pride.

"'Ear, you're too young," Bill whispered. He had the good sense to keep his voice down before introductions were made to the seamen at the table. A few minutes' conversation revealed my unfortunate circumstances of arriving too late to catch the ship I had been allocated to everyone. It resulted in forfeiting the chance of a cruise liner and I had to wait for an alternative. The men round the table laughed with each other and assured me it was normal. In fact, all four seamen sitting at the table were in the same situation.

"We're having a game of cards. It's pretty serious stuff mate. If you don't mind we'll carry on," Bill said as I sat on the bench beside him.

"Will it be okay if I watch?" I asked. Nobody at the table objected and within a few seconds it felt comfortable being in their company.

Shortly after the game restarted, Bill's name was called out. He wasted no time getting his kitbag before leaving with a cheery wave and a good luck shouted to me.

When my name eventually filtered through the smoke-laden noisy atmosphere, it sounded so distant and strange it almost went unnoticed. A minute later, however, with a kitbag over my shoulder, a chest swelled with pride and a swagger in my step, I headed toward the wharves. A great ship of the line, a huge oceangoing tanker waited for me on the other side of the river. It was difficult trying to suppress the excitement inside but I slowed down in an effort to prove to anyone watching, there walked a man of the sea, full of confidence and about to take on the world.

"Oy!" A heavy voice boomed across the yard.

I looked about before seeing the unshaven face of an enormous seaman staring angrily.

"Who me?" I asked timidly.

"Yeah you squirt. Where does yur think you'm goin'?" The question sounded harsh and unfriendly, even intimidating.

"Going to join my ship," I replied firmly in as deep a voice as the fear inside allowed. That answer drew men out of hidden corners like a magnet draws pins across a smooth surface. Suddenly a circle of giants formed around me. They were ugly hands-on-hips giants who looked as though they would demand a fight with anyone or anything and required no rhyme or reason to start fighting. "Fee-fi-fo-fum, I smell the blood of an Englishman", filtered into my brain as I looked up at the surrounding faces. The look in their eyes left no doubts they were men who meant business. My kitbag was lowered to the ground.

"Goin' to yur ship eh?" a deep voice asked angrily.

I felt it was an appropriate time to show a little deference and humility before responding with, "Yes Sir. I've just joined the Merchant Navy, it's my first ship." This respectful answer was supported by my widest smile.

A hand the size of a dinner plate with bananas for fingers reached down while a voice that should have belonged to King Kong growled, "Let's see yer papers?"

These were pulled from my tunic pocket and handed over. A muttered conference between the giants towering above me took place. "Tioga!" someone exclaimed, "That ol' rust bucket will never make it across the river." One or two Jolly Green Giants laughed while others muttered like rolling thunder in agreement.

I considered the spokesman's remark as a very disparaging one to make about someone's first ship and totally unwarranted. Besides, what would he know anyway, just because he'd been in the Merchant Navy for years and was about fifty times bigger than me, it didn't mean he knew everything.

"The Tioga be in dry dock 'avin' 'er bum scraped so 'tis," someone else up there chipped in.

"First ship eh?" the original giant asked while looking on my upturned face.

"Yes Sir," I said adding a little enthusiasm to my reply.

"The lad ain't goin' nowhere, 'sides be 'is first ship."

It was impossible to see who was doing the talking because their faces were high above with the sun directly in my eyes. Some more muttering sounding like distant thunder followed. Then a voice directed toward me said, "Follow us." With the command given, we marched off with me taking two strides to their one. Those giants led me straight through the picket line. We were seven men of the sea. To be perfectly correct, it was one small under-aged delinquent accompanied by six of the biggest men on the planet. Nonetheless, those men represented my introduction into the Merchant Navy. Having escorted their charge through the picket lines, the contingent of giants about turned at the ferry terminal and walked away laughing amongst themselves.

The waiting room at the terminal was almost empty. An old salt, looking for the world like a sack of potatoes, occupied a bench seat in the corner. I never hesitated to sit beside him. My bum had only warmed the woodwork for a split second before he spoke in a voice that sounded like a coffee grinder struggling to grind some beans. "What ship mate?" the old man of the sea asked.

"The Esso Tioga," I replied with some pride and confidence. After all, with six of the biggest men in the world as my escort, there was no reason to fear anyone.

"Ah well now, I'm be cook aboard same so you must be the cabin boy."

"Steward," I corrected. There seemed little point in training for six weeks to earn a title only to have it taken away by a total stranger. Being new at the game, did not mean my title could be taken away. The lumpy human moved closer. He had sloping shoulders, a huge pot belly, a round battle-weary face with a double chin covered in salt and pepper bristle. That old man of the sea had obviously been around. His eyes sparkled with mischief, much as my own did when confronting strangers, and he held out a hand. I gripped it tightly to impress my shipmate.

"You can call me Cookie, 'tis easy to remember an' I be cook anyway."

I attempted pinning down the accent but the mix must have come from every country in the world with nothing specific enough to identify. "My name's Paul."

"That be a fine name but in this game we 'ave proper names as befitting us. I think I'll call 'ee Nipper, yep that'll be best for 'ee."

My first friend, on my first ship, in a new career had just given me a new name. It sounded pretty good and fitted my physique. My bad start was finally turning out to be a reasonably good one.

"Do 'ee smoke Nipper?"

"Yes I do."

"Have one oh these." Cookie handed over a packet of Capstan Full Strength.

His offer was declined. "No thanks Cookie, I prefer my own.

The man resembling a sack of potatoes burst out laughing. It was a deep coarse chuckle that struggled to escape. It gave the impression he was on the verge of choking until he took a deep breath to settle a quivering body. "Ha, you'll do Nipper, you'll do."

The second time he called me Nipper still sounded a little strange yet acceptable, since my stature was indeed small and there appeared nothing demeaning or callous in the name. I settled back to roll a cigarette before handing the tin to Cookie and watched him show off by rolling a cigarette with one hand.

"Neat," I said and smiled.

An out of use by dated face grinned. "You'm alright Nipper, when you be as old as me it'll come easy."

"How old are you Cookie?" I asked, testing the sound of my new friend's name.

"I'm too old. 'Ow old be you then?" My companion looked me in the eye and rubbed his five o'clock shadow. Although from the length of the bristle, it must have been five o'clock several days ago. It seemed obvious he saw straight through my guise. That sideways look cut right to the heart of the matter.

Nights in the Forest

It became necessary to take a page out of Uncle's book. I took a deep drag before blowing out long and slow. It gave my mind long enough to come up with a suitable answer. "Old enough."

There was that burst out laughing again. It sounded reminiscent of someone with whooping cough. He was still chuckling, which sounded like someone choking, when we boarded the ferry to take us to the other side of the river.

Esso Tioga was a small, relatively old coastal oil tanker. True, it could never be considered as a large ocean-going tanker or an elegant cruise liner, except she had a beauty of her own. Cookie led the way up the gangplank before making straight for the galley where he made a quick check through the lockers before putting the kettle on and said, "Is you 'ungry Nipper?"

"Starving," I replied.

"Arr well now, let's get some practice on working together. It's what we'em goin' to get paid for." Cookie rummaged about banging saucepans, tins and utensils until the kettle boiled. "Make the tea Nipper," he called out with his head inside a locker.

There was no need to make a second call on that one. I found an enormous brown china teapot and put plenty of tea leaves with boiling water into it in preparation of a brew. I gave the brew a good stir before placing the pot, with two big china mugs, a bowl of sugar and a tin of condensed milk on the table. We sat down to drink, smoke and talk while the meal in the oven cooked. It felt absolutely wonderful. My adventure had begun but there was little to do while the seamen stayed on strike. The Esso Tioga had a specific role to play by plying the UK coastline. I considered her the first stepping stone in what would be a long illustrious career at sea. Crossing oceans and visiting foreign ports would come soon enough. Obtaining some experience on a small ship would hold me in good stead on a much larger one. Captains and crew would view me as an old hand who had been around.

After a refreshing large mug of tea, Cookie took me on a tour of the ship. He started pointing out this and that as we went. A door was opened, we both peered in as he said, "Saloon, 'tis where Captain an' 'is officers eat." My tour guide held me by the shoulders while looking directly into my eyes before adding, "'Tis where your duties be." We moved past the Captain's cabin where I would take him his morning tea.

"Who wakes me up in the morning?"

"I does," Cookie answered.

I pondered that answer for a few moments as we moved toward the crew's quarters until it occurred to ask the obvious. "Cookie!" I exclaimed softly to attract his attention, "If you're already up, why don't you take the Captain his tea?" It seemed a perfectly reasonable and logical question to me.

Cookie stopped dead in his tracks before turning slowly to face me and growled like a junkyard dog. "Cos that be the cabin boy's duties an' I be the cook."

That answer seemed fair enough so I nodded but restrained from correcting him on my title. I continued following my newly acquired leader down an alleyway until the pathfinder came across an open door and stood to one side. "Crew's quarters, a more motley bunch of rats you ain't never goin' to see," Cookie said. He pushed me through the door and introduced the crew. Each man nodded acknowledgment of my presence with a wink or smile.

The first thing that hit me was the smell. Six men were in that room with everyone emitting all the usual human odours of sweat and farting while smoking did nothing in producing a pleasant aroma. The ashtrays overflowed with cigarette butts and a scattering of coins and dog-eared cards littered the table. A small single bar electric fire reflected heat into the small room without any ventilation. Every man at the table looked pale with a fine sheen of sweat covering their faces. My thoughts and impressions were interrupted by a voice.

"This be the Chief," Cookie said laying a hand on the man's shoulder.

The chief looked through me with pale blue, watery, lifeless eyes that were identical to those of Old Pigface. I may as well not have been there and an immediate dislike between us developed in that instant. A minute later Cookie and I left the crew laughing amongst themselves while dealing another hand of cards.

Nights in the Forest

"The Chief's not very friendly, is he Cookie?" I stated on our way back to the galley.

"He be a funny bloke but 'e knows 'is job."

I shrugged off that snippet of information because I was far more interested in an answer to my next question. "When do you think we'll be sailing?"

The cook scratched his chin while answering that question with, "Arr well now, if'n you ask I that every day I'll be right when I tells 'ee soon."

Cookie's comments were correct because the next day the strike ended. Suddenly, the Thames River docks became alive with vibrant activity. It seemed that everyone on every ship was in a hurry. When the captain came aboard, every crewman aboard Tioga smartened themselves up, moved quicker, said "Aye aye" and spouted all sorts of nautical jargon. It reminded me of sailing ship movies where crewmen went for'ed or aft, secured the sta'bourd or port line, below or above decks. The boatswain would shout orders and men would jump to obey. There would be lots of har hars, shiver me timbers and men scrambling up rigging to lower sail. However, there was none of that aboard the Tioga.

Within minutes of our captain coming aboard, the ship's hawsers were removed and she began moving backwards (astern) down the slipway. Seconds later, I felt the sensation of being afloat. Even in still waters one can experience that wonderful feeling. The throb of engines, pumps working, horns blowing, with vibrations rippling through her hull, the propellers on Tioga pulled us astern for a few seconds. There followed a mighty shuddering as the props started thrusting in the opposite direction and we stopped going astern. Tioga began moving forward. We were finally under way.

"Take the skipper 'is coco mate," Cookie whispered. A big china mug brimming with frothy brown liquid was shoved under my nose. "'E be up on the bridge, be a good chance to see 'im up close."

Tioga motored toward the estuary amid a flotilla of ships eager to get on with the commerce they were built for. On the bridge our captain stood with hands firmly clasped behind his back. He looked very authoritative in black jacket and peak cap. It would have been difficult to tell him apart from a police officer. It took me a couple of seconds before summoning up enough courage to speak. I took a deep breath and muttered, "Cup of cocoa, Captain."

The man turned slowly to look down at me, reached out and took the mug from my hand, gave a small grunt, then turned to face forward.

The helmsman looked at me, smiled, then shrugged. He gave the impression of reminding me that after delivering the captain's drink, did I have nothing better to do than stand there gawking. I smiled back, casually walked over to check the compass before shaking my head very slowly and muttering while leaving the bridge to return to the galley.

Although I had the smallest cabin aboard, at least a single berth afforded some privacy with a porthole for ventilation. The only fault was its position on the ship. It had been built directly over the main pump, which made it impossible to get any sleep with the constant pounding. The metallic throbbing worked its way into my head so that I tossed and turned with a brain incapable of accepting the noise. The steady unrelenting motion of the ship also got to me and a seemingly longer than usual night ended with another thumping sound. Through the mists of sleeplessness and overwhelming nausea a voice called my name. I rolled off my bunk to open the door.

Cookie reached in and ruffled my hair. "Come on Nipper, you'm late."

I felt sick, tired, and totally disillusioned, apart from that, it was still pitch dark so had to ask what time is was.

"Time the Captain were on deck. Look lively Nipper, to the galley quick sharp."

I dressed quickly before heading for the warmth of the galley where Cookie handed me a big mug of tea. "Oh thanks mate," I whispered before pursed lips pouted in readiness to suck up the first hot reviving sip.

"Oy! That be for the Skipper not you," came the hissed command as a hand shot between my lips and the mug. "Now, you get yurself to 'is cabin afore you'm any deeper in the shit."

With bleary eyes, a mouthful of fur, a weary body requiring rest and feeling sick to the stomach, I staggered toward our illustrious captain's quarters. The door was opened carefully. A stealthy walk took me toward the bedside locker where the mug of tea was gently placed before slowly backing out the cabin. I was almost certain the man moved just before the door closed. Having accomplished my first task of the morning, it only took a few seconds getting back to the galley, sit down and breathe a sigh of relief.

"Captain get 'is tea?" Cookie asked.

"Yes," I replied quickly. The excitement and tension woke me up. My heart pumped undiluted adrenalin through my veins and gave me an appetite.

"You be ready for breakfast then."

"Oh yes please Cookie, I'm starving."

"Get that into yur belly," he said as a mug of steaming tea appeared.

I made numerous grateful comments while sucking noisily at the sweet liquid. The fur in my mouth dissolved, my head cleared like magic and suddenly the world turned into a better place. My duties had started. All those weeks at the training depot were going to be put into practice. The table in the saloon was laid as it had never been laid before. Even the officers commented on the effort, which inflated my pride to explosive proportions. Later in the day Cookie and I were having lunch when he put me right on something and the reason for the captain's displeasure in my performance.

"You didn't wake 'im. He overslept, ain't nothing more upsettin' fur a skipper who be late fur 'is own watch."

There was no option but to respond to the criticism by saying sorry and I would do better next time. It seems that nothing had changed. After all, why was it my fault if the man did not wake up when he was supposed to?

"You 'as to be firm Nipper," Cookie began. "Go in, put the mug on 'is table an' say somthin' like, morning Skipper, loud enough to wake 'im." He leaned forward to continue the lesson at close quarters. "Draw the curtains an' say, 'tis a good day fur a sail or some such verse."

I listened intently, repeated the sentence once, then again but a little louder in a determined effort to get it right.

"Arr that's it, you'll 'ave 'im eatin' out of yur 'and in no time at all."

Having my efforts rewarded and complimented by Cookie cheered me up and compensated my faults. However, during the night not only did that pump keep me awake but there were concerns how my future in the Merchant Navy rested on a mug of tea being delivered correctly. Cookie's words kept rolling around in my head the way Tioga rolled about on the ocean. I must have dropped off for a few seconds. The horrifying dream of our captain eating my hand loomed large in my subconscious. I was stamping my feet in agony and protest before a thumping on my door woke me.

By the time the second mug of tea was in my hand, I was in a bad mood. There would be no more pussyfooting around. The captain was just a man without any need to be afraid of him. He would pay dearly for invading my dreams and eating my hand. All I needed to do was what Cookie told me and everything would be fine. Those words were repeated over and over during my long walk down that corridor in firm resolute steps. The only consolation I allowed myself was that if anything went wrong, it would be Cookie's fault, not mine. The door was flung open. It crashed noisily against the bulkhead. I strode steadfastly toward the bunk, slammed the mug down, a little of the tea spilled over but hell what did that matter, then switched on the bedside lamp and noted the captain's eyes were wide open. "Good morning Captain," I said in a clear firm voice full of confidence, if a little high in the octave department. "Lovely day for a sail," I added in a loud voice from the other side of the cabin while drawing the curtains back in a swift noisy move to reveal an early morning sky black as pitch.

Nights in the Forest

Before I left the cabin, our glorious captain had propped himself up on one elbow, his eyes and mouth were wide open. I shut the cabin door firmly before walking briskly back to the galley where Cookie waited for me. There remained no doubts in my mind. I had just completed a good job. Not even the king of Siam could complain about it.

"'Ow did 'e go?"

"You were right Cookie. I did just what you told me. When I left he was sitting up with his eyes open." I saw no reason to comment about his mouth being wide open as well or the stunned look on his gaunt face.

"Arr, that be good Nipper. I'll 'ave a word with 'im afore the day's out, see if'n 'e be 'appy."

After serving breakfast to the officers, the cook and I met up in the galley to enjoy our own. He handed over a mug of tea while whispering softly, "Nipper we still 'as a problem."

My heart sank faster than the Titanic.

"Captain ain't 'appy."

"What!"

"You did too good a job Nipper, you 'as to moderate yur callin' card."

"But I did exactly what you told me," I responded ardently with the word "you" being very firmly emphasized. "It isn't my fault."

"Arr you did right enough mate. But a touch too much enthusiasm, I believe were the skipper's very words", Cookie told me sympathetically before adding, "We 'as to practice lad, we 'as to practice."

Part of the morning was spent doing just that. I stepped in and out of the galley with Cookie pretending to be the captain. Various levels of sound were practiced with me saying "Good morning Captain, lovely day for a sail," until Cookie finally said, "'Tis as good as any, I see no reason for complaint on that performance. Nipper you got it right."

The third morning saw me up dressed and ready before Cookie knocked on my door. Not only was I tired but exhausted. It had been three nights without sleep. With that pump thumping

265

its way into my dreams and the apprehension of achieving a simple task, things were not easy. Serving the skipper with his morning mug of tea was a really tough job. My mind became a jumble of confused thoughts. If the skipper's mug of tea was served cold, did it constitute an offence punishable by walking the plank? What would happen if I tripped and poured scalding hot tea over our sleeping skipper? Who would be at fault, me, Cookie, the ship's movement or the helmsman?

My moment came. The mug was handed over with reassuring encouraging words that everything would be fine. The cook directed me down the corridor. My heart thumped louder than that pump under the bunk. A tremble developed in both legs. I grasped the door handle while struggling to compose and steady myself with a mind going over Cookie's instructions. I pushed the door open, it creaked, that was something it had never done before. I stepped into the gloom to face the captain sitting on the edge of his bunk with a funny look on his face. His eyes were bloodshot after they stopped blinking. That much was clearly visible, especially when the light came on. I held out the mug and said, "Good morning Captain," in a subdued voice. He took the mug as our eyes locked in on each other. His were definitely bloodshot, the whites and eyelids were tinged with red. Wild staring eyes are very unnerving to a youngster. I reached up and very slowly drew the curtains while our eyes remained locked together. "Nice day for a sail," I muttered quietly. It seemed inappropriate to raise my voice in such a confined space, besides the man was as wide awake as any man I had ever seen.

The captain grunted in what seemed like an acknowledgment but there was no way of telling what it meant. There was no certainty about anything anymore. I backed out the cabin and gently closed the door before turning and running like a scalded cat back to the galley. On my arrival Cookie seemed more anxious about the event than me. He sat me down, handed me a mug of tea, ruffled my hair, looked into my puzzled eyes and asked a very simple question. "What happened?" He rubbed the stubble on his world-weary face as I explained the events of the last minute. His brow creased in confused concentration until realization spread across his face. He snapped his fingers and exclaimed, "Of course!" before adding, "By the 'eck Nipper our worries are over."

"They are?" I said with a feeling of excitement about his declaration. There were no doubts about me feeling a profound sense of relief.

"Of course!" my overgrown friend said gleefully before continuing, "Captain be so afraid of 'ee comin' into 'is cabin, he's awake afors you'm arrived. He ain't ever goin' to oversleep again. Not while you'm on board anyways." Both of us were still laughing as we prepared breakfast for the crew.

Things went along a lot easier after that. With a renewed level of confidence I could relax and sleep despite the noisy pump. The settling in period had passed. Fear of the captain turned to respect and whilst it never became necessary to wake him again, the occasional grunt or "morning" was enough to keep me happy. However, a festering thorn remained in the shape of a pale-faced, watery-eyed chief engineer. After Tioga docked and while being loaded, the crew were watching television in the confines of a small cabin. I could not see the screen from my position without putting my feet up on a chair and leaning precariously to one side. The chief had been giving me a hard time with some intimidating stares from the day we met. His attitude passed beyond any understanding because I did nothing to provoke that kind of treatment.

"Get your feet off the seat!" The order could not have been directed toward anyone else. Those watery blue eyes were looking directly into mine. I shifted about until both feet dangled over the edge. That was not good enough. Any attempt to appease the man seemed to present an opportunity to have another go at me in front of the crew. "I told you to shift your damn feet," he repeated in a raised voice.

"I did, Chief, they're not on the seat."

Apparently, that reply had not been good enough because he responded angrily with, "Don't answer me back or I'll smack you in the gob."

Anger bubbled to the surface and suppressed my fear as other crew members looked at the chief. They were unable to see his reason for such an angry verbal attack on me. Asking him what he was so angry about resulted in the chief standing up, pushing his chair over, and displaying an intimidating gesture. Any doubts about his intentions of looking for a fight were dismissed. Like all cowards or bullies, he picked on the smallest person available. If nothing else, my nature did not allow any backing down, no matter what the odds. Perhaps it was foolhardy but nature is a hard thing to suppress. I looked about me for a weapon feeling certain an attack was imminent. With nowhere to run in the close confines of that cabin, defence became a priority. My hand closed round a milk bottle as the chief pushed a crewman aside. Everyone in that room heard the crash of glass on the bulkhead. Suddenly! Without being able to comprehend how, I was holding a jagged broken bottle in front of me.

The sight stopped my aggressor in his tracks and he bellowed a stream of obscenities at me. His pasty pale face turned red with rage while I remained staunchly committed to defending myself without a flight path. The chief picked up a chair. The small room emptied itself of crewmen who were leaping over the table to get out.

"I'm going to smash yur stupid poxy face in," my aggressor proclaimed.

He would have done it, except a hand came down on his shoulder. "What be up?" Cookie demanded.

"Mind yur own damn business," the chief replied.

I had never seen my friend become angry or use force until that moment but noted the knuckles on his hand turn white. The chief winced under the fingers closing tightly on his shoulder. Cookie hissed into the only vacant ear, "I be makin' it my business mate. Now! You be a good chap and put down that chair." When the chief hesitated, Cookie's free hand grasped him by the elbow and the chair fell to the floor. "Be real easy fur 'ee to pick on Nipper 'ere, why not pick on me." Cookie spun the man round, pinned him against the bulkhead and drew his face up so close, their noses were touching. My saviour began a tirade on the

Nights in the Forest

man pinned against the bulkhead. "If you're lookin' fur a fight there be plenty of room on the stern. Tell 'ee what Chief. You can 'ave first punch but 'ee best make it a good un cos if'n I get's up, you'm dead!" His eyes blazed with manic hatred. It was fantastic to see such a happy twinkling eye turn into a vicious animal's stare. A long silence followed before the chief's eyes dropped. He pulled away and was rubbing life back into his shoulder as he skulked away.

Cookie's cold stare looked at me. "Put that damn bottle down and get yourself back in the galley, we 'as work to do," he growled. I followed along the alleyway as he continued talking. "You best keep out of the Chief's way Nipper, that man don't like you."

"Good, cos I don't like him either," I replied and sat down. My friend smiled. The anger had left his eyes, but when he had inadvertently revealed the hidden strength in his hands, it made a lasting deep impression on me.

After Tioga was loaded with oil, we made our way up the turbulent Irish Sea. I stood on the bridge, fascinated by the ship diving beneath the waves until her decks were awash before heaving back out again. Each time she plunged through a big wave, vibrations rattled through the hull. Back in the galley, Cookie called to follow him onto the stern and in the open where furious winds beat against our faces.

"Hang onto the rail," Cookie shouted as the wind slammed the door shut.

Tioga fell into a trough, then her stern dipped. Suddenly water started swirling around my feet. A big hand grasped my shoulder to steady me but the grin across my mouth stretched from ear to ear and hurt my face. Freezing cold wind screamed in my ears while rain stung any exposed skin like hundreds of bees protecting their hive. Huge waves hurtled toward us threatening to swamp the little ship. It turned into my best five minutes since joining the Merchant Navy. The ship punched her way through waves until she reached Belfast to discharge her tanks of oil. We remained in port overnight with some of the crew going ashore while others, including myself, remained on board. In the morning we turned around and headed back down the Irish Sea for Southampton. A great sense of satisfaction swept over me with a feeling of having achieved something. My first voyage had been completed, and returning to England was the beginning of another. The weather abated and this allowed Tioga to ride high on empty tanks and move easily through the water. The helmsman was alone on the bridge when I went up to have a look around. I stood beside the man in control of the ship for several minutes before asking if he would let me have a go. He looked around, saw no one about and moved aside so the junior crewman could stand behind the wheel. My ultimate dream was realized. An overwhelming sense of power enveloped me while standing behind the helm and steering the ship down the Irish Sea.

"Hold your course," the helmsman whispered and pointed at the compass.

I remained at the wheel for several minutes before footsteps on steel stairs prompted the helmsman to push me aside and resume his position.

The captain came in and looked at the pair of us standing side by side facing forward. My heart sank in the dead certain belief he knew exactly what I'd just done. Guilt flooded me, particularly when he looked directly into my eyes.

"Cup of cocoa please, steward," he said.

"Aye, aye Captain," I replied before beating a hasty retreat. While the milk heated up in the galley, I gave Cookie a gentle shove to wake him. I had to tell someone what happened. He muttered something but did not appear to wake up. I made myself busy with the cocoa while talking to Cookie about my turn at the wheel in whispered excited tones. He gave no indication of being awake or listening to what was being said until my friend suddenly jumped up. He looked out a port hole and growled, "What country be that?"

"Ireland," I answered.

"Thank God," Cookie sighed before sitting back down. "Be a terrible joke you'm playin' on me sayin' things like that."

Nights in the Forest

"But Cookie it's true, you can ask the helmsman when he comes down."

"Ach, he'll deny it even if it were true." A lumpy hand waved me away in a nonchalant manner.

"It's true honest. I steered the boat for several minutes."

"Ship, you lubber, this be a ship," he corrected and sat still while staring into space shaking his head. "All my years at sea an' I never 'ad a go at the wheel." The cook's long sad face turned toward me as he continued muttering, "An' here you is a pipsqueak who don't know nothin' an' you've done more'n me already."

"You've never steered a ship?" I asked incredulously.

"Never," he replied.

"Don't believe you."

"On me word of honour, 'tis true so 'tis," he responded with hand on heart.

I whisked up the cocoa contemplating Cookie's last remarks before leaving my friend blowing plumes of smoke from his Capstan Full Strength. Later that evening after dinner, we sat talking till late with the stove insulating us from the cold. My comment about the temperature caused Cookie to make a caustic remark. He leaned across the table and said, "Cold you say, ha, this ain't cold Nipper. I'll tell 'ee a story about cold." His big nose almost touched mine. Both eyes were as big as saucers when he concluded with, "If'n you 'as the stomach fur it." Without a doubt Cookie had a great way of telling stories. He could set the preliminary atmosphere to promote the story before it began, any resistance to it failed me and I nodded.

"Well so be it then matey," he declared. "'Twere well north of 'ere. Arctic circle so 'twere an' I wasn't much older than you at the time." He took a long drag on a Capstan as his eyes glazed over. His head shook ponderously slowly and the teeth in his head made a terrible grinding sound. Whatever awful memories haunted him, came flooding back and were about to be revealed. "'Twere cold Nipper, real cold. These 'ere bones is still stiff from it all these years later." He leaned forward again, his eyes were wide while deep furrows carved their way across his forehead.

"The wind were blowin' somthin' fierce so 'twas. Ice formed on the riggin' an' mast." At that point Cookie took a drink before wrapping both arms around himself as if to protect him from the cold still surrounding him from all those years ago. "Skipper calls out, all 'ands on deck, an' we 'as to clear the ice an' keep it cleared." He shook his head slowly from side to side. "Man but 'twere cold an' we 'as to Nipper. 'Twere life or death. You does know what 'appens when ice forms on riggin' an' deck, don't 'ee?"

My head moved from side to side, I think my eyes must have been as wide as his when he continued in a hushed voice, "When 'tis two foot thick on deck, ship comes top 'eavy so we 'as to keep it off. They riggin' wires an' masts were festooned we icicles. Festooned I tell 'ee, festooned!" He leaned forward again with his eyes rolling toward a hand held above my head. I followed the gaze to watch the index finger on Cookie's hand draw circles. "Ship turns turtle Nipper, she turns turtle."

The thought sent a shiver down my spine. I took another drag on my own cigarette before Cookie continued with his story.

"Ahhh, but we shovelled an' chopped all night. Shovel an' chop, shovel an' chop, no rest, no food nor a drop oh drink passed me lips. Tons of ice I shovelled over the side Nipper, so I did, tons of it." The effort of telling the story drained him. He slumped into the chair wheezing. A long drag on the cigarette followed before sucking noisily on some tea. Cookie took a deep breath then continued. "Come mornin' the storm had passed an' we were safe but a mate oh mine 'e went over the side that night an' another, well, 'e froze to the spot."

"Froze to the spot, how can a man freeze to the spot?" I queried and gulped.

Cookie's head fell forward in an agonizing nod. With his face pressed against the table, a distraught voice whispered, "Ah well now, 'e took a rest Nipper an' died on account 'e stood still too long." Glaring eyes flashed into mine, a large fleshy hand clasped into a fist and shook under my nose as he declared, "'Angin' on the riggin' so 'e was. Still standin' an' dead as a nit, so 'e was." Cookie took another break, sucked noisily at his tea then another long drag on his cigarette stub while I did the same. "We 'ad to use an axe to break 'im free," he hissed through clenched teeth and reached across to place a hand on my shoulder. The angry hiss turned into a hushed whispered conclusion. "An' you call this cold."

I couldn't answer because his story had chilled me to the bone. After falling asleep that night, my dreams were inundated with frozen corpses dangling from the rigging of old sailing ships. In the background a voice kept yelling "Festooned, festooned." I was glad to wake up in the morning, serve the captain his tea and return to the warmth of the galley.

We were a day from Southampton when the skipper called me to his cabin. The awful sensation prickling up and down my spine brought back memories of being summoned to the headmaster's office. Something had to be wrong. I wondered if he had forgotten the problems we encountered at the beginning of the voyage. The journey down that corridor to his cabin was the longest I'd ever taken.

The captain stood in a classical stance with both hands clasped firmly behind his back looking out a forward porthole. A long silence elapsed before he finally spoke. "How old are you son?" It doesn't take a genius to know, captains do not ask that sort of questions unless they already knew the answer. Somehow, the truth about me had leaked out and the game was up.

"We had a call from the harbour authorities. It appears you are under age and unfortunately I will have to let you go."

"Aye Captain," I said softly.

"Son, we had a bumpy start but you've proved your salt." He held a hand out to his under-aged, shortest term ever served crew member. "When you are old enough and still of a mind to, let me know, I'll be happy to have you aboard."

We shook hands. Tears began welling up as I hurriedly went down that damn corridor to the cabin to lie on my bunk where the tears were allowed to flow. I banged on the bulkhead and cursed the person who betrayed me. My mind focused on those who knew my whereabouts. The first thought was of Billy going to see mother and informing her where I was. On the other hand, perhaps Uncle told her for some reason. I realized that Bill would not have returned from his overseas trip yet. Therefore, there remained no option but to conclude it must have been Uncle. A knock on the door brought me out of some vengeful thoughts.

Cookie came in. "I 'eard matey, Captain just told me." He rested a hand on my shoulder and could see I'd been crying. "I thought you might be a bit young when we first met and figured maybe it was me getting old."

"Like you said that day Cookie, you are old."

"I understand why you'd want to join the Merch but 'ow did you manage it?"

"Manage what?"

"How did you manage to wangle yur way into the Merch?"

What a question. My eyebrows shot up, since the answer seemed so obvious. "I lied."

"You lied."

"Yeah, I lied."

Cookie's eyes rolled back as he started laughing. It quickly resorted into a snorting hysterical choke as he screamed, "He lied, he lied," while sinking slowly to the floor.

Seeing my friend putting on such a performance made it impossible to remain in the depths of self-pity. I shouted at him to get up because he was acting like a big kid.

"A big kid," the man on the floor said while pointing at me. He took a long deep snorting breath, and then screamed before bursting into hysterical laughter again. A few moments later, the fit of amusement being suffered by my friend became contagious. It took hold of me until we were both shaking from it.

That night in the galley after everyone had been fed, Cookie told me about his dreams and how one day he would be cook on the Queen Mary. I honestly felt he wasn't the sort. His lifestyle was as a cook aboard the Tioga, which would always be his type of ship. He knew it, but everyone must have a dream. Next morning after docking at Southampton and while the mooring lines were being secured, Cookie and I had our last meal together. After eating he looked across the table and said, "Captain says they be waitin' fur 'ee on the dock. Be time to go."

"If I'm going to be handed over to the police I want you to do it, no one else."

My friend was taken aback by the demand. He started shaking his head and mumbling almost incoherently, "I ain't handin' no mate oh mine over to the police," and looked sideways at me with the double part of his chin disappearing as he held his head high in a defiant gesture. "'Twouldn't be proper an' you 'as no right to ask."

The stubborn streak inside me rose to the surface when I said, "You don't, I'll make a run for it. I'm not being handed over unless a friend does it. We are friends, aren't we Cookie?" Our eyes became locked in silent combat.

The big ugly coot sat there for a minute contemplating the issue, but my eyes remained firmly on Cookie's when he spoke. "Be a fine thing for a shipmate to demand." The insubordinate posture crumbled like a digestive biscuit in hot tea. He stood up and came round to my side of the table. "If'n they be waitin' fur 'ee an if'n I be doin' this deed, then let it be done." Cookie strode out of the galley with his head held high.

I followed my friend down the gangplank with a kitbag over my shoulder to face the police escort. Cookie raised himself to his full height and so did I because neither of us had done anything to be ashamed of.

A large black Wolseley without markings, a siren or lights attached stood behind the police sergeant and constable. They were standing at ease in white shirts and black trousers with peak caps shading the eyes scrutinizing me. An attempt at creating a new life for myself had caused them a considerable amount of trouble, apart from costing everyone involved a significant amount of concern. So the sergeant informed me.

"Have a good time did we?" the constable added.

That condescending remark irritated me into wishing I was about ten times bigger so the stupid man could be taught a lesson. However, size was not in my favour and I responded in the only way left. "Better than you'll ever have," I replied and dropped the kitbag on his foot.

Cookie's face took on a stone-like appearance, although his eyes never hid the despondency and sadness in them. They were reflecting the distinct look of despair. Those outlandish stories he told me were appreciated, so were the free cigarettes and defensive moves on my behalf. The patience in teaching me, supporting my attempts to overcome any failings couldn't be measured. We had become close, yet our new friendship was being cut adrift. It would have been alright for me to cry, since that's what boys did. But with the whole crew watching, Cookie couldn't show any emotion.

"I got nothing to give 'ee mate," he said as we shook hands.

"You've given me more than anyone else could," I responded.

"Well at least have a fag on me," my big friend muttered as a crumpled half packet of cigarettes was stuffed into my Merchant Navy seaman's blouse breast pocket. A wave to the watching crew raised one or two fingers in response. I turned and walked away with enough pride left not to allow the crew to witness my falling tears. At that moment I had every intention of returning to the sea. However, the circumstances in my life remained in constant change and my objective of returning to the Merchant Navy never materialized.

As the police car sped along the road toward home, memories brought a smile to my face while pulling out one of Cookie's cigarettes. I popped it into my mouth and lit it.

"You can't smoke in the car, besides you're too young," the sergeant said.

I nipped it out and tucked it behind my ear feeling it would be an awfully long trip home. We stopped for a cup of tea, which gave me a chance to light up under the disapproving looks from my escort. I felt certain they would be the type of adults who were conditioned to disapprove of anything and everything. They were narrow-minded with tunnel vision and no spirit. Their life's ambition never deviated from what they'd been trained for, which was, restrain anyone different to them and their way.

Mother performed in her usual hysterical way, while Uncle had a hard time looking me in the eye. That fact alone provided enough evidence, as if any were needed, it was him who betrayed me. After two nights, we were finally alone and it was time for the inevitable confrontation.

"All traitors should be hung, drawn and quartered. That's what happens to them in the navy."

"You are too young to understand," Uncle replied.

"Traitor."

"I must live with your mother," he murmured.

"Traitor."

"She can make life very difficult for me, you must understand," he tried.

"Traitor," I persisted.

"What can I say, I very sorry." It was a pathetic attempt at appeasement.

"Traitor," I whispered in his ear while walking past. Cookie taught me that trick. You whisper an insult into your enemy's ear, it possesses an ability to sustain a long-lasting effect, and provides a deeper lasting impression than a shout.

The word quickly got around about my exploits at sea and the fact my career in the Merchant Navy had been cut short by police intervention. The supervisor at Starfield, Old Pigface, refused to have me back, claiming I had a disruptive influence on the other children. The long list of disruptions presented to the board must have been impressive because they complied with his request. There were some people in authority I could have spoken to about what really went on at that place but hells bells, why spoil a good thing for others. Destiny reasoned I should return to Corsham Secondary Modern. Being an escaped convict who served time at sea by telling lies to become a seaman before being recaptured elevated me to hero status among my peers. During that euphoric period, almost anything I asked for was given to me. Boys thought my escape was on a par with the man from Alcatraz. Girls wanted me to kiss them because, that's what girls wanted from criminals.

During my absence, John had been made a school prefect, also known as a monitor. That was a big deal for him and he wore his polished, almost flat badge with pride. He took the responsibilities of his uplift in status very seriously. However, for what appeared no better reason other than my return, the headmaster took John's prefect badge away. The head never even gave me the chance to influence John's behaviour. As far as anyone could tell, it was nothing less than vindictive speculation or a pre-emptive knee-jerk reaction to something that might happen. Whatever influences those teachers were able to apply on John was lost in that one unnecessary move.

John blamed me but it only took him a couple of days to realize it had nothing to do with me because I hadn't done anything wrong – yet! Nonetheless, John's rebellious stage blossomed at that point and it took far less persuading in getting him to come fishing, swimming or hunting.

The call of the forest was getting stronger and there was little if anything that could be done about it. Uncle and I were not on speaking terms but the ice was broken by mother when she dished up the morning breakfast – porridge! The glutinous cement-like mass landed on the plates with a distinct thud. Uncle and I stared at the solid pile of nutrition. We were left contemplating which would be the most appropriate weapon to attack it with. Uncle's face was a picture as mother stood over him with a pot in one hand ready to dish up second helpings before we cleared the plates.

"Eat up boys, there's plenty more," she said happily.

"I've had enough mum, but keep some for Uncle, he's not working this week and will be home for lunch." Indigestion for breakfast and lunch with a very strong possibility for dinner as well. That should teach him to betray me. He looked into my eyes pleading for mercy. I started to laugh. A few seconds later, Uncle followed suit. Mother joined in, although I felt certain she had absolutely no idea what we were all laughing about.

After the breakfast incident things between Uncle and I returned to normal in a very short space of time.

Chapter Fourteen

The Gun

Uncle was the only person able to understand. Perhaps he saw a reflection of himself in me when he was a boy. We almost always got on well and had even been seen going hunting together, although I preferred being alone during those trips to the forest.

After my enforced return from the sea there remained an untamed spirit of adventure dominating my heart. This feeling was constantly on the lookout to satisfy that lust, despite most of my hunting gear being confiscated again. I remained sitting and fostering a deep depression that settled in my brain when something occurred to me. The perception of something one looks at is almost entirely dependent on one's position or outlook. How could anything be determined one way or the other? The small bore shotgun was considered by the authorities as a lethal weapon. However, the bow and arrows still hanging on my bedroom wall were not considered dangerous enough for removal. From any point of view, a very odd system of reasoning must have been ruling the human race. Perhaps the ruling party considered those arrows were not dangerous because they were homemade, quite clearly, they'd never seen them in action. Some had been designed with very elaborate hunting heads and as such were positively lethal. I spent many hours practicing to become a very capable archer when using that device for hunting.

Uncle recognized my gloom and sensed the desperate feeling of being trapped and invited me to sit with him one evening. "We are having time for some talk, a little drink and a smoke eh," he said.

We began discussing what could be done to remedy the situation. Uncle had recovered the small bore shotgun, which I used many times and whilst it may have been reasonable, it never made an effective long-range weapon. The conversation continued while another glass of homemade spirit helped to deaden my lips, tongue and finger tips until Uncle waved a finger as he spoke. "You know, I hear a farmer he die." That short statement gave Uncle my undivided attention for as long as he needed it, particularly when he added, "This man, he maybe have plenty guns und I am hearing his vife she sell them."

My attention became avid. "So where does she live Uncle?"

"That I not know," he replied and shrugged before adding, "but am finding out from vork in the morning eh." He looked at me across the table and began rolling a cigarette.

I said nothing until Uncle had the makings in his mouth and alight. Smoke streamed from his nostrils as I reached for the tin knowing how best to look cool under such circumstances, although it never fooled Uncle. The long silence finally broke with me asking if he was thinking of buying one of those guns. Without looking up, I lit my own cigarette, took a long casual drag and waited for a reply.

"Yes maybe this will be good, and maybe it will not be so good. First we must look and see."

That "we" in the sentence picked up my heart rate. Curiosity centred on finding out where the woman lived and when "we" would be paying her a visit. I leaned forward to pour another two glasses of Uncle's potent brew but said nothing. He was a man of few words who gave them when they were ready to come out. The second glass was followed by a third before Uncle finally decided to break the silence. He looked at me and said, "I shink maybe ve goink her to sheeing tomorrow eh."

"Yes, that sounds okay Uncle, anything you shay," I said. My glass was raised to touch his fourth before taking a drink. That home-brewed spirit never took long to affect Uncle's speech, which did not surprise me. My own tongue and lips were being numbed by the effect and it required concentration to deliver a simple sentence without slurring.

I found it difficult to sleep during the night and by morning remained in bed listening to Uncle preparing for work. It would be a long wait until his return from Smith and Lacy, the builders' yard in town. That company was responsible for building a considerable number of the houses in Corsham and more than a few in Chippenham. It wouldn't surprise me if that firm had assisted Noah to build the ark; they'd been around long enough. Later that afternoon while taking Lassie for a walk, I spent some time talking to her the way dog owners do when they're alone with their pet. Any number of secrets can be revealed in the certainty they will never be heard by anyone else. After lunch I settled in my room to wait and read the latest book I managed to "find". It was Lady Chatterley's Lover. From what I managed to find out about it, the one in my possession was the unedited version. Publication of the original had been banned for several years as sexually offensive and immoral. Without having the other copies to compare, there's nothing I can say about them. On the other hand, the one that held me fascinated for hours helped pass the time. Man oh man, that gamekeeper certainly got up to some naughties with her ladyship. Chasing her through the woods and planting forget-me-nots in her pubic hair certainly got my imagination working overtime. Mind you, she never resisted or refused him either. That book was kept in my own secret place, despite knowing mother and Uncle were illiterate when it came to reading or writing.

When Uncle eventually returned he seemed more interested in a cup of tea than telling me what he managed to find out about the guns and their whereabouts. Pestering him with the same question over and over again made no difference. He just kept giving the same answer. "Ve are going in a minute." His attempt at stopping my harassment and keeping quiet while he finished his cup of tea, did not work. My questioning persisted until I was relieved to hear him say we would be leaving in a few minutes. I went to my bedroom to retrieve a jacket before waiting by the motorbike.

The still warm Norton Dominator's big engine restarted with a single kick. I climbed on behind Uncle. The bike accelerated away for the farmhouse no more than a few minutes' drive down the road. Uncle steered the bike down a lane to a big house set among a group of enormous English oaks and Spanish chestnuts.

The large solid looking building had dogs in residence and they came charging out barking a welcome.

We dismounted and I fondled the dogs behind their ears while Uncle knocked on the door. A solid brass knocker boomed through an empty hall. A short time later the door swung open and an old woman peered out. The smile on her face told us we were welcome and when she asked, "Can I help you?" it confirmed it.

"Lady," Uncle began, "we come because we hear that maybe you are having a gun for sale." He hesitated for a second, and then remembered his manners. "My name is William Klosko, this is my friend Paul." Our introduction included a short respectful bow without a click of the heels.

"Well," the old woman responded softly, "you two better come in so we can talk." She stepped aside and beckoned us to enter. Her accent carried a soft cultured tone and when passing her, she also smelled good and the instincts inside me felt secure enough to make up my mind to like her. Uncle and I were shown into the dining room where its size and structure would leave a permanent impression on my mind. In fact, the whole house had a solid feel about it. There was a cool atmosphere with soft natural lighting. The room, we were led into, had a huge table in the centre with half a dozen matching chairs surrounding it. Apart from a couple of large leather armchairs in front of the fireplace, the big polished table held pride of place.

We intruders on that peaceful domain sat facing each other at one end of the table while our hostess excused herself to fetch some refreshments. Uncle and I sat in silence soaking up the rare ambience of the room. Low ceilings with heavy wooden beams were impressive but there was timber everywhere. The table itself must have weighed more than a ton and across the fireplace was a huge beam that represented the mantel.

Big flat, shiny from wear flagstones represented the floor with their only covering being an old woollen rug between the two leather armchairs. The whole room contained a softness about it, despite being made of solid wood and stone. Uncle also became aware of the atmosphere. He looked impressed and it showed in his eyes and on his face. The moment I got up to walk around, the sound of footsteps coming toward the room stopped me.

Our hostess came in carrying a tray with an elegantly shaped ornate teapot, three fine bone china cups and saucers plus an enormous fruit cake. That was something I might get a chance to eat once a year at Christmas. And yet here we were about to be served some for afternoon tea.

"Would you like milk and sugar, William?" the old lady asked.

I looked about for this William before realising it was Uncle when he answered in a very polite voice, "Oh yes please, Lady."

The name William struck me as funny and I immediately began thinking of ways it could be used to get at my companion in some way. I watched closely as our hostess' long bony fingers clasped the teapot handle and poured hot golden liquid into the first cup. When it had been filled, she held a small silver spoon over the sugar bowl and said, "One or two?"

"Ah yes, two please, Lady."

"There you are, William, how is that?" she asked, holding out the cup to him.

"That is very good, Lady," he responded while peering at the contents. He put on his best smile before stirring the brew. The sound of silver tinkling against fine bone china made a perfect accompaniment to our surroundings.

The old woman's eyes turned to meet mine for the first time. They were clear blue and sparkled with life. I looked back holding my ground. Her face creased into a smile. "How do you like your tea, Paul?"

"Same," I heard myself say and watched her pour, put two spoonfuls of sugar into the cup, add a little milk then hand over the cup and saucer.

"There you are, young man."

"Thanks." I could not think of anything else and started stirring the tea before taking a sip, to discover it was the best tea I ever tasted.

The woman proceeded to cut the cake to release a fresh aroma of fruit that flared up my nostrils and made my mouth salivate.

She must have seen the size of my eyes and took it for granted that a question like "Would you like some?" would be silly.

A large lump of heaven landed on a small plate in front of me. I wasted no time delivering it to my mouth, which was opened as wide as it could to accommodate that slab of joy. My eyes closed in anticipation of the flavours about to infiltrate millions of taste buds – they were not disappointed. Real cherries, real fruit and nuts held together in a rich cement of paradise. Uncle and our hostess were watching me when my eyes opened.

"You like eh," Uncle said.

The only reply available was to refill my mouth while nodding, after all, it's rude to talk with your mouth full. Meantime, the oldies sipped their tea while making small talk about the weather before the old lady started reminiscing about how long she'd lived in the house with her former husband. I saw a tear welling up in her eye.

Uncle quickly changed the subject to where he came from. "I from Poland, come to England from war," he said with inflated pride.

"I had a son in the war," she responded in a desperately sad voice. "He was a lot like you, very similar and would have been about your age by now."

That was an idiotic subject to open up on. Once the oldies started talking about wars and who they lost in them, it could go on for hours. I recalled my father constantly harking on about it with other old soldiers. How brave they'd been and if it hadn't been for them at this or that battle, we would all be speaking German by now. Needless to say, father and his mates managed to defeat the Germans all on their own. From what I read about it, the weather had as much to do with defeating them as anything else. That aspect of warfare was controlled by God who, so it's been claimed, was on our side. As for the Americans, well no one mentioned either their efforts or those of the Russians who actually blunted the German advance.

"I fight the Germans," Uncle declared inflating his chest. However, his boast can only be described as being somewhat liberal with the truth because we both knew he had been con-

Nights in the Forest

scripted into the German army. The only fight he put up was the one to get out of the army. Credit where credit is due, he did manage that but only by surrendering at the earliest opportunity. Nevertheless, I supported Uncle in getting the subject round to guns. My mind screamed at him to divert the subject onto the reason for our visit but my efforts were not doing any good. None of my telepathic messages were getting through.

"My son fought them too but he never came back. They buried him in France," the old woman said quietly in response to Uncle's puffed-up pride.

He was struck dumb for a few moments before reaching out to reverently hold her hand and whispered, "I very sorry, Lady."

The kind of talk they were embarking on belonged to grown-ups and tragic love stories in women's magazines. Whilst it may have been interesting to them, the subject was somewhat removed from what we came to discuss. I had to get their attention away from talking about the war. "Did your husband have a gun?" I blurted out. The question may have been delivered too loudly for the sombre circumstances because both adults turned to look at me. The old woman looked at me in an inquisitive way, Uncle with a hostile glare. Maybe I had broken some sort of unwritten code or perhaps it was true that children should be seen and not heard. However, their conversation was beginning to bore me to the point of getting impatient.

"He had a lot of guns," the old lady said gently.

That woman seemed to understand but the sound of the past tense being used had me worried. Maybe we were too late. Perhaps the dream was destined to die before it had a chance of being born. The real question and purpose of our visit remained on my tongue but the look in Uncle's eye told me to back off.

"Can I have another piece of cake?" I asked, feeling like Oliver Twist requesting more. In his case, the corresponding remark was an exclaimed "More!" but not so in my case.

"Well of course you can," a gentle voice said and the woman quickly pushed a plate full of cut pieces across the table. "Please, help yourself to as much as you like. I always bake far too much and it's good to see a young man with a healthy appetite." She turned back to Uncle who quickly removed his hand from hers.

I continued watching them while eating that deliciously rich dark brown cake in silence and picked up the crumbs and real cherries that fell onto the plate. Those that didn't fall out of their sugar-coated burial ground were enticed into doing so by my finger when nobody was looking. The grey-haired lady carried on talking to Uncle about how the table served as the gathering point for the family. They always met round it for Christmas, weddings, christenings, celebrations, and how it had always been a happy room. I could understand what she was saying during that deep personal conversation. She did most of the talking while her listener obliged with an occasional nod or an "Oh yes, Lady," to indicate his ears were open.

During their chitchat I slid off the chair and moved away toward the far side of the table where a Carver chair stood, on which the arms were leather bound. It looked like a throne and most probably was in its own way. I ran fingers along soft-to-the-touch leather and looked down the table. Facing me was a small silver-framed photograph of a man. I reached out and caught the reflection of my outstretched hand on the polished surface as the picture was pulled toward me. The round rugged face had a ruddy complexion. A full set of teeth grinned while they clenched a briar pipe but it was his eyes that caught my attention. They were still alive, quite obviously, it was the farmer who died recently. I could tell right away that whatever hardships that man faced, he overcame them with strength from within. The eyes glinted.

"Put that down boy," Uncle said in a stern voice.

"It's okay, bring it here, will you Paul," the lady said. The picture was handed over and she showed it to Uncle.

"He was a fine looking man," Uncle said in a flattering tone before adding, "A real gentleman. Yes?"

The subject of the gun had slipped away. My instincts told me something must be done about it and the best thing I could think of was to blurt out, "I'll bet he went hunting a lot. There must be lots and lots of rabbits and pigeons around here."

"Oh yes, he loved to go shooting," she said lovingly before redirecting her eyes back to Uncle. "Do you go out shooting much, William?"

My mind started racing with, "Go on Uncle, now's the time to tell her you can't because you don't have a gun," as hard as I tried but those telepathic thoughts did not transpose themselves to Uncle's mind. He immediately started going on about his days in Poland as a young boy. Since my telepathy obviously did not work, it was time to leave them alone and take a walk round the room.

I studied the windowsills and the thickness of the walls. The place had been built to last several lifetimes with a huge fireplace at one end. One could almost put a full-sized tree in it. I walked into the opening and looked up the chimney. From a small person's point of view, it looked very impressive. The big Chesterfield leather armchairs on either side of the fireplace were inviting me to try one. Glancing across the room, I saw the Lady and Uncle in close conversation and seemingly oblivious to my whereabouts. I sank into one of those welcoming leather armchairs. The padding was still firm, although the seat area had given way just a little; the gorgeous aroma remained. It seemed strange that the pleasant pungent tang of leather was still obvious after so many years.

I stroked the arm feeling its strong soft texture. A worn patch demonstrated a different colour where my hand rested and where many hands had been before. I looked at the mantelpiece above me where a pipe stand filled with old pipes stood. Among the row was a mottled well used briar. There was no mistaking it as same one in the photograph.

I imagined the farmer sitting in the chair on a cold winter evening, full to the brim with delicious fruit cake. He would have a contented smile on his face and having a smoke in front of a roaring fire. The fragrant smell of pipe tobacco still hung in the air, the farmer's presence lingered. However, it was a friendly aura and not in the least intimidating. I half-expected the man to walk in, sit down with a relieved sigh in the Chesterfield opposite and light up his pipe. The thought made me feel like a cigarette.

I got up and returned to the table where I was pleased to hear the old lady asking Uncle who the gun was for.

"It is for me, Lady," Uncle replied shyly.

It would have been quite obvious to anyone seeing the colour of his face, that answer was an out and out lie. Uncle was quite good at telling lies but had to be half drunk to manage it comfortably without blushing. It also made a great deal of difference if the person asking him questions was in uniform. Under our current circumstances, the lovely lady was gentle in her manner, very eloquent in her speech and within salubrious surroundings. She had a huge advantage over him.

The old widow turned to face me standing next to her. Our eyes locked into each other's once more. Those eyes peering at me were as sharp and bright as diamonds. If superman had X-ray vision, his eyes never compared with the old woman's, who could read thoughts. I barely heard her say, "For you, is it?" One could tell she was confirming Uncle's lie and letting me know that she may have been old but still retained the use of her facilities or intuition. The old lady knew who the gun was really for.

Uncle cottoned on quickly and managed to retrieve a portion of self-respect by saying, "Oh yes Lady, for me but to teach the boy how to shoot also." His intervention at that point sounded like a good one.

"He is much too young to learn about guns," our hostess responded while maintaining eyeball to eyeball with me.

My thoughts began racing at that objection, and although I retained my stance with her, I found it increasingly difficult to maintain any resistance to that woman's overpowering eye contact.

"It is better to learn early how you must use a gun, don't you think, Lady?"

Mentally, I applauded Uncle for such a tactful verbal move. It seemed as though he had turned it around. Fortunately, our hostess' eye contact with me broke as she turned to face Uncle. I confess to breathing a sigh of relief.

Nights in the Forest

"You may be right but I do not like guns. They killed my son you know." Although beating Uncle down with cold eyes, her voice turned into a cutting edge.

My heart sank into my shoes with a mind unable to get away from the thought of "here comes another long war story". However, Uncle managed to avoid it by first agreeing with the old lady and then suggesting that her man, Mister Henry, must have liked to go shooting.

The lady remained silently facing him. A tense moment passed until her stern uncompromising face creased into an open smile. The glint in her eye turned to a sparkle. Just the mention of Henry put the light back into her life. "Oh my, yes, he did love his shooting," she sighed. At that, the lady of the house stood and walked toward the door.

Uncle and I watched her slender figure disappear. We continued waiting in silence for a few moments then looked at each other. Uncle shrugged his shoulders and lifted his eyebrows. From where I sat there didn't seem to be anything better than having another piece of cake while waiting. Several minutes went by as we sat staring at the walls. I licked my fingers but curiosity was driving me crazy. Playing it cool sounds easy but take it from someone who knows, it isn't. I reached forward and picked up the picture of farmer Henry to study the face. It looked as though he was grinning at me, which was more or less exactly what I expected from him.

The sound of footsteps clipping smartly over stone prompted me to replace the picture. From that moment I've never been sure if Henry didn't wink or if it was a trick of the light playing across the glass. I blinked before turning to see the old lady walking toward us while ceremoniously holding the gun out at arm's length. Even from my position I could see it was a big one. Uncle stood to take it from her hands.

"It is a very fine gun, Lady," he said with a reverent quiver in his voice. I hoped he would remember who we'd come to get the gun for.

"It was Henry's favourite. He used to take it with him all the time," she replied with a faraway look in her eyes. The woman paused to look at the picture of her late husband on the table before continuing. "I thought all the guns had been disposed of but found this one was in the tool shed where he used to hide for some peace and quiet."

A long silence followed while we held a minute silence. I looked at the frail, lovely and terribly lonely woman. She looked remarkably elegant in a long cotton flowery dress with a fine leather belt tied around the middle. Even the delicate silver buckle seemed perfectly fastened around her slim waist. The tall grey-haired woman made no secret of the fact that she was still very much in love with Henry and desperately missed her man. She picked up the picture and held it close.

Uncle broke the silence with a whispered question. "How much do you want for the gun, Lady?"

"What!" she exclaimed. Then snapped out of her daydream and concluded with, "Oh no, no. I don't want anything for it." The frail-looking woman held Uncle's gaze until he looked down. With that final victory accomplished, she turned and walked away leaving us to find our own way out.

We were roaring along the open road before my pent-up emotions erupted with a loud "Yahoo!" Uncle responded by dropping down a gear and opened up the throttle. He had his own way of shouting yahoo.

After reaching home we took a really good look at the newly acquired shotgun. Uncle got his tape measure to find out exactly how long it was. When standing beside it, I could just see over the barrel on tiptoe. The Webley and Scott single barrel twelve gauge had a thirty-six inch full choke barrel with the butt containing balancing weights inside. It possessed a self-ejecting mechanism and was hammerless. In my eyes nothing could compare to its beauty.

"Ve try her out ven I coming home from vork eh."

"Yes," I said.

The old lady never had any shotgun cartridges for it, so Uncle decided to buy some. The differences between a small bore shotgun and the twelve gauge were worlds apart. That night the gun was cleaned till it shone like new before it came to bed with me. Early next morning while Uncle was preparing for work, I reminded him about buying some shells for the gun. "You won't forget the ammo, will you," I whispered.

"You must go to school or I am to you not giving them," Uncle replied.

I stepped back in horror. Uncle was resorting to emotional blackmail. That was a new aspect in our relationship and not like him at all. It made me wonder why he should care if I went to school or not. What if it happened to be a nice sunny day, did he expect me to sit in a boring classroom? Obviously the time had come to reason with him. "What difference will one day make?" I pleaded.

"You must go to school, not trying for tricking me," he said with an index finger waving at me. The lenses in his steel-rimmed glasses made his crossed eyes looked twice as big. "When I am home coming I vill knowing if you lie to me, eh, eh. Your mother wants you at school, so you go. Okay!"

It became clear as crystal. Mother had Uncle by the short and curlies. He had to do whatever she wanted. If he refused to comply, whatever conjugal rights he had would be retracted. There was nothing new in that part of their relationship. It worked on more than one occasion. There was no alternative but to agree with some reluctance. "All right then Uncle, I'll go to school for all the good it will do."

With a roar of the engine and a wave, he disappeared round the corner. I remained true to my word and went to school. For all the good it did, I may as well have stayed in bed or gone fishing. My body may have been in the classroom but my mind was elsewhere in the forest hunting with my new gun. By lunch time I had enough. There was no point in staying so headed home.

"You're home early, dear," mother said on my entry into the kitchen.

"Yeah, we had a half day today," I lied casually.

Mother had a hard time finding bad in anyone and would believe just about anything. My guilty feelings at having told mother a white lie were suppressed by anticipation and thoughts of hunting. In the confines of my bedroom I practiced pulling the gun to my shoulder with Lassie as my only audience. She wagged her bald tail every time I shouted, "Bang!" Over and over again, flying pheasants, pigeons and rabbits were given a lead with what I considered their speed and distance to be. The afternoon's practice went much quicker than anticipated and at five thirty I waited impatiently at the garden gate, despite knowing Uncle would be late. Although he normally got home just after five, he would have gone into Chippenham to buy those shells. Waiting for his return became harder by the minute.

Mother had tea ready at the usual time but my appetite no longer existed. Apart from which mother's cooking promoted a suppressed desire to eat. Anyone wanting to lose weight only had to live with us for a while. Not that there wasn't any food available, mother just had the uncanny knack of producing inedible food from perfect ingredients.

Eternal vigilance was eventually rewarded by the sound of a big motorbike approaching the bend. It pulled me out of my daydream. A blip on the throttle signed Uncle's signature. The expectation we would at least be trying the gun today made my spirits soar. Uncle parked the bike and took his own sweet time about it. A few minutes later, we were sitting at the table before he decided to tell me he purchased some shells for the gun. An orange-coloured box was placed carefully on the table. I reached to pick the box up. Uncle pulled it away and demanded to know what I'd learned at school. He obviously wanted to test me with a few questions. I was ready for him. My time in the Wolf Cubs held me in good stead. Be prepared, they said. Without hesitation, I responded immediately with, "Ten sixty-six and the battle of Hastings."

"Ha!" Uncle exclaimed and waved my answer aside with a casual wave of his hand before adding, "Every von is knowing about ten sixty-six und battle for Hastings."

"Well, what do you want to know about it? Go on, ask me any question you like," I challenged. Most people probably knew, the battle took place in ten sixty-six but not much else.

Uncle stuffed his mouth full of indescribable food to give himself time to think. He washed it down with a gulp of tea that made his eyes water. After taking a deep breath, he removed his glasses and blinked. The sight made me wonder if the hot tea or the lump of food making its way past his gullet on its way toward his unfortunate stomach caused that reaction. With the food he ate and homemade spirit he drank, there were no doubts he would end up with ulcers. Uncle blinked away the tears in his eyes before asking me, "Who won?"

"The Normans," I answered quickly. Although anyone could see, had I said the American Indians, Uncle would still have nodded.

"Okay, that good," he said while spearing another lump of something on his plate. He stared at it with the curiosity of a cross-eyed cat. He rolled the fork. It gave an alternative angle to view it from but there were no revelations in what it might be. His brow wrinkled. Something to do with hunger pangs decided for him. With a casual shrug and quiet whimper, both eyes closed, his mouth opened wide. The unknown morsel disappeared.

"They beat the Britons who were on top of a hill," I continued in an attempt to press home my advantage. It was, after all, something that he taught me by saying things like "always pursue an advantage; if you have to fight make sure you make your punches the best you have; do whatever is necessary; the end justifies the means" and other awe-inspiring words of wisdom.

"Yes, yes, okay," Uncle mumbled through a mouthful of unknown food. His jaw worked in double time as he waved me to stop the anticipated volume of useless information being imparted on him.

The signal was ignored, I continued with the dialogue in a raised voice. "King Harold was the English king. He was the king of England."

A loud gulping sounded. A distraught Adam's apple bobbed. Another gasp of air was followed by, "Yes, yes, I am knowing zis." Watery eyes focused on another morsel of food disguised with lumpy gravy on the end of a fork. He hesitated, his mouth opened as his eyes closed. A half-expected "God have mercy on my soul" never came.

From where I sat Uncle could have been saying his prayers although, even if he had, it would not have prevented pressing home my advantage. "He was killed in the battle, did you know that?" I asked in an excited voice.

Another hurried gulp sounded. Then a "Yes!" exclaimed in an irritated tone. He preferred to finish eating before talking. Another forkful of indescribable food had already been speared before that too disappeared into an open mouth. A drop of brown gravy dripped onto his shirt. His eyes opened and bulged as he swallowed hard. There was a race on to get the agony over as soon as possible.

"Shot in the eye with an arrow!" I exclaimed with enthusiasm rapidly developing in my voice as I pointed at Uncle's right eye. Had my finger prodded any closer, Uncle would have been in the same condition as poor Harold. In true Norman fashion, I pressed home my advantage by repeating, "In the right eye, right in the right eye. What a piece of bad luck. Right in the right eye, Uncle, what do you think of that, eh, eh? I can even tell you the time of day if you want."

Uncle shook his head while chomping frantically at the food but was unable to say anything until it was washed down with another gulping swallow of tea. I saw a tear welling up in his eyes before he answered. "Okay, okay, so you are in school going today, I am believing you."

"At three o'clock on March the tenth in ten sixty-six, the Norman archers peppered the English and got Harold in the eye. I'll bet you didn't know that, did you, eh, eh!" I felt certain neither Uncle nor anyone else knew about that fabricated piece of information.

"Yeah, yeah. Okay, zis is enough," he cried. They were the only English words that came out of his mouth at that point. The rest was some gibberish in Polish.

That was just as well because I almost ran out of any knowledge on ten sixty-six and all the stuff that went with it and was even prepared to providing further fictitious elements to the story no one had ever heard about. So, Harold lost, so what! I remained quiet and waited till Uncle put his mug of tea down before asking the only question on my mind. "When can we test the gun?"

Nights in the Forest

His inflated chest sank. He looked defeated and ready to surrender. "Soon as I am finishing eating boy, giving for me de chance," Uncle pleaded through a mouthful of food.

Mother put down a plate full of food in front of me. There was a temptation to ask what it was but thought her answer would spoil my surprise. I decided to wolf down whatever it was and leave the table while Uncle finished rolling a cigarette. I stood at the door cradling the gun in my arm and calling out, "Hurry up, we should go before it gets too dark."

We reached Top Wood at six thirty, which gave us about an hour before dark. Uncle pinned the first cardboard target on a tree before taking twenty-five paces from it then looked at me. "I am trying first, okay." As a matter of fact, I did not like that idea at all but it would have sounded childish to object, after all, Uncle found the gun and bought the cartridges. He'd even been willing to pay some money for the weapon. I nodded reluctantly before handing the gun over and stood back.

Uncle steadied himself while taking aim at the target. It seemed an awfully long time before an explosion of the first shot ripped through the woods and echoed across the fields. All the rooks took off from the surrounding countryside as the whole area erupted into life. We stood stock-still staring at each other.

"Holy cow!" I exclaimed.

"Tak, tak," Uncle added in agreement, ejected the empty cartridge and concluded with, "Now ve must going and see the target." He walked quickly to the cardboard on the tree to inspect it and saw the pattern of shot was very tight. It seemed reasonable to assume we could go further back and still put plenty of holes in the target.

A few minutes later, I stood at a distance further than ever when attempting to shoot at anything. The small bore shotgun and BSA air rifle were close-range weapons, not like the one in my hands. Uncle provided little help in lifting my confidence by saying things like, "be careful, hold it tight, mój Boże, it kicks like a donkey." I'd never been kicked by a donkey and was therefore unable to imagine a comparison.

"Hold it tight, keep both eyes open, line the barrel with the target and squeeze the trigger," were his final instructions. They were nothing more than I had been using with the other shotgun. The gun did kick, more like a full-sized horse than a mere donkey. The sensation that enveloped my entire body felt incredible. The power pounded through it with a single jolt. I took a deep breath, opened the breech and the empty shell ejected in a puff of beautiful aroma; gunsmoke filled my lungs. Excited fingers closed on another shell to drop into the open breech before the gun snapped shut. Man, it felt good.

After examination, the target still had a close pattern and what remained of the daylight was spent putting up fresh targets and moving further back. Uncle made me practice loading, bringing the gun up, pull the trigger and reloading with empty shells ten times before allowing me to fire the next live shot. By the time I fired that last shot, the target was barely visible in fading daylight. My shoulder felt like a solid bruise, my ears were ringing so loudly I barely heard Uncle say he'd seen enough. "It time ve go now," he said a few minutes after the last shot echoed through the trees. We collected the last target as proof of the gun's ability to maintain a close pattern at a distance before setting off for home. Both of us were very pleased with the results.

"You know boy, that a very powerful gun. It vill kill rabbit from von hundred metres, maybe more."

I nodded in agreement and knew it would be hard waiting to find out, but before that happened, someone would have to buy some more shells. Uncle refused, since, as he put it, he had done more than his fair share. That represented a problem I had not anticipated and immediately began thinking about who to approach for odd jobs that would bring in some money.

The significance of that weapon would make its presence known much later. The influence it had became the starting point in developing my growing-up stage. It became the controlling factor on my wild inclinations and started enforcing responsibilities from the first day I used it.

Chapter Fifteen

The Great Hare Shoot

Mother, Uncle, their mutual friend Victor Pilchard and I were sitting at the table eating dinner, discussing world events and putting them to rights. Victor, who happened to be my friend Kipper's father and had a very strong West Country accent, asked Uncle if he would like to go shooting with him. Vic was West Country through and through, Wiltshire born and bred with an accent needing a translator during conversations with those not familiar with it. The same could be said about Uncle's Polish accent. Any dialogue between them sounded like the United Nations without an interpreter.

"Be a faarm infestid we 'ares." (There is a farm infested with hares.) "It'd be farmer's wish we 'as te clen 'em out, does 'ee wana cum wiv I?" (It is the farmer's wish that we clean them out. Do you want to come with me?)

"Ya," Uncle replied, "Zis vould being goot but tomorrow is not so goot a day for me. It is to vork I may going." (Yes. That would be good but tomorrow is not good for me. I have to go to work.)

When thinking about it, there's little wonder I grew up with a confused state of mind. There was Vic communicating in a heavy Wiltshire accent requiring some concentration to make out what he said. Uncle would reply in a heavy Polish accent that few could understand. Whenever mother was drawn into the tête-à-tête, she slurred after one drink of Uncle's homemade spirit and had a hard time understanding herself, never mind what the men were saying. She answered or asked questions in Maltese sometimes, which always prompted Uncle to start speaking in Polish. On such occasions confusion reigned while everyone remained happily talking at the same time. To top it all, none of the three could read or write yet they all had a wonderful time. Whenever any reading or writing needed to be performed, they looked to the only educated member of the family still at home.

"Arr well thaan, I be goin' on me own so I is. 'Tas gota be tumorrer fur sure." (Ah well then, I'll have to go on my own so I will. It's got to be tomorrow for sure.) End of translation lesson.

Uncle poured another drink all round. Mother had already consumed two glasses and looked at everyone through bleary eyes with a perpetual silly grin on her face. She was about to have a third but already had problems staying on the chair by beginning to slide off it. The silly grin widened while a slurred muttering in her native tongue sounding like "Wahda, tnejn, tlieta" blurted out. (I think that's Maltese for one, two, three.) The glass was raised and before anyone could stop her, the contents were emptied down her throat in one swallow and the glass replaced unsteadily on the table.

"I'll go with you Vic," I piped up. It was a golden opportunity for Vic to fulfil an earlier promise and I had no intentions of missing it without making a point of trying.

"You must going to school," Uncle interrupted in an attempt to spoil it for me.

I swung round to mother on the edge of her seat but much closer to the edge of oblivion. "Mum can I go hunting with Vic in the morning?" I asked in a loud voice just before she slipped off her chair.

"Oh cosh ya can shon, why notch," she slurred thereby negating Uncle's objection. They were the last words mother uttered before she went totally limp and passed out. I often heard the expression "drinking someone under the table", but never witnessed it before. Victor and Uncle put her to bed. After a few minutes they returned to the table and resumed the discussion.

"I knows 'e cun shoot but do 'e 'ave a gun?"

"Of course he can shoot," Uncle said coming to the aid of his protégée with a thumb pointed at an inflated chest as though it was enough in anyone's language. He leaned across the table whispering, "I am teaching him myself, an' sink he maybe good like me." He turned and winked at my approving face.

Nights in the Forest

Vic looked at me then back at Uncle. "Arr, but do 'e 'ave a proper gun?"

"Go fetch gun boy," Uncle instructed while maintaining eye contact with Vic.

I rushed out the room to fetch the newly acquired weapon. Up till that moment it had remained a closely guarded secret. We felt it unnecessary to let Vic or anyone else know about it. I came back into the kitchen and handed the gun to Vic.

"By the 'eck!" he exclaimed. In Wiltshire, that expression refers to being just about as impressed as one got. "By gum lad, 'tis a big un fur sure." Victor's solemn statement was announced while handling the gun with loving care.

"The range she is goot too," Uncle said before adding enthusiastically, "I have seen boy shooting von rabbit from more zan von hundred metres."

"An 'undred?" Vic queried.

"Maybe more," Uncle assured Victor before taking another sip of potent brew.

Meantime, a rapid search of my memory banks ensued in an attempt to recall when we'd been shooting together. Or for that matter, when I last shot anything from one hundred metres. The difference between one hundred metres and one hundred yards was not that much. To be perfectly frank, the only conclusion drawn from that statement could not be anything less than a creative description of the truth. Also known in white man's language as a downright lie or as the American Indians say, he speak with forked tongue.

"Well," Vic continued, "hare shootin' be a two man job so 'tis. Mebe I'll give 'e a go." I became elated with numerous promises not to let him down. Victor smiled at my enthusiasm and looked me in the eye. "Be an urly start, afore daybreak."

"You no vorry, I get boy up und him ready even for ven you is going eh," Uncle assured him.

Victor nodded, and then drained his glass. A long moment of silence elapsed while Uncle refilled our glasses. "To zer hunt," he shouted.

"Bottoms up," I added raising my glass.

"Arr, an' up yours," Vic yelled as all three of us united in the toast. The firewater was downed before three glasses slammed onto the table.

That firewater came from a homemade still Uncle built using a gas bottle and set the whole thing up in the pigeon shed. Its output maintained an almost unlimited amount of pure alcohol for himself and a select number of trusted friends. The brew came from an old secret formula from Poland with the main ingredient being root vegetables, mostly potatoes, which were chopped up and mixed with yeast, sugar and lemons. The mash then fermented for a couple of weeks before being stilled off. Raw alcohol was then flavoured with any kind of fruit juice, according to the drinker's preference. I think the Irish country folk do the same thing. Their name for the brew is poitín. In the United States they called it moonshine or hooch during their period of prohibition. Attempts at enforcing the no alcohol legislation simply provided crooks with an opportunity to produce an illicit brew that everyone wanted. Uncle would have been in his heyday.

Consuming small amounts of the stuff was prone to opening up the mind to a whole new world that swayed for no apparent reason. It also made the lips go numb and the speech slur. The secret recipe from Poland had the amazing effect of giving the drinker an ability to provide a three-dimensional story, also known as exaggeration. It also contained a source of knowledge to answers that would cure every problem of the world.

I was incapable of matching neither Uncle's nor Victor's capacity and consumption rate so retired early and set the alarm for three thirty, since Vic promised to pick me up at four. It would take us about half an hour to get to the farm where we would prepare for the hunt before sunrise. The numbing effect of alcohol soon had me heading for the land of nod with the voices in the kitchen slowly fading into the distance.

My eyes opened just before the alarm went off. It was a strange phenomenon and something I never understood. Had the clock not been there, I may have slept on and been late but as long as the alarm had been set, I always woke just before it went off. I sat up in pitch darkness and drew back the curtains to see a clear starlit sky. There were no doubts in my mind it would be a marvellous day. I dressed quickly, went to the kitchen and put the kettle on, made some tea before packing some sandwiches into my hunting satchel. The gun was propped up in a corner and a new box of shells on the table with twenty-five high velocity number four shot also packed into the satchel.

Hares are apt to be good-sized animals that would take some stopping. Experience had shown number four shot carried well and had plenty of stopping power.

"Sum oh they 'ares be real big uns," Vic told me last night. Nonetheless, he felt sure a combination of number four high velocity shot travelling down a thirty-six inch barrel on full choke would do the trick. "That'll knock a bludy 'orse down so 'twil."

At four o'clock Uncle blundered into the kitchen and staggered toward the teapot and almost burned his hand. "You is already up!" he exclaimed softly.

"Yes, up and ready to go. Vic will be here any minute," I answered as he poured himself a cup of tea. We sat talking in whispers for a few minutes, drinking tea and having a morning cigarette until the sound of Vic's old van was heard outside. I made ready to leave. Uncle held me by the shoulder and looked me in the eye. "Remembering vat I am tell you und don't forgetting to bringing me home a nice big von, eh, eh." The tea and cigarette did nothing to mask the odour of alcohol drifting up my nostrils.

I threw the satchel over my shoulder then picked up the gun before turning to say, "Don't worry Uncle, if there are half as many hares out there as Vic claims we'll be shooting plenty. I promise we will have meat on the table for dinner tonight." With that declaration made, I headed for Victor who was pleased to see me and thankful he didn't have to wait as we climbed into the old Austin A40 van. I waved to Uncle as the vehicle shuddered on a slipping clutch before it accelerated away.

The old van had an extremely noisy engine, which made conversation very difficult and was probably the reason why Victor hardly said a word. The engine fumes, mixed with a leaking exhaust, coming through a hole in the floor, blended with the tobacco Vic and I were smoking. It necessitated leaving one of the windows open to prevent either of us from asphyxiating. The aromatic combination produced a smell sensation that buried itself into the recesses of my memory.

We arrived at the farm half an hour later after Vic negotiated the old van along the long potholed unsealed driveway. The vehicle came to a halt just as the farmer's wife emerged out of a ramshackle cow shed. "Be a good mornin' fur it boys," she said in a quiet cheery voice.

"Arr that it be and we 'as tu keep movin' 'tis gettin' light a'ready so 'tis," Vic responded. It was his way of avoiding a conversation he didn't want. Besides, he was right, the sky in the east had already become paler compared to the west. There were more important things to do than stand around chatting to a farmer's wife at four forty-five in the morning.

I retrieved the box of shells off the back seat and began pouring them into a pocket when Vic asked where my gun belt was. There wasn't much that could be said to that question but tell him that I never had one and just put any shells in my pocket. I held it open for Vic to peer into.

"There be a spare un in back oh van, bis cun use 'im if'n 'ee want," Vic responded as he began walking away and heading for open fields while I ducked into the van, found that cartridge belt and ran after him pulling it on and asking where we were going. He pointed his Browning Automatic shotgun at the purple shadow of a hill already visible against the onset of pre-dawn light and said, "They be on tuther side oh thaat 'ill."

I started pulling shells out of my pocket and pressing them into the gun belt as we continued walking at a brisk pace. "How are we going to do it?" I asked.

"Be a big field needs ploughin' an' that'll scatter 'em so we'em 'ere to clean 'em out affor it be too late," he replied as we pressed on. My question remained unanswered. A cool breeze suddenly announced the sun's imminent arrival. I looked over my shoulder to confirm dawn was about to break, which always happened quickly during summer.

Nights in the Forest

"You 'asta go up thar young un," Vic said when he stopped at a corner and pointed his gun in the direction he wanted me to go. "An' wait fur my signal. I be walkin' toward 'ee an' flush 'em out, be up to 'ee then." With his instructions on how we were going to do it given, he walked on toward his corner. Vic put a lot of faith in my abilities and it made me wonder what Uncle had told him when they were alone. I picked up my pace and my heart started beating harder. The important thing for me was to be in a good position before the sun came up. During the drive to the farm, I acquired a strong determination to put on a good show.

I continued up the hill, kept well back from the hedgerow and kept low, but moving quickly with my eyes constantly looking from left to right. A hare was spotted well within range but I disciplined myself to stay with the plan. Near the top corner of the field, a convenient gap appeared in the hedge. A tree filled most of the opening but it represented an ideal spot. I nestled close to the hedge with the gun loaded and ready. A wide expanse of a dark green hillside unfolded in front of me. The land dipped away to my left. As Vic suggested at the outset, it was a big field with numerous tufts of grass providing good hiding places for hares.

In the distance, Vic could be seen climbing over a gate. Once over, he stood still for several minutes and waited for enough daylight to shoot by. Within those few minutes the sun crested the horizon and cast long shadows of trees from one end of the field to the other. I spotted a movement well down the field but close to where Vic was standing and hoped he'd seen it. At least one hare had picked up the scent or sight of a human predator.

Vic raised his gun and waved it from side to side. That prompted me to stand up and expose myself but I wasn't sure if Vic could see me in the shadow. My gun was raised in acknowledgment before easing back into cover. The safety catch was moved to the "off" position with the softest click. I became a very willing partner in what could only be described as "the culling". My ability remained to be tested.

At the other end of the field, Victor set off at a slow deliberate walk and began zigzagging across the field to drive whatever hares were there toward me. In the meantime, I waited with a loaded gun and bated breath. My mind became full of Uncle's instructions with my own doubts about how good I really was. Being aware of having to judge the distance, in my mind I set up a field of fire that could be managed and no matter what the temptation, wouldn't shoot outside it.

In those few minutes of waiting, the area on the ground had been measured and fixed in my head. Anything coming inside it would be within range but it was also important not to shoot at anything too close. The pattern of shot with a full choke had proved to be very small from close range. I needed to give the target time to run a distance that would give the gun and me the best chance of making a kill.

Victor continued moving up the hill toward me. Suddenly, a hare bolted. Vic managed to dispatch it easily but the sound of the discharge had a startling effect. All the hares still under cover and hoping to be avoided changed their minds. All of them seemed to panic at the sound. They began scattering in every direction for safety and cover.

One animal had its head down and moved directly into my field of fire. The gun came to my shoulder, I held my breath, then allowed instinct and training to take over. The first boom, including the recoil and the visual sight of the hare tumbling head over heels as the impact of shot hit it, were the last things I clearly recall. Much of the following few minutes reverted into a blur of reload, aim, and fire in rapid succession, as hare after hare came into the killing range.

After the first nervous shot, a cool determination procured from disciplined training took over mind and body. It fixed itself to the job in hand and put me into automatic mode. One after the other they came, dozens of them running hither and thither in confused panic. The numbers, speed and the different directions they ran, made it difficult to select a target. However, once they were inside the killing area, I didn't miss.

Along with my own single shot rapid fire, Vic's automatic weapon pounded the early morning air. One would be hard pressed to blame the local populace within earshot for thinking a war had broken out. As Vic closed the distance between us, the panic among the animals became more frantic. They doubled back and forth until they were heading directly into one gun or the other. They were caught in a cross fire with nowhere to go.

Several entered my designated area at the same time and some quick decisions were made. I began selecting the easy targets first, those running from left to right were picked off but one came straight at me. I knew there was no chance of pulling it down and aimed at an alternative target. By the time I fired and reloaded, the hare had passed between my legs, making good speed across open ground behind me. After stepping back and swinging my body round, I lifted the barrel over the obstructing branches in a single fluid motion. The gun barrel traversed toward the target and followed the animal until it turned a right angle in its zigzag course. I squeezed off a shot and saw the target crash to the ground. The whole shooting match was over in about two minutes or as fast as one could load and fire twenty-five cartridges. In any case, I ran out of ammunition but felt sure another three or four hares could have been killed if more cartridges had been available. The last empty shell smouldered at my feet as my hand ran over an empty belt.

I cleared the gun before sitting down to roll a cigarette and wait for Vic to join me. I watched him check for any wounded animals that needed finishing off as he came closer. The area resembled a battlefield with corpses littered everywhere. I hadn't counted the total, since things were happening too fast to keep a tally as shot after shot was fired. There had been twenty-five shells in my belt to begin with and I was not aware of missing any but fired a second shot at a wounded animal attempting to escape. Following the country code means finishing off a wounded animal that's still able to run. It must be killed regardless of the temptation and there had been plenty of that. As far as I could figure, there must have been twenty-four of my own kills plus the number Vic managed to bring down. From the noise and number of rounds he fired, there had to be a fair number to add to my own.

Vic sat next to me, rolled himself a cigarette and lit it before he spoke. "Thaat be one 'ell oh a gun young un."

"Yeah, that's the best bit of shooting I've ever had, thanks Vic," I said through a cloud of exhaled cigarette smoke.

"'Ow many did 'ee get?"

"Twenty-four," I replied.

"By the 'eck, I ain't ever seen the like afore."

We were sitting in a hedge smoking, watching the sun rise and surrounded by empty shotgun cartridges. I felt mentally drained yet at the same time euphoric. We'd done a really good job. A few hares escaped but another hunt would sort that out. I took a drag and blew a long stream of smoke before asking Vic how many he shot.

"Ah, 'bout a dozen mebe more," he replied softly.

"Fantastic wasn't it?"

Vic didn't say anything, he just nodded. We finished our smoke before standing to start clearing up the empty cases.

Carrying the kills back to the van proved hard work and took over an hour. All the animals were in the back of the van, except one. Victor lifted the dog hare by its hind legs to compare it against my height. The animal must have been over four feet long and by Vic's estimate weighed more than sixteen pounds. It was certainly the biggest hare I ever saw.

The farmer's wife invited us in for breakfast while we were stowing our gear. The sun was well up when we headed for the kitchen. Eating was the last thing on my mind during that very early morning start. However, the excitement of the shoot and the last hour's effort, with a reminder that breakfast was on the stove, stimulated my appetite. Suddenly I became very hungry. Once inside, the warmth and smell associated with country kitchens filled my being. Smoked bacon, fresh baked bread, eggs fried in butter and well-brewed hot sweet milky tea all mingled to tantalize the senses.

Victor and I sat at a big table that had not been highly polished but the hardwood surface was scrubbed clean. In fact, all the wood in the kitchen was plain and unvarnished. The table was almost white with the kitchen range black as pitch and shone like glass. The impression it gave was of a practical, homely, comfortable place. Whilst it never had the same atmosphere and grandeur

Nights in the Forest

of the other farmhouse Uncle and I collected the gun from, this place had a friendly welcome of its own.

"Won't be mor'n a minute, you boys must be starvin'," the farmer's wife said as she continued creating a meal with the accompaniment of clattering pots and pans.

"Arr, I weren't 'ungry afore I cum in 'ere missus but the smell oh your cooking be 'aving a powerful effect on me appetite."

I could not have put it better myself and a moment later, the farmer came in, although he wasn't the typical image of a farmer. All the farmers I knew, up till that moment, had been ruddy-faced, well-built men with a cheerful disposition. The farmer who sat at the table was a skinny man. He had a long mournful face and looked like a real misery guts and not a bit like his wife whose happy cheerful disposition lit up the room.

"Mornin'," he said softly while removing his dirty Wellington boots before sitting at the table to silently watch his wife.

A big brown china pot of tea was handed round while he cut large chunks of steaming fresh baked bread and piled them onto a plate. Lumps of homemade butter were meted out to each person while his wife lifted an enormous skillet off the stove. All of a sudden, the reason for all that frying sizzling beautiful smell came into view, before us was the biggest frying pan ever seen. It was full to the brim with eggs and bacon simmering in butter and bacon fat.

"Help yourselves, boys," the farmer's wife said.

With our plates loaded Victor and I waited for the farmer to start. Manners were something I learned at home that became part of country life. In fact, the head of the house would start any proceedings at a meeting round the table and nothing was more important in life than eating. As soon as every plate had been loaded, the farmer bent his head and put his hands together while my hovering knife and fork were laid gently back onto the table.

"Lord, we thank 'ee fur this grub, amen." It was very short and to the point. The man said it all in one sentence and looked up at me. "Eat up, eat up," he commanded as though we were at the start of a race.

No further words of encouragement were needed. For a full five minutes, the only sounds heard in the kitchen that early morning were the noises of hungry humans enjoying their food.

I'd never seen a breakfast like it before, empty plates were refilled, chunks of fresh crusty bread smothered in butter were used to mop up bacon fat and egg yolk on the plates. Everything was eaten with relish and compliments to the cook were emitted between mouthfuls of food with, "oh arr, thaat be good, more please, by the 'eck", all blended with the clattering of knives and forks on big white china plates.

During second helpings things slowed down. Our host took a deep breath, sighed in satisfaction then sucked noisily on his tea before leaning back in his chair. "'Ow did yur do then Vic?"

"Good," was the muffled response through a mouthful of food.

"I 'eard a lot oh shooting, mustav been missing mor'n a bit from the noise yur were making."

Vic continued chewing quickly while shaking his head, then took a gulp of tea to help the food down. After all, it's bad manners to talk with one's mouth full. He held up a hand indicating an answer would be forthcoming soon after he swallowed. A second sip of tea did the trick while everyone at the table waited in anticipation. Vic looked over the rim of his tea mug. "'Twere the best bit oh shootin' as ever I did see." He paused to chew some more, smack his lips, then wash down whatever remained with another noisy gulp of tea.

"'Ow many did yur get?" the farmer asked.

"Dunno, lost count," Vic answered shaking his head before turning to me. "'Ow many, young un?" Another mouthful of tea needed gulping down while his free hand wiped a patch of good-looking bacon fat on his plate with some bread. The lump of bread soaked in bacon fat, butter and egg yolk was pressed into his mouth as his eyes closed.

I put on my best let me think face, which gave Vic sufficient time to finish chewing while doing a rough count in my head. "Well, I think there must be about thirty-six, maybe more, I'm not sure."

Nights in the Forest

"Thirty-six!" the farmer exclaimed as his mug came down on the table. "'Ee were only shooting fur no mor'n a few minutes."

"Arr, best bit oh shootin' as ever I did see," Vic repeated while nodding and stuffing the hole in his face with more food. Manners seemed to have been temporarily forgotten during the interim period.

The farmer looked away from Vic, turned his attention to me and said, "'Ow many did 'ee get?"

"I shot twenty-four before running out of ammo. I could have got a few more, but there were no shells left," I replied concluding with a nonchalant shrug of my shoulders.

"'Ave 'ee got an automatic like Vic then?"

Victor interjected at that stage by shaking his head while holding up his hand. He required a moment or two before answering on my behalf. "No, no, no, lad 'as a single shot weapon. Best bit oh shooting as ever I did see."

At that moment, I realized Victor had been talking about my shooting not the general score. It made me acutely embarrassed but a feeling of pride swept over me the same time as a flush came to my face. I turned away from the admiring looks.

"Now then, you two stop it, you'm embarrassin' the boy," the farmer's wife said much to my relief.

Breakfast continued at a leisurely pace once it settled down with a second mug of tea, honey on crusty bread and a cigarette to finish off. It was just as well we sat and talked for half an hour while the dishes were being washed and put away. I felt dead certain that with a stomach so full my legs had no chance bearing the excess weight. I loosened my belt, so did Vic and the farmer. My belly felt tighter than an overripe watermelon ready to burst.

Victor insisted on showing off the evidence of our successful shoot in the back of the van but the farmer turned down the offer of one. "I 'as 'ad enough 'are to last till the day I dies, but I thank 'ee anyways." He turned to me, put his hand on my shoulder and looked me in the eye. "'Ee cun cum 'ere shooting whenever 'ee wants, don't 'ave to ask, jus' cum."

I thanked him and climbed into the van. Not only did I have a first class shotgun, I had a fantastic morning shooting and actually had a farm to shoot on with permission from the farmer. There wouldn't be any need to go poaching anymore. It was almost too good to be true. Things had taken a turn for the better and they were in my favour.

Victor drove slowly along the rutted dirt track causing the van to sway alarmingly under the excess weight. Once on the main road to Chippenham, Vic and I discussed how our good fortune should be distributed. A dozen were delivered to the old folk's home, which had to be the one place where jugged hare would be appreciated. Victor kept two for himself while I chose to keep the big dog hare and a smaller one. The rest were sold to butchers and game shops in Chippenham. The money we made was more than enough to replenish the ammo and tobacco many times over.

When Vic dropped me off, I thanked him for the greatest morning in ages, lifted my two hares and went inside. I hung the big dog hare in Uncle's shed before preparing the small one for the pot. Everything had to be ready before mother and Uncle came home.

With spirits so high, I could hardly wait to tell them how successful my morning had been. By the time I sat down with a cup of tea, mother came through the door. She was immediately taken to the shed to look at the dog hare. Mother couldn't believe the size of it, a hand went to her mouth while she muttered something under her breath about having never seen such a big rabbit. There was no point in trying to explain the difference to mother, it was enough to see her so happy.

When Uncle came home, I decided to play it cool. We talked about the hare in the pot and Uncle praised my ability to hunt and bring home some meat. After a smoke I led Uncle to the shed and showed him the big one I brought home especially for him. Several excessively crude Polish swearwords were used as he gazed on the monster hanging in the shed before Uncle reverted back to English. "I am ask you bringing me a big von, not a horse." He stood there with hands on hips before putting his arms around me to give a hug.

"Victor said we'll have to let it hang for some time before we can eat it," I commented while prodding the carcass.

"He is right boy, zis von will be tough. It must a little rotting first eh. Ven I finish vis him it vill be the best." Uncle concluded his claim with a flourish of a hand and a kissing of the finger tips.

We returned to the kitchen where the pot bubbled gently as more vegetables were added to the meat. Uncle and I sat down to light up cigarettes.

"Tell me again, from the beginning," he said leaning across the table.

I reached for the bottle and poured us both a good measure. I was about to retell the story and would try very hard not to exaggerate the distances, my extraordinary skills or the number of hares I shot. But hells bells, it was a time when a little embellishment was justified.

Anthony Corbyn

Chapter Sixteen

My Nemesis

The winter months progressed toward the end of the year, more snow had fallen and I wanted to go hunting but mother wasn't keen on the idea. She pleaded with me not to go and claimed it was much too cold. Mother convinced herself that I would freeze to death out there.

"Mum, it's warmer in the snow than the frost, you tell her Uncle," I responded.

As an experienced hunter himself, Uncle had to agree. "Tak tak, this is correct vat boy say. You must not worry," he assured her.

I went on to explain that although snow may be wet, it was still warmer than frost and freezing winds. She shrugged and seemed reassured when persuaded by Uncle that everything would be all right.

"You take gun as well as bow eh," Uncle said as he watched me assembling the hunting gear.

"Yes, I must get some practice with the bow, it's been too long since it was used. Anyway there's always the gun," I replied while looking down the shaft of one of my hunting arrows. Time was running out. It would be my last Christmas of freedom because next year, the real world would finally catch up. I already had a job to go to. The wages from my short career in the Merchant Navy had been used to purchase a second-hand car. A Standard Flying Twelve stood in the backyard. It resembled a classic 1930s hoodlum's car with running boards and big headlights on the wings. Although I was not old enough to drive, and therefore unable to get a licence, paid no insurance or road tax, it made no difference. Those minor legal infractions weren't going to stop me doing what I wanted. Most lessons had been performed by driving round the estate. The old vehicle had no suppressors and it caused numerous complaints regarding the disruption I created by driving past any house with a television. During the evenings I tempted fate by going out on the main road. Darkness had a number of advantages with one being, nobody could see who was behind the wheel. A good steady drive consisted of going up the Bradford road to Fiveways and down the other side. The steep hill towards Boxfields provided the car with enough momentum to pick up speeds of sixty miles per hour. The kingpins were in very poor shape and at that speed the vehicle had a tendency to wander. Needless to say, my night driving became quite good, despite being limited by the amount of petrol I could afford to buy. By the time I left school early next year, the vehicle would be available for driving to work. From my point of view, entering the adult world required one to be ready in every sense of the word including the independence to come and go.

There were no pressures to do anything but my own thing. Although no one would come looking, I had no intention of returning home until I wanted. My school satchel, bow with quiver of arrows were looped over my shoulder before setting off with Lassie who was thrilled at the prospect of going on a hunt again.

A few flurries of snow had fallen but there was hardly enough to cover the ground, although I noted some snow clouds gathering and knew there would be a heavy fall soon. Temperatures during the day were still warm when compared to the freezing nights we had experienced over the last week. My thoughts about staying out overnight soon turned to considering the best shelter instead of camping in the open or under a lean-to.

The haunted house came to mind and it was central to the area I normally hunted in. That place would be comfortable and Lassie would be good company as long as she behaved herself. By midafternoon I set off and planned to be close to the game early by staying in the deserted farmhouse overnight.

On reaching the haunted house, it was already getting dark, since winter nights in the forest arrive early. The house had been filled with winter feed and bedding for the farmer's stock. Most of the rooms were piled high to the ceiling with bales of straw but one room at the front had already been half emptied. Like all the other rooms, it contained a fireplace on the outside wall. I immediately set about securing the house with my top priority being the removal of any potentially combustible material away from the fireplace.

I took Lassie for a final walk down to the river and stopped on the small stone bridge to gaze into dark tranquil waters. The still water close to the bank held crystals of ice that would grow during the night. The temperature made it much too cold to go swimming but memories of long summer days spent splashing about in the nude with my friends came flooding back. It was also the spot where I sank a whole battle fleet with two homemade cannons and an air rifle, those events were still vivid in my mind. The night was almost silent but for a gentle tinkle of water over the tiny waterfall.

The shadows and the house held no fear anymore and as for the ghosts, if there were any, they were welcome to join me. I studied the trees topped with a dusting of snow that highlighted their silhouettes against the dark sky. Although it was heavy with cloud, the breaks of moonlight cutting through were lighting up a magical landscape. A gentle breeze rustled the trees to shake a shower of white onto the ground. A clear reminder it was getting late and colder. I walked briskly back to the house with Lassie close at heel.

A short while later, a tin of beans rested on a bed of hot embers while I toasted some bread. Lassie remained lying under a blanket of straw drooling at the smells and watched every move. Supper that night was hot toast dipped in beans and tomato sauce served up on a tin plate during a cold winter night in a haunted old farmhouse. Food never tasted better and Lassie naturally had her share.

After a smoke, I rolled up in a blanket, with Lassie at my back and a small fire flickering in the hearth. Within a minute my eyes closed and I slipped into the deep peaceful oblivion of sleep.

My dreams were of hunting, fishing and running free across wide open fields and chasing naked girls into the fresh spring waters of Penny Pool. There were daring deeds at sea with Cookie and me braving huge icy storms, and me outrunning the police on the back of Uncle's motorbike. Each dream superimposed itself onto another with me wearing a trilby hat driving the Standard Twelve while Uncle stood on the running boards firing the new shotgun from the hip just like they did in the Eliot Ness gangster movies. In the back seat, a ginger-headed pregnant girl smoked a Woodbine while the bank manager whom we had just robbed bore a striking resemblance of Old Pigface. He was shouting at me the way he always did. The dreaming concluded with me holding a shotgun above my head in a victory salute.

When my eyes opened, it was still dark but the dawn couldn't be far off. The small fire had gone out, although the embers were still hot. They were brought back to life with a little dry straw and a match. With water collected from the stream it didn't take long to make a cup of tea. Lassie and I shared the hot reviving nectar with some bread and margarine.

When approaching daylight started turning the dark skies grey, I extinguished the fire. Nothing attracts attention more than a wisp of smoke coming from a deserted chimney. Time pressed me to get on. All the hunting gear including the big gun was stowed away in a safe place under the bales of straw. I donned my heavy jacket and called Lassie to heel. The time came to practice hunting with a bow and arrows.

It had never been my intention to go far but found myself drawn toward Deer Forest. On the way I came across a flock of rooks scattered across the ground. Their black bodies against a white background were an attractive proposition and certainly a challenge to any hunter's skill with a gun, never mind a bow and arrow. I ducked down and began crawling behind an almost barren hedgerow but my stealthy moves weren't good enough. The rooks spotted me and were soon circling high above squawking their warning to everything in the area that a hunter was about.

They were circling overhead like vultures when I decided on trying a long shot, knowing it would be useless to aim at any particular bird. The arrow flew straight up through the middle of the flock. The rooks had no trouble avoiding it and appeared to be laughing at the futility of the attempt. Nevertheless, they forgot or perhaps never knew that what goes up must come down.

Nights in the Forest

The pulling strength of seventy-five pounds forced the arrow out of sight into the clear sky. However, on the descent it managed to gain sufficient speed to catch one of the rooks unawares and struck a wing to lodge itself deep into flesh and bone. The jet-black bird screeched in pain as it fluttered to the ground like a rag doll. Even as it fell, another arrow had already been fitted in readiness for a second try. When the quarry hit the ground I released my second shot to ensure the kill. Many hours of practice had proved effective and my arrow pinned the bird to the ground.

Both arrows were removed and wiped clean before being replaced in the quiver. The rook was attached to my belt while Lassie watched and wagged her bald tail. We continued roaming together for the rest of the day although the hunting remained poor. We eventually headed back toward the house before the fading light of dusk turned to darkness.

During our return across open ground I spotted deer tracks in the snow. The tracks were fresh, I knew some snow had fallen during the night but the prints were clear. Had I taken more care, perhaps they would have been spotted earlier. I circled round trying to pick up the direction the deer had taken with the intention of following but the light began fading fast. I knew it would be hopeless to continue, which meant breaking off the hunt and heading for the farmhouse. The brisk walk kept me warm, despite the wind picking up with the snow clouds gathering high above. Even as I approached the house and crossed the small bridge, the first heavy flakes started drifting down.

My fast walk slowed to a stop. Through the open doorway of the old house I could just make out a silhouette through the gloom. A man sat on a bale of straw next to the fireplace. My heart pounded. I hesitated to enter the house but all my hunting gear was hidden in there, besides there was nowhere else to go. I stood still for several moments taking deep breaths and slowing my heartbeat down. A question loomed in my mind. "Who the hell is he?" With little alternative, I took a final very deep breath and advanced the last few paces across frozen ground.

The stranger stood up and peered through squinting eyes. "I thought 'ee might cum baack," he said in a deep, heavily accented

West Country voice while leaning against the stone mantel. There were no threatening moves although my heart continued pounding against my ribs. Lassie stood beside me, she gave a long deep growl of warning but stopped when my hand touched her head. No one moved. There weren't many times when I asked a question. However, on that occasion it came from a dire necessity to know who confronted me. "Who are you?"

"More to the point, who be you? 'Tis you thaat shouldn't be 'ere," the stranger responded.

I stood my ground looking the stranger up and down. He wore a cloth cap, a long waterproof coat buttoned up from the neck that reached down to his ankles and a pair of heavy leather boots. Feet that big usually belonged to policemen. I gathered he must have come through the back door, since I detected no footprints out the front.

"I 'asn't done nothing wrong," I said slowly with an appropriate accent, after assuming the man had to be the gamekeeper.

He pulled out a pipe as flurries of snowflakes drifted through the open doorway. I moved cautiously into the room. The sudden rush of fear subsided, my heartbeat calmed. He resumed his seat and seemed not the least bit angry but relaxed as he puffed at his pipe, looked in the bowl, frowned, then at me and Lassie. "You be 'im baint yur!" The statement was clear despite the accent falling through the floor. "Thought you'd cum baack tonight," he added slowly before taking another few short puffs on his pipe.

"What dus yur mean?" I asked. Join him, were my first thoughts. Get on level terms had always been Uncle's advice. Use whatever you can to gain an advantage. Putting those sound reasonings into practice seemed like a good idea.

The pipe smoker looked at me then Lassie. "You be thaat yung un as is al'ays running away, ain't yer?" He drew hard on the pipe but the only objective he achieved was a gurgling sound. Another match flared as the stranger made a second attempt at getting his tobacco to light. Gurgle puff gurgle, then three puff, puff, puffs followed in quick succession as the tobacco lit. Each puff proved the attempt worked.

Nights in the Forest

While he was busy getting restarted, I pulled out my own makings to make a cigarette and knew it would be stupid to deny the truth to his question. The man may have had an accent considered by many as typical country yokel but underestimating his intelligence would be a big mistake. "Ain't never caused no 'arm," I said looking him in the eye while lighting my cigarette. A long plume of smoke billowed out before I concluded with, "Not down 'ere at any rate."

The gamekeeper nodded. He accepted my reply and seemed happy that his suspicions as to whom had entered the room were confirmed. "Bin lookin' fur 'ee fur two years." A smile touched the corners of his lips while his head shook slowly from side to side. The original tension and suspicion in the atmosphere simply dissolved.

"Arr, an' I bin avoidin' you fur the same time," I said while easing off my belt to sit. "You almost stepped on me once." The belt and items attached were dropped beside the bale.

The gamekeeper spotted something and pointed his pipe at the bundle of black feathers. "What be thaat?"

"Just a rook," I replied while carefully removing the bow slung across my chest as the man watched.

"How'd 'ee get it?"

"Bow an' arrer."

"Bis casn't shoot a rook we a bow an' arrer."

"Can if'n you'm lucky."

Lassie had been standing to one side but came over to join the meeting and get a scratch behind the ear. She was a useful distraction for no better reason than her strange appearance.

"'Ere, yur dog's got a bald tail," the gamekeeper stated and pointed his pipe stem at Lassie's naked appendage which at that stage began wagging viperously.

"Silly bitch chases it, then eats the 'airs," I said laughing.

The man sucked on his pipe. More gurgling sounds came from the bowl as a tiny puff of smoke emerged from his lips. "You shoot any o my pheasants?" The question came softly, almost nonchalantly, as though it didn't matter.

Anthony Corbyn

A long drag on my cigarette was required before answering. I flicked ash into the fireplace. "No mor'n I needed to eat, mostly rabbit, pigeon and rook," I replied kicking at the bundle of black feathers at my feet.

"Ah, thought so." A smile of confirmation touched his lips as he brushed an exaggerated moustache with the back of his hand. The two years of wanting to know and the satisfaction of having the knowledge confirmed, was obviously very important to him.

"Never did any damage though, always left things the way I found them." I had relaxed enough by then to forget the accent, but refrained from an attempt at putting it back.

"Arr, I knows thaat, 'tis why I took no offence," came the slow drawl.

We sat smoking in silence for a few moments listening to the wind as large snowflakes swirled through the open doorway and hole where the front window used to be. The outside world became a turmoil in what looked like a blizzard. The ground softened to become white and smooth; the small bridge could not be seen through the flurries. I leaned against the wall in an attempt to get comfortable. My eyes became accustomed to the dim light while the gamekeeper and I carried on a conversation. We were country boys who represented no threat to each other and whilst never having met before, in reality we knew each other for two years. Our conversation centred on the weather, good hunting, shooting and fishing. Actually, we had a lot in common. When the time came for the gamekeeper to leave, he stood up, put the pipe in his pocket and moved to the door. We stood side by side looking at the blanket of snow covering the landscape. The wind had dropped completely and allowed the remaining snowflakes to fall gently to earth.

The gamekeeper said, "Bis casn't stay 'ere for long," as he looked over the white carpet of snow covering the bridge.

"I know, I'll be gone soon enough."

"You just make sure you'm careful." He looked about at the bales of straw, nodded a goodnight and left.

His dark shape slowly disappeared into the white landscape and I wondered how far he had to go. Clear size eleven footprints would be all that were left in the morning to provide the only evidence of his departure. At least an hour went by before I decided to light a fire. The hunting equipment and gun were still there but a lingering doubt remained in my mind. Had the gamekeeper found them and waited? Perhaps that's how he knew I would return.

While the fire crackled, the rook was plucked and cleaned while fresh snow melted in the bean tin for tea. Within a few minutes, the bird began roasting over the fire on the end of a stick. Most people I knew wouldn't eat rook because of its stringy texture and strong flavour. They rated it as vermin and included in that description were rabbit and pigeon. To me, it represented good nourishing food and also meant something for Lassie to eat. After all, she needed feeding as well. We hadn't eaten for hours and once cooked, the rook tasted absolutely wonderful. While I ate the flesh, Lassie got the carcass, which she devoured noisily. The cooked meat was enjoyed with bread and margarine. A cup of tea with a cigarette rounded off the evening meal. I felt as though the world was my oyster.

My opposite number had been confronted and found to be okay. The feeling that a circle in my life was about to close and become complete surrounded me as Lassie and I snuggled up under the blanket. As sleep began to envelop me, the gamekeeper's last words invaded my subconscious thoughts. His small trusting concession to stop for the night would not be taken advantage of.

Realization that the area known as Deer Forest was well outside my normal hunting ground prompted me to surface before dawn. I set off to where the deer prints had been spotted. I considered an extensive search across the valley before returning home. Although it wasn't light when Lassie and I left, the whiteness of snow and clear sky made movement easy. The gun would remain strapped to my back because it wasn't going to be used on that special day. No gunfire would be heard from me, not on that occasion. A powerful bow and quiver of hunting arrows were the only weapons available for the hunt.

Anthony Corbyn

It took over an hour to find the area and the evening snowfall had covered it under a white blanket. I began to circle in the hope of coming across some prints. A small white sheet was draped over my head and shoulders then belted in at the waist to provide some camouflage. Despite it, I knew it was movement more than anything else that might give me away. No tracks could be seen for miles. I despaired at ever being able to find anything at all, let alone fallow deer prints. My spirits reached a low ebb.

Suddenly! There were small prints, crisp and clear. I crouched to examine the spoor while pulling Lassie closer to whisper in her ear, "Be a good girl." The small backpack and gun were slipped off then pushed under a hedgerow close by. The tracks led over a low crest at one end of the hedge close to a small group of trees. Lassie was made to stay before I crawled to the corner. Through a gap in the sparse hedge, light brown and white spots caught my eyes. The animal stood less than twenty yards away. With my bow loaded, I began raising myself very slowly, using the nearest tree for cover. The small deer was totally unaware of the imminent danger. It simply continued to graze quietly on a patch of grass not covered by snow.

I stood fully upright with the bow string pulled all the way back. The feathered flight touched my cheek. An open eye followed the shaft down to the cutting edge of the hunting arrow levelled at the shoulder of an easy target. The deer's head came up to present a perfectly still posture. It was impossible to miss the most beautiful animal I ever saw as it presented itself in perfect profile. Just a small movement of the fingers was required to bring a dream to reality.

Uncle would be so proud. He would claim the honour, since it had been his influence that prompted me to become a hunter. Mother would be thrilled at all the meat and make valiant attempts at cooking it. A successful hunter's homecoming would be mine. News of the event would spread far and wide. I would become a hero.

In spite of all that, the air in my lungs flowed out. The pressure on the bow string eased as my arm relaxed. I sank to the ground and sat there for several minutes watching the deer continue to feed. Early morning sunlight threw long shadows of the animal onto the crystal clean white ground.

It made no difference that my reason for not killing that fabulous creature was impossible to understand. The kill was mine anyway, since the certainty in my mind left no doubt. The fact I never actually killed it was of no consequence. The sense of satisfaction was overwhelming as I looked along the hedgerow to where Lassie waited. In no time at all, with a satchel over my shoulder and Lassie walking beside me, I started looking for a special place to make my final visit, if it could be found.

The landscape looked very different to the way it did in summer. Everything had turned white, even the trees carried crystal clear chandeliers hanging from their branches. The air was crisp and clear as Lassie and I wandered aimlessly across snow-covered fields.

Midday saw us standing at the edge of a small clearing where a large oak stood in the centre. Its barren winter branches reached out to cast pale shadows over the ground. "This is the place," I said aloud and sat down pulling Lassie closer.

It seemed such a long time since a pheasant kill had taken place from the very same spot. My mind wandered back to the day when my persona become part of nature and had even become an animal. I relaxed, sat back and rolled a cigarette, hunting for the day ended. The exhaled cloud of smoke hung on the still air and moved across the ground like a ghost as memories filled my mind. Events of the past two years had finally caught up and yet I continued running, still looking for that something but not knowing what or where it could be.

Uncle told me at the beginning of my quest, that one day my searching would stop because whatever I was looking for would stop me, when I found it. He was absolutely right and my being delved into the daydream and felt the warmth of its memory. A cock pheasant cried out, my eyes misted over as they fixed on the opposite side of the clearing. The midday sun, although weak, melted the icicles in the trees in a scattering of drips. A mist formed close to the ground as it often did at that time of year in such prevailing conditions. Something in the mist moved, something dark and shiny, its colours glinted in pale sunlight. I blinked and wasn't sure what it might be. Something on the ground seemed to flutter and disturb the film of mist. My eyes were staring at the spot when, in the far distance, that pheasant cried out again but only his echo answered.

I stood up, wiped my eyes, yet the mist remained. The air became totally still, nothing moved. There were neither sounds of birds singing nor any breeze whispering through the branches surrounding me. A magical spell was taking place as the cock pheasant's ghost returned to walk his land again.

My best arrow was loaded onto the bow and pulled back hard while aiming at the big oak tree. The aim held good for a long deep breath before the arrow was released to whistle across the open space. There was a clear thud of impact. The shaft quivered. Long wide flights were the same array of colours as those on a pheasant's neck picked out by the sun. I stood back and heaved a sigh of relief.

There's an old country saying that goes "If you leave something of yourself behind, one day you will return to claim it." As a rebel, time had run out, but as an older rebel the spirit lives on.

The arrow remains lodged firmly in solid oak and I often wonder about a time long ago when I spent days and nights in the forest.

♦ ♦ ♦

About the Author

Anthony Corbyn (1945–2011), whose novels were initially published under the pseudonym **Anton Bonavia**, was raised in Malta, Egypt, Germany, and in England. As a young man, he enlisted in the British Army and was sent on a tour of duty to Malaya, which included operations in Borneo, before he was stationed in Aden, southern Yemen, during the Aden Emergency.

According to his own accounts, he subsequently fought as a mercenary in Burma (Myanmar) and in the Angolan Civil War.

Later, he obtained a qualification in food technology at Salford University, Manchester, and pursued a career as technologist and company executive in the food processing industry in the United Kingdom, which included numerous business trips to many European and other overseas countries.

After accepting a job offer from an employer in Australia, he boarded a sailing yacht and, with a motley crew, sailed halfway round the world to get there. Here, Anthony Corbyn continued working in the food processing industry and pursued his passion for sailing. At the same time, he prepared several manuscripts, mainly of an autobiographical nature.

While on another long sailing trip, his yacht "Endymion" struck a coral reef in the Red Sea and sank in October 1998. After drifting in a dinghy for three days, he was rescued by a fishing boat and eventually returned to Australia.

Anthony Corbyn

After retiring, his intended circumnavigation of the globe ended in New Guinea when his yacht "S. V. Shiseido" foundered at the southern coast of Papua province in June 2010 and he was detained by the Indonesian authorities as a suspected spy.

Returned to England, he married Antoinette, his teenage sweetheart of the early 1960s, and bought the sailing yacht "Irascible" which the couple only enjoyed for a short time.

Anthony Corbyn died in November 2011 after suffering from cancer.

All Titles by the Author

Lothario's Diary
Dorrance Publishing Company, 2007
Paperback (currently unavailable)

Amoral Infidelity
AuthorHouse, 2008
Paperback

The Endymion. A true life adventure voyage
Anton Bonavia and Chris Ryu (editor)
Ryu Group (Amazon Kindle), 2011
eBook and paperback

Issue of Contempt. A narrated true-crime mystery
Anton Bonavia and Chris Ryu (editor)
Ryu Group (Amazon Kindle), 2011
eBook and paperback

Illicit Seductions. A true story of crime, love and betrayal
Anton Bonavia and Chris Ryu (editor)
Ryu Group (Amazon Kindle), 2011
eBook and paperback

The Endymion. A Voyage of a Lifetime
2nd revised edition
Red Point Publications, Caithness (Amazon Kindle), 2020
eBook and paperback (currently unavailable)

Ausstieg ins Abenteuer. Fünf Männer allein auf See
German Translation of "The Endymion"
Red Point Publications, Caithness (Amazon Kindle), 2020
eBook and paperback (currently unavailable)

Anthony Corbyn

Issue of Contempt
2nd revised edition
Red Point Publications, Caithness (Amazon Kindle), 2020
eBook (currently unavailable)

Verhängnisvolle Fehleinschätzung
German Translation of "Issue of Contempt"
Red Point Publications, Caithness (Amazon Kindle), 2020
eBook (currently unavailable)

Nights in the Forest
Red Point Publications, Caithness (Amazon Kindle), 2024
eBook and paperback

Nachts allein im Wald
German Translation of "Nights in the Forest"
Red Point Publications, Caithness (Amazon Kindle), 2024
eBook

Thirteen Platoon. A Tour of Duty during the Aden Emergency
Red Point Publications, Caithness (Amazon Kindle), 2024
eBook

Dreizehnter Zug. Gefährlicher Einsatz in Aden
German Translation of "Thirteen Platoon"
Red Point Publications, Caithness (Amazon Kindle), 2024
eBook

Hunter's Moon. A Fighting Retreat from Angola
Red Point Publications, Caithness (Amazon Kindle), 2024
eBook

Jägermond. Tödliches Abenteuer in Angola
German Translation of "Hunter's Moon"
Red Point Publications, Caithness (Amazon Kindle), 2024
eBook

Soldier's Eclipse (Historical fiction)
Red Point Publications, Caithness (Amazon Kindle), 2024
eBook

Der Soldat aus der Zukunft
German Translation of "Soldier's Eclipse"
Red Point Publications, Caithness (Amazon Kindle), 2024
eBook

Printed in Great Britain
by Amazon

8e64ff4c-be0f-4407-93cf-37f9abd48288R01